# Mañana Forever?

ALSO BY JORGE G. CASTAÑEDA

*Compañero*

*Utopia Unarmed*

*Limits to Friendship*
(with Robert Pastor)

*The Mexican Shock*

*Perpetuating Power*

*Ex-Mex: From Migrants to Immigrants*

# Mañana Forever?

*Mexico and the Mexicans*

# JORGE G. CASTAÑEDA

ALFRED A. KNOPF    NEW YORK    2011

THIS IS A BORZOI BOOK
PUBLISHED BY ALFRED A. KNOPF

ISBN: 978-0-375-40424-5
LCCN: 2011925522

Jacket design by Jason Booher

Manufactured in the United States of America
First Edition

*For Josefina Santacruz,*
*who accompanied me through much of this marvelous voyage*
*through the past and to the future*

# Contents

# *Acknowledgments*

Many acknowledgments are in order. First, to Ash Green, my editor at Knopf, who convinced me to write this book and not another, and who kept me on as one of his writers after retiring from everyday editing. Then, to those who helped me enormously with research: Lourdes Zozaya, Dafne Tovar Múñiz, Andrea Ballesteros, Elisa Estrada, Mariana Celorio, and José Alberro, who did his best to get my statistics right, and most of all, Emma Vassallo, without whom this book would simply not exist. Then, to those who ploughed through the entire manuscript and on occasion tore it apart, but always improved it: Dudley Ankerson, Cassio Luiselli, Joel Ortega, Alan Riding, Manuel Rodríguez, and Federico San Román. Then, to those who read parts or most of the text, and provided relevant, insightful, and productive advice, most of which I tried to follow: Claudio Lomnitz, Andrea Oñate, Andrés Rozental, Guillermo Sheridan, and Marcela Tovar. And finally, two special thanks: to my sister Marina, for thinking up a great title, if I say so myself, and to Alejandra Zerecero, who proofread, researched, edited, and patiently put up with my many moods and manias.

# *Preface*

Few countries have devoted so much time and energy as Mexico to dissecting and debating, to hailing or regretting their "national character." Our obsession with who we are, and why, is endless and constant. It is not only ours. The number of foreign "regards" of Mexico is lengthy indeed: from Ambrose Bierce to Walter Lippmann, Cartier-Bresson to Jacques Soustelle, from D. H. Lawrence to Graham Greene, from Oscar Lewis to Tina Modotti, Edward Weston, B. Traven, and Leon Trotsky, from Sergei Eisenstein, Luis Buñuel, and Elia Kazan to John Reed and Jean Le Clézio. Mexican poets, novelists, anthropologists, sociologists and journalists, politicians, and painters have all delved into the Mexican soul, hoping to discover the Rosetta Stone that will finally decrypt and reveal the unpolished jewel of Mexican identity that so attracts admirers, discourages skeptics, and systematically fascinates and thwarts academics.

This is not a book about the Mexican national character, but about some of the country's most distinguishing origins or features, and their consequences. It is about their contradiction with the daily reality of a society ever more removed from an initial series of national traits that rendered it so endearing and frustrating to Mexicans, no less than to foreign visitors, travelers, retirees, or adventurers. It is essentially an attempt to explain Mexico to Mexicans, and to Americans. It seeks to explain why the very national character that helped forge Mexico as a nation now dramatically hinders its search for a future and modernity. While clearly in a country as regionally, ethnically, and socially diverse as Mexico such generalizations are perilous, shared cultural, historical, and geographical experiences do nonetheless create shared characteristics. A discussion of national character as a whole has obvious limitations and is inevitably superficial, leading to a turgid academic debate that this book seeks to avoid. As recently as 2007, Alan Knight, the outstanding British historian of the Mexican Revolution, pointed out the difficulties and contradictions of working with notions such as a Mexican "national character," preferring terms like "objective and subjective national identities." We have no dog in that fight, and will limit ourselves to working with the terms used often interchangeably here.[1]

The traits we will address are not exactly those stereotypes understandably offensive to Mexicans: lazy, irresponsible, violent, or despondent. Nor are they mannerisms often linked to Mexicans though hardly restricted to them: machismo, a different sense of time, or a special feeling of uniqueness embodied in what José Vasconcelos called our "cosmic race." Furthermore, this contradiction between the cultural traits and the reality of the country is by no means its only obstacle to full-fledged modernity. But it is, in our view, the most crucial. Others have written about the lack of a democratic tradition, corruption, the enormous concentration of wealth and power in the hands of very few, the negative impact of living beside a neighbor such as ours or, conversely, the poorly exploited benefits of contiguity with the United States. The purpose of this exercise, as the Coen brothers' Big Lebowski might have said, is to determine what "ties the room together." It is the disconnect between Mexico's national character and its current reality.

The book is organized by contrasts. One chapter seeks to describe, substantiate, and probe a particular trait of the national character; the following chapter attempts to confront that trait with the description of a central feature of modern Mexico that contradicts and invalidates the previously depicted trait. It hopes to show how that specific trait is no longer viable in today's Mexico, and has become a major obstacle to its progress. Each trait is derived from three "fonts of wisdom": the classics, the numbers, and the author's own experience. What makes the three sources appropriate and useful is, precisely, their diversity.

First, the classics. Rarely has a country devoted so much intelligence, hard work, speculation, and soul-searching introspection to identifying its identity. As far back as a century ago, and as recently as two decades past, the examination of the Mexican soul has consumed poets like Octavio Paz, novelists like Carlos Fuentes, essayists like Jorge Cuesta, Alfonso Reyes, Samuel Ramos, and Salvador Novo, dramatists like Rodolfo Usigli, psychoanalysts like Santiago Ramírez and Jorge

Portilla, anthropologists from Manuel Gamio and Miguel León-Portilla to Roger Bartra, Mauricio Tenorio, and Claudio Lomnitz, sociologists from Guillermo Bonfil to historians like Edmundo O'Gorman. They have nearly always disagreed on details, devoting interminable pages to highly specialized—on occasion arcane—polemics, yet at the same time their research and reflection have had the same fundamental object. They cannot be lumped together into one single corpus of theory or description, but viewed from outside the specialists' realm, they share enough conclusions so as to suggest something of a consensus. We shall select and study a few of those consensual traits—acknowledging that there are many others, far less unanimous—by taking the experts' common viewpoints at face value. In many aspects, though not in all, they got it right.

A second set of sources are the mountains of data that the classics partly lacked to buttress their ruminations, insights, and intuitions, but which would have confirmed them, had they been available. This is not so say that they based their views only on hearsay and impressionistic analyses—there was that, but also intuition, travel, study, experience. Still, Mexican society was, until the mid-1980s, a very opaque one from just about every point of view. Over the past twenty years or so, however, it has been dissected by innumerable polls, surveys, focus groups, microstudies, sponsored and carried out by public and private agencies, universities and marketing firms, political consultants and parties, international agencies and local scholars. The National Statistics Institute, founded in 1985, has only recently compiled comparable historical surveys, while national household income and spending studies are less than thirty years old. After years of living without polls other than for certain very specific marketing purposes—why bother with election polls when there are no real elections—Mexico has become a pollster's paradise, partly thanks to the advent of modernity and democracy, partly perhaps as a result of a certain narcissism. There is no relation between the data available to the classics—even the most recent among them—and that which any student or candidate for office can retrieve today from almost infinite sources. This information is not always easily or accurately comparable in time and space; series are not uniform; regional perspectives are often unavailable; and, inevitably, there is a great deal of self-serving information culled from leading questions or foregone conclusions. Similarly, there are valid doubts and objections regarding the reliability of Mexican polling firms, especially in view of their relative youth and inexperience. This explains why we often quote or refer to several polls simultaneously, and why the data we cite should always be seen as indicative of trends, not as precise measurements. Nonetheless, this trove of facts provides the speculation of the classics with the type of solid statistical foundation that they were partly deprived of before, and which either would have made their ingenious intuitions impossible if wrong, or more reliable if right.

Finally, there is the vantage point of the author. It is the lot of millions of my compatriots now, before, and in the foreseeable future to find ourselves in a curious internal/external position. The latter lends itself to eternal ambivalence, which encourages insights and discoveries that others, too far removed or excessively entrenched in everyday life, cannot easily acquire or achieve. More than 11 million native-born Mexicans reside abroad; 300,000 to 400,000 depart every year, more or less for good; the country's leading businessmen, intellectuals, scientists, writers, and artists have almost all studied, worked, lived, and triumphed partly outside their birthplace. But with a few notable exceptions that I would never hope to emulate, these remarkable and simultaneously detached Mexicans have not devoted their talents to crisscrossing the country, studying it, and organizing the product of their study in a layman's volume such as this. Most Mexicans who have never left the country are too close to perceive and admit its weaknesses; those who permanently settled in the United States are in all likelihood too distant and critical of their homeland to penetrate its mysteries and be captivated by its enigmas. So a lifetime of traveling throughout Mexico, lecturing at universities, writing in the local media, visiting small communities, and speaking with social activists and professionals, all the while teaching and writing in the United States, may lend this author the possibility of seeing what some others do not. A nomadic childhood and university studies in the United States and France may also contribute to this perspective.

## An Outline

The first chapter describes one of the most neglected attributes of the Mexican ethos: an acute individualism and stubborn rejection of any type of collective action. It is contrasted with the thrust of the second chapter, that is, the emergence of Mexico today as a middle-class society, which by definition imposes limits on that individualism, and a growing reliance on collective endeavors. The third chapter returns to a classic feature of the Mexican soul: a powerful reluctance to engage in any type of conflict, a reverential respect for form and appearance over substance and content, and a constant effort to disguise feelings, interests, ambitions, and aspirations. This is challenged in the fourth chapter with the advent of representative democracy from the mid-nineties onward; the incompatibility of the necessary attributes for coping with authoritarian rule (during nearly five centuries) is coupled with the requirements of rough-and-tumble, transparent democratic politics, warts and all.

Chapters 5 and 6 delve first into the Mexican penchant for introspection, and fascination with history and the past, as well as fear and rejection of the "other," especially of the "foreign other," of which Mexico has always been a "victim." This, once again, is a trait recurrently described by the classics, ever since they began to write and reflect upon the Mexican soul, and which thoroughly contradicts contemporary reality. Despite its closed-off, monopoly-dominated markets, Mexico's economy is one of the most open in the world today;* Mexico is one of the world's main tourism destinations; remittances from its population abroad represent one of the largest sources of its hard currency earnings. More importantly, few countries in the world have as close, complex, and multifaceted relationship with another, as Mexico does with the United States.

The seventh chapter is dedicated to the Mexican tradition of absolute disregard for the law, both for justified and understandable reasons and other unacceptable ones, and to the patrimonial approach to government service and Mexico's world-renowned corruption, summarized by the marvelous admonition "*El que no transa, no avanza*" ("He who doesn't trick or cheat gets nowhere"). Conversely, Chapter 8 examines Mexico's need today to build a set of judicial institutions that guarantees the rule of law, and secures personal rights to property and

* We will refer often to Mexico's open economy; by this we mean from a foreign-trade perspective and not that it is fully open to private investment, competition, and new entries into markets.

due process. This clash is more current than the previous ones, since Mexico is already, up to a point, a democracy, a middle-class society, and an open economy, but is nowhere near to becoming a nation of laws. If anything, drug-trafficking and drug wars have distanced it from this goal in recent years, even if corruption has in all likelihood diminished. It is a crucial clash, because the resistance to living by the law, and as well as the traditional justifications for not doing so, are perhaps even more deeply entrenched in the Mexican psyche than other attributes of the national character.

Finally, in an almost desperate plea for the viability of change, and in an equally desperate search for a strong reason not to discard it, we will try to ascertain whether Mexicans in the United States, when placed in a different context, become different. There is almost a real-life, real-time experiment under way, involving millions of Mexicans about whom we know a great deal and can discover much more, who have decided, or been forced to decide, to transport themselves into an environment that is even more contradictory to their national character than the country they left behind. Mexicans in the United States live, work, marry, and settle in a context that, as much as they may attempt to make it resemble or replicate the one "back home," is radically different from the country they left days, months, or years ago. Can Mexicans change, overnight or gradually? Can they adapt to settings so dissimilar to the ones they were born and grew up in? Is the modernization of Mexico possible when taken to the extreme—i.e., when peasants or students or children are uprooted and moved north—supposing it is desirable? Or, phrased in a more positive light, can Mexicans acquire the traits of a new national character, one truly compatible with their double nationality and double new reality: at home and abroad? These are the questions to be addressed in the last chapter.

## Where and What Is Mexico?

The dysfunctional relationship between the classic traits of Mexico's national character and its contemporary economic, social, international, and political landscape is well illustrated by one of the few relatively long-term statistical series regarding Mexicans' values and beliefs com-

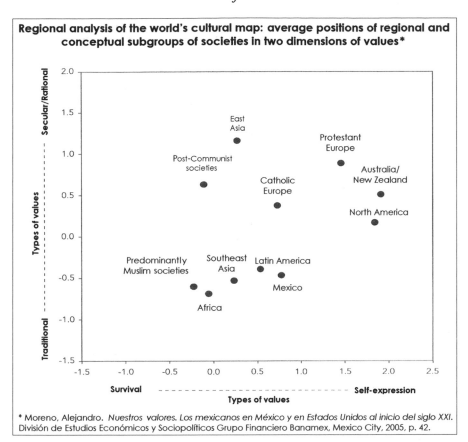

**Regional analysis of the world's cultural map: average positions of regional and conceptual subgroups of societies in two dimensions of values***

* Moreno, Alejandro. *Nuestros valores. Los mexicanos en México y en Estados Unidos al inicio del siglo XXI.* División de Estudios Económicos y Sociopolíticos Grupo Financiero Banamex, Mexico City, 2005, p. 42.

pared with the rest of the world's. In that series, which stretches from 1981 through the beginning of the new century, the nation's values were plotted on a graph where the horizontal axis tracks changes between attitudes of survival and those of self-expression.* The former is considered by the team of social scientists who drew up the tables as "premodern," and the latter as "modern." The vertical axis also shows movement from traditional ("premodern") to secular/rational stances ("modern"). From this perspective, Mexico falls clearly in the group of lower- and middle-income, emerging, or poor countries from Latin America, Southeast Asia, Africa, and the Islamic world, where traditional and survival attitudes prevail. It is not bunched together with the industrialized, "modern" nations from the North Atlantic, the post-Communist societies in

* The data for Mexico are for 2003; the World Values Survey of 1995–2000 as well as the European Values Study for 1999 provide similar data for other countries.

Eastern Europe (now part of the European Union), or the prosperous East Asian ones (such as Japan, South Korea, Taiwan), where attitudes and values are of "self-expression" and "secular/rational." But by its other features—Gross Domestic Product per capita, total exports, literacy, urban population, proximity to the United States, emigration, among others—it is clearly more part of that world, generally grouped together in the OECD, the Organisation for Economic Co-operation and Development (to which Mexico nominally belongs), or in the cluster of countries from Eastern or Southern Europe. It is closer to Poland and Portugal than it is to Peru or Paraguay.[2]

That said, this contradiction, which constitutes the central premise of this book, does not rest on an underlying culturalist, essentialist, or ontological bedrock, or on a revised formula of what academics would call cultural determinism. The nation's traits have changed over time, as its citizens adapted to constantly evolving external and internal circumstances; they are not set in stone. The foundational "shock" represented by the Spanish Conquest and the decimation of the pre-Columbian civilizations by disease, forced labor, and war are viewed in most historical and anthropological literature as an initial event. But that event, while it may have created the mixed race, or "*raza mestiza*," did not engender a permanent essence, always present and immovable whatever the environment. It unleashed a process that over time has been influenced by other surrounding conditions, other moments, other factors. There is an original sin, but the sinners have changed, the sins have been modified, and the ritual of expiation and repentance has also been transformed. Least of all is there, in this endeavor, any predilection for the existence of a "Mexican essence," of an "us versus them" mentality, of a supposedly superior Mexican substance victimized and violated by the "other(s)." Obviously any invocation of a national essence or ethos poses this risk, and while hopefully the author can avoid its pitfalls, others could, and indeed have, made use of such arguments for political purposes. Our approach is sufficiently removed from any insinuation of cultural determinism in that it explicitly posits that a number of historical, economic, social, political, and international factors have made Mexico a modern nation, despite its culture, not as a result of it. But until now, when this series of traits has become an insurmountable obstacle, culture was more an effect than a cause. In the importance attached to what is generally referred to as "culture," there is perhaps a certain proximity to views such as Gunnar Myrdal's and Arthur Lewis's; in the rejection of "culture" as a permanent factor of underdevelopment lies a strong distance from authors such as Lawrence Harrison.[3]

There is no question, as many scholars—most recently Roger Bartra and Claudio Lomnitz—have suggested, that the previous political system utilized the notion of "Mexicanness" to install and impose its own definition of patriotism, nationalism, cultural, religious, ethnic, and even linguistic identities. And maybe it would be preferable to throw the baby out with the bathwater and cancel the idea of differences that can be subsumed under a single concept; it might pay off to accept the full, logical consequences of Nobel Prize–winning economist Amartya Sen's multiple-identity thesis. Except that even in the European Union, together with India the most diverse federation of identities, cultures, origins, and expressions in today's world, the local or national factor subsists, perhaps because the legal one does. Or maybe, and more likely, it's the other way around: the separate juridical existence of the nation-state, even absent a national currency (in most cases), a local market, and certain other swaths of statehood, could stem from the persistence of the national character of any one of the twenty-seven members. Messing with Mexicanness is a perilous enterprise, but suppressing it out of an overzealous reverence for certain currents in modern anthropology may be excessive . . . for now. Mexicanness remains a worthy subject of study, if due attention is paid to the regional, social, and ethnic diversity of modern Mexico, to the multiple-identity theses of many scholars, and to the evidently ideological nature of many of the components of Mexicanness, whether new or old.

Nor does this text subscribe to a neo-Weberian, Protestant ethic/ Catholic essence approach, where the basic difference between South and North America, and the enduring characteristics of the latter, stem from the nature of the Conquest: by Northern European, Protestant, and ascetic settlers in one region; by Spanish, Catholic, swashbuckling *conquistadores* in another.* This dichotomy is not entirely illusory and had its influence on Mexico's cosmogony for the past two centuries. If

---

* Perhaps the first expression of a similar view was formulated by the British empiricist philosopher David Hume in his essay "Of National Characters": "the same set of manners will follow a nation, and adhere to them all over the globe. . . . The Spanish, English, French and Dutch colonies, are all distinguishable even between the tropics." David Hume, "Of National Characters," quoted in Sebastian Edwards, *Left Behind* (Chicago: University of Chicago Press, 2010), p. 25.

anything, the juncture at the destination is as crucial as the one at the point of departure, but in both cases it only explains (insufficiently) how and why things began, not how and why things have been ever since. The search for a single origin of the current status quo is as futile as the quest for a unique essence of all things Mexican. One of the classics we shall quote frequently, Emilio Uranga, was often referred to during his prime as the "smartest" man in Mexico, before he drank himself to death. Before he did, he wrote a brilliant, now out-of-print essay titled "The Ontology of the Mexican," which demonstrates that there is in fact no such thing. There are the traits of a people, transformed through the sophisticated interpretation of the classics, from stereotypes to "character," and which made it possible for a Mexican nation to emerge and survive, though never to thrive nor flourish, despite brief moments of economic glory in the nineteenth century. Which is where we are today.

### A National Character?

What do we or anyone mean by national character? It is a strange thing. Everyone knows what it is—or at least believes they do—and yet few can actually define it, generically or in any other fashion. Descriptions are bandied about incessantly: the French are this way and that; the people of China collectively feel, think, or hope for this or that; Americans are . . . whatever; the Arab "Street" reacts one way or another to one event or another. Most of these generalizations almost always envelop more than a grain of truth, and can also be offensive, stereotypical, or downright false, particularly as more and more heretofore "homogeneous" nations become increasingly diverse, or, in some cases, polarized to the extreme, leading to bouts of national introspection. The generalizing psychobabble and sidewalk psychoanalysis often resorted to in this domain either boils down to an insightful anecdote, or reaches such a degree of abstraction as to be meaningless. The relevance of the issue, however, appears greater than ever. French president Nicolas Sarkozy (the son of Hungarian immigrants) called for a national debate in his country in 2009 on "What it means to be French": a question that, in France at least, would have been unthinkable just a couple of decades ago, and that unleashed a national paroxysm and discussion that confirmed the relevance of the question. We understand national character to mean the package of cultural traits, practices, and enduring traditions, shared most of the time by most Mexicans, that make Mexico different from other societies, whose traits and practices make them, in turn, different from Mexico.

We do not equate this national character of a society or of the dwellers of a given territory with the notion of national or cultural identity: a much more sophisticated, useful, and simultaneously contradictory concept. Partly in contrast to Sarkozy, then British prime minister Gordon Brown called for an analysis of national identity early in his premiership, linking it to the need for immigrants to take a citizenship test, showing they knew what the British national identity was. The two notions are not the same. One—character—is often viewed as a watered-down version of the other—identity—but in fact springs from quite different cultural, anecdotal, and anthropological sources. Identity is used frequently in the struggle of subnational groups against discrimination or in favor of greater equality; character can come to signify just about anything, and often does. Ultimately, national identity is a concept that *defines* a nation unto itself, in an ontological, historical, fundamental manner: it is what makes a nation . . . a nation. National character is, partly, how a national society *views* itself, and how it is viewed by others. Some societies identify their national "uniqueness" with their national "character," as opposed to their history, their religion, their creed, their language, or their ethnic origins (Americans with the rule of law; British insularity; Mexican festiveness, the self-attributed main trait chosen by 72% of Mexicans in 2008, having a choice of ten options).[4]

National character, then, is a much simpler, more malleable, and superficial notion than national identity, but it is also one that can be more easily described, surveyed, probed, and quantified. Anthropologists may have in part abandoned it, but that does not mean that in less academic work it cannot be useful, although it is clearly not devoid of internal contradictions. But national identity is too. As Sen has most recently noted, it is far from unified; it can be, or become, plural or diverse, particularly under the impact of globalization or significant immigration as several European nations have experienced. Few societies can boil their national identity down to a single feature—religion, language, ethnic origin, history, creed—but almost all encompass diversity. In the case of national character, though, and precisely as a result of its simplicity, one can cherry-pick traits, setting aside others without excluding any of consequence, and without subsuming a national identity to any single trait or small group of them.

The enigmas are countless. Countries of immigrants face problems when invoking a national character: whose is it? In a classically relevant quip, Octavio Paz wrote (although some have attributed the original sin to Jorge Luis Borges) that "Mexicans descend from Aztecs, Peruvians from Incas . . . and Argentines from boats." Unless it is a creed, a myth, or a common sense of themselves, citizens of immigrant nations often have to forge a national *identity* without resorting to a national *character.* Americans can all (more or less) agree that they belong to a nation of laws, but it is not easy—nor is it often attempted—for them to find and glorify a character binding together the patchwork quilt that is American society today: English, Irish, Italians, Poles, Chinese, Africans, Mexicans, and so on. Brazilians face a similar challenge: is there a common character to a few Portuguese explorers, a large number of African slaves, a huge group of Italian immigrants, and smaller cohorts of German, Jewish, and Japanese ones, and to the *feijoada* pot they all forged over the years? Or are there simply—and crucially—a number of common tastes, talents, and traditions that, together, built a national identity: soccer, music, a frontier spirit, and an endless optimism and cynicism about their collective and individual future?

Nations of emigrants, like Mexico is today, on the other hand, encounter alternate challenges in defining themselves, and dealing with the differences and similarities between national characters and identities. When is a diaspora still a diaspora? Can emigrants retain the traits of a previous national character, their sports passions, cuisine, music, dress, and customs, while acquiring another national identity, along with another nationality? How long can the home country continue to count its sons and daughters abroad as nationals, when they serve in the armed forces of another state, pay taxes to another government, and vote in other elections? Or can national character and identity be split so smoothly that everyone is content with the persistence of the first and the dissolution of the second? These questions find fewer and fewer answers in the real lives of tens of millions of present-day emigrants all over the world, as they did with others who sought foreign shores over the last several centuries.

No resolution of the question of national identity is ever permanent. From our perspective, what matters most is whether the specific forms each solution entails are functional to the "success" of the country: whether it thrives and grows, protects and feeds its people, educates and heals them, respects their human and civil rights, and allows them to choose—more or less freely—how and by whom they wish to be governed. Those solutions—partial, total, lasting, or ephemeral—must meet the test of functionality. Occasionally, the traits of a national character get in the way of constructing and conserving a working, lasting national identity, as in the case of the snappy slogan many Latino demonstrators chanted during the 2006 marches in the United States against immigration restrictions: "We didn't cross the border; the border crossed us."*

## *H1N1*

This initial digression into the meanders of pop anthropology has a purpose: to attempt to define what we will be talking about, and to place it in an appropriate historical and universal context. Before moving on to the heart of the matter, a relatively recent tragedy in Mexico can perhaps exemplify the meaning of what we are getting at. In April 2009 an outbreak of so-called swine flu or H1N1 occurred in Mexico, rapidly spreading to the United States and the rest of the world. By the time it was controlled and matters returned to relative normalcy, nearly one hundred people had died in Mexico (mostly in the capital), and somewhere around ten thousand cases had been detected across the globe, chiefly in the United States and Mexico. Subsequently the illness surfaced just about everywhere, though with a lower mortality rate. Mexican authorities were rightly praised for their epidemiological and medical handling of the crisis, by everyone from the World Health Organization to Barack Obama. One year later the WHO acknowledged it had exaggerated, and the Mexican government was moderately criticized for the type of measures it took, including trying to bring patient fever down even when many epidemiologists considered fever to be a form of defense against the illness.

* In fact, very few of today's Mexican-Americans' ancestors were in Mexico before 1847, and certainly Mexico's loss of two-thirds of its territory has very little to do with contemporary mass outmigration.

But many in Mexico, and also abroad, wondered why, in two nations that are for practical purposes communicating vessels, that experience more than 1 million individual border crossings and 15,000 truck crossings every day, with 11 or 12 million Mexicans living in the United States and 1 million Americans residing in Mexico, did the illness generate such different consequences and policy responses by both countries? Why did Mexico shut all schools and universities for upwards of a week, lock down economic activities and commerce (including restaurants) in several large cities, cancel movies, concerts, soccer games, and virtually force the entire population to wear ineffective face masks, while Obama suggested people wash their hands, and went out to dinner with his wife and his VP for burgers? Why did nearly one hundred people die in Mexico during the first days, and only six (one of whom was Mexican) in the United States, with three times the population? Why did schools on the U.S. side of the border remain open, while those to the south were closed? Was the virus unable to cross the river, or climb over George W. Bush's wall?

There was, and still is, only one nonconspiratorial, sensible explanation for this gap. It lies in the Mexican health authorities' almost intuitive wisdom and accumulated experience, which led them, early on, to conclude that without raising the alarm decibels well above what the epidemic intrinsically merited, Mexicans would not pay attention. Why? Partly because of skepticism with regard to anything derived from government, but also because of a series of cultural, historical, enigmatic traits that many had already detected in local health habits. Self-medication is the most remarkable one—controlling for GDP per capita, Mexico is probably the most self-medicated society in the world. But others are nonexistent prescription drug regulations, indefinitely postponing a visit to the doctor, either because private ones are too expensive, or public ones require endless waits or are unavailable, or, more likely, because Mexicans don't like doctors and prefer resorting to traditional or homespun remedies dissonant from the country's educational and income levels. The government had no choice but to exaggerate the danger of H1N1; otherwise no one would have taken the matter seriously. It subsequently argued, perhaps with some hyperbole, that this "overreaction" saved thousands of lives; the authorities were nonetheless correct in assuming that this individualistic, incredulous attitude had to be factored into policy. It was, and it led to the accolades across the globe.

But it also led to an economic disaster. Mexico is a leading tourism destination. It receives nearly 20 million visitors per year (90% from the United States); the tourist industry is one of the economy's largest sources of hard currency, it is one of its largest employers (2.5 million jobs), and contributes a little less than 10% to GDP. The only "medical" way to manage the crisis was probably the one the government adopted, but economically the costs were staggering. In the months after the outbreak, cruise lines eliminated Mexican ports of call, U.S. airlines cut half of their routes, hotels suffered on occasion single-digit occupation rates, the entire world identified Mexico with "Mexican flu," hundreds of Mexicans were quarantined abroad, and the economy contracted 10% during the second quarter of 2009, partly as a result of far fewer working days, but also because of tourism shortfalls.[5]

The authorities knew their people, and responded to an emergency in the light of the national character. That character proved costly and dysfunctional in this episode. The government didn't know, or didn't acknowledge, that this response would prove to be undoubtedly more onerous for the country than the epidemic itself. Had they toned down their reaction, and responded gradually, day by day, the pictures of thousands of Mexicans wearing face masks that circled the world would not have been taken, the damage to the country's reputation would have been smaller, and the economic cost might have been reduced. But most people would not have reacted in an orderly manner, and instead of one hundred dead, there might have been two or three hundred, or more. Given the hand it was dealt, the government did the right thing: the problem was the hand, and that is what this book is about.

# Mañana Forever?

## CHAPTER I

# Why Mexicans Are Lousy at Soccer and Don't Like Skyscrapers

The most salient traits of Mexico's national character are part of a maelstrom of differences and similarities with other countries. These can serve as an initial tool of comparison, highlighting attitudes and practices that make most Mexicans similar to themselves, and different from others. We can start with anecdotal evidence of a Mexican tragedy, familiar to every one of the country's sports fans, if only unconsciously but with pain and sorrow. And quite rightly too.

During the 2008 Olympic Games in Beijing, Juan Villoro, one of the most distinguished members of a new generation of novelists (he was forty-eight in 2010, whereas the deservedly acknowledged dean of all living Mexican writers, Carlos Fuentes, turned 82 in May 2010 and published his first novel more than a half century ago), as well as one of its most articulate sportswriters, reported an oft-cited factoid about Mexican athletic performance. He regretted that, once again, Mexico had fared poorly in China, but that, also once again, it had failed less miserably in individual sports than in collective ones. Tae Kwon Do and diving were the only competitions in which Mexico, a nation of 110 million inhabitants and a per capita GDP of nearly $15,000 in purchasing power parity (PPP), obtained any medals (two gold in the former sport, one bronze in the latter).[1]

Villoro was restating an empirically demonstrable conclusion about the country that Alan Riding in his 1985 classic, *Distant Neighbors,* had already noticed. The Mexican, he lamented, "is not a team player: in sports, he excels in boxing but not in soccer, in tennis but not in basketball."[2] He was referring to a crop of stellar boxers from the past (Rodolfo Casanova, Kid Azteca, Vicente Saldivar, Rubén Olivares, and Pipino Cuevas) and, prophetically, Maromero Páez and Julio César Chávez in what was then the future, as well as to tennis stars Rafael Osuna and Raúl Ramírez in the 1960s and 1970s. He might also have referred to another individual effort where Mexicans' performance is outstanding, though some might not label it a sport: bullfighting, in which Mexico repeatedly challenges the Spanish as the best and the bravest. Since the former *New York Times* correspondent wrote this lapidary generalization, it has been repeatedly confirmed. Mexico has never gone beyond the quarter finals in the soccer World Cup, though it's the only "Third World" country to have hosted the "*Mundial*" twice. It has also never come close to the Dominican Republic, Puerto Rico, Venezuela, Panama, or Cuba in supplying stars to Major League Baseball, despite the success of Beto, or Bobby Avila with the 1954 Cleveland Indians and Fernando Valenzuela with the 1981 Los Angeles Dodgers. And it has always fared poorly in international baseball competitions, including the Olympics. We are systematically bested either in the local team Caribbean "Series," or in the national team World Baseball Classic, despite being an incomparably larger and wealthier nation than those mentioned above.

Our two outstanding athletes of the 1980s, 1990s, and early twenty-first century, Spain-based soccer striker Hugo Sánchez and 400-meter sprinter Ana Gabriela Guevara, were both highly individualistic stars, while the country has continued to disappoint its fans at every international soccer tournament and Olympiad. Since the 1900 Olympic Games, the first in which Mexico participated, it has won a (sorrowful) total of fifty-five medals (gold, silver, and bronze), of which forty-seven came from individual competitions, and eight from collective ones.[3] And in 2010, Mexico's only remaining world-class athlete was Lorena Ochoa, by many rankings the number one woman golfer in the world: once again, a highly individualistic competitor, in a highly individualistic sport.

The great soccer clubs of South America, founded at the end of the nineteenth century or the beginning of the following one, were brought to the New World by the British, and copied many of their features. Teams like River Plate (established in 1901) and Boca Juniors

(1905) in Buenos Aires, Peñarol (1913) in Montevideo, Colo-Colo (1925) in Chile, and Palmeiras (1914), Flamengo (1895), and Santos in Brazil (1912), which half a century later became Pelé's home team, were essentially social networks. They all had members, some with greater responsibilities than others. A few could actually enjoy a nonsoccer career in the club, and discounted or free and special access to games. But they also obtained many other benefits: sports facilities, other social activities (fund-raising for certain causes), schools for members' children, and children's leagues as well as soccer farm clubs. In a nutshell, these were not just sports clubs, like in the United States, but social clubs where immigrants (mainly Italians in Argentina, Uruguay, and São Paulo) interacted and formed the equivalent of self-help societies.[4]

This has practically never been the case in Mexico, or at least not until 2003, and only just. The oldest soccer teams, Mexico City's América and Necaxa, or Chivas in Guadalajara (established in 1906, although professional soccer only began in Mexico in 1943), were just that: teams. There were no members, let alone benefits, other activities, or social networks. So much so that some of them have actually changed cities (like baseball and football teams in the U.S.). At most, there were more or less organized cheerleaders, who occupied specific seats in the stadium. Only in the last few years, or a century ago in the case of the Atlas and Pachuca teams, have a couple of teams (América and Guadalajara, mainly)—and previously, the National University's Pumas, founded as a professional squad in 1954—established something like what the South Americans set up a century earlier, especially children's and youngsters' leagues and sports facilities.[5] Granted, there was no comparable immigrant or British presence in Mexico at that time (or at any time, for that matter), but the explanation is insufficient. More likely, Mexican fans don't like to socialize collectively. They prefer to watch games at home on television (since the 1960s), or to limit their devotion to going to the stadium—not less, but not more. Were we to push this point, we could take it as far as wrestling. Perhaps nowhere, not even in Middle America, is the "sport" or "game" as popular as in Mexico.

If one goes back to the pre-Columbian era, there is confirmation of this individualistic trend, as well as evidence of how weakness in collective sports was aggravated but not invented by the later Spanish conquest of other peoples in what today is known as Mexico. A collective spirit did actually exist in Mayan, Nahuatl, and Mexica religious-athletic communities, but just barely.* It was limited to certain rituals, land tenure regimes, and military activities. According to deciphered inscriptions at the ancient sports arenas of the Chichén Itzá archaeological site in Yucatán, at the Taltilco sites near Lake Texcoco, in San Lorenzo, the oldest Olmeca site, in present-day Veracruz, and mainly at the Tajín site, also in Veracruz, where most of the other depictions or stadiums probably stemmed from, the famous *"juego de pelota"* or "ball game," was both collective and individual. Two teams, originally representing the underworld and the heavens, played against each other to determine the fate of local life and civilization, but there are frequent references to the teams being identified only by their captain on the playing field. At the Tajín site, there is a bas-relief where, as Octavio Paz describes it, one can clearly discern the human sacrifice of the captain of the defeated team; in another depiction at the same site, we can see a decapitated player, with seven serpents springing forth from his mutilated trunk; there is another beheaded figure in Chichén Itzá. Although not all archaeologists agree, according to many, the captain of the losing team (and only he), once defeated, was promptly decapitated by the leader of the winning team. The individual nature of the competition was thus emphasized by the highly individual nature of the consequences of losing.[6] Perhaps the captain represented a team, and paid for the failure of all of its members, but that is the point: the punishment was individual, even though representational.

At a similarly anecdotal level, but by no means insignificant one, the first "Mexican," in the current sense of the word (in the sixteenth century, only the Aztecs were Mexicans), may not have been, as legend has it, Martín Cortés, the second marquis of the Valley of Oaxaca, Hernán Cortés's son, begotten by his interpreter-mistress and concubine, Marina or La Malinche. In fact, the "first Mexicans," in the sense of the first *mestizos*, were Spanish expeditioner Gonzalo Guerrero's offspring, born a decade before on the eastern coast of Yucatán; what's more, Cortés had two sons, both named Martín, one out of wedlock,

* The name Mexico comes from the Mexica civilization, which, according to the foundational mythology of Mexican culture, settled in Tenochtitlán, where after roaming through the northern desert for many years, they found an eagle eating a serpent.

by Marina, the other by marriage with his Spanish wife, who inherited the noble title.

But the truly first Mexican was probably Marina herself, a Mayan Indian who was able to gain Cortés's trust, translate and explain to him the nature of the challenges he faced, console him when things soured, and encourage him when they turned for the better. All in all, she became not only the mother of his children and the woman who shared his bed, but, most importantly, his closest political and cultural advisor. She had initially learned to translate from Mayan to Nahuatl, and later on from Nahuatl to Spanish thanks to her contacts with previous *conquistadores* on the east coast of the Yucatán Peninsula. However Indian she may have been at birth, Marina "became Mexican" once she put in practice what millions of her descendants have done ever since: seek and find individual solutions to collective problems. Here the two terms were magnified to the extreme. The individual solution ended up consisting of sleeping with the enemy, and the collective problem was none other than the cataclysm that hit Tenochtitlán and the entire region we know now as Mexico, when it was conquered and decimated by the Spanish. La Malinche simply used her considerable talents and charm to make a virtue out of necessity, and extricate herself splendidly from quite a mess. Other Mexicans followed her path over the coming centuries, though seldom with her success or cynicism.

## The How and Why of Mexican Individualism

The self-evident conclusion of the sporting conundrum is that Mexicans are highly individualistic in their athletic achievements, excelling in personal competition, but failing pathetically in associative sports.* This behavior, however, is found not only in sports but in multiple endeavors of a similar nature. Mexicans tend to be mediocre performers in collective efforts, and resistant to any type of collective action. But maybe we have a point: as a Mexican student pointed out to me during a lecture I gave at Rice University a few years ago, where I mentioned

---

* It is worth recalling: the word "soccer" comes from "asSOCiation football," i.e., this is by definition a collective sport.

this unscientific correlation, perhaps we do well to stay away from col-lective exercises. Our collective efforts—the struggle for Independence between 1810 and 1821, the Mexican Revolution of 1910–17, the student movement of 1968, even the democratic transition of 2000—have not exactly been resounding successes. Why insist on failure?

Villoro speculates that we excel at tasks that demand solitude and suffering, like literature and Tae Kwon Do. He may be right, but his assertion begs the question: why are Mexicans solitary and desirous of solitude? The initial response may have more to do with the question of individual versus collective action, and with a peculiarly Mexican ver-sion of the prisoner's dilemma. The latter, as most second-year eco-nomics majors know, is a metaphor used extensively in game theory and microeconomics to illustrate the contradictions of collective action (whether it is preferable for two or three prisoners to work together and have a high chance of a mediocre deal for their eventual freedom, or for each one to work alone for his or her escape or liberation, with a small chance of a much better outcome). The Mexican response is the classi-cal allegory of the crabs in a bucket, which may also exist in or apply to other countries, but which every inhabitant of Mexico, young or old, knows well and quotes incessantly. Mexicans, it goes, are like crabs in a bucket, all trying to escape from their eternal captivity; if by chance one of them is close to reaching the rim of freedom and survival, it is dragged back in by its brethren; they would prefer to see it die with them than to live without them. While the parable can be also read to the contrary, that is, reflecting Mexican collective action against an individual crab who becomes the object of proverbial Mexican envy for its success, it is probably more accurate to see it as an expression of individualism.

This dislike or mistrust of collective action is not just anecdotal, or a figment of armchair psychoanalysis. Now that the nation has emerged from the authoritarian political system of the past and inte-grated its economy more strongly with the United States, labor union affiliation has fallen dramatically, for example, though it was an inte-gral part of the cliental machinery of the old one-party PRI (Partido Revolucionario Institucional) regime, and often mandatory as well as rewarding for workers. It is much lower than current levels in other Latin American societies, like Argentina, Brazil, Bolivia, and Chile, and closer to countries like the United States; from 1995, toward the end of the old era, to 2006, it dropped from 22% of all workers to 16%, whereas countries in the rest of Latin America were all around 20%.[7] Likewise, the propensity of Mexican civil society for participation in any type of association—charitable, religious, communitarian, educational—is sadly inferior to that of other nations in the region. In Mexico, in 2009, with a population of 110 million, the Center for Philanthropy counted 10,704 formally registered nonprofit organizations, of which about half enjoyed tax-exempt status (that is, donations made to them could be deducted from taxable income); the equivalent figures for Colombia were more than double, with less than half of Mexico's population.[8] Part of the reason may lie in Mexicans' skepticism regarding the use of their monies, which may not be as philanthropical as promised. According to the Center for the Study of Civil Society at Johns Hopkins University, the nation with the highest percentage of charitable donations in the world as a percentage of GDP is the United States, with 1.85%; Latin American countries like Argentina, Colombia, Brazil, and Peru are in a middle category (excluding donations to churches), and in a list of forty societies worldwide, Mexico ranked last, with 0.04% of GDP.[9]

In the United States, there are approximately 2 million civil society organizations, or one for every 150 inhabitants; in Chile there are 35,000, or one for every 428 Chileans; in Mexico there are only 8,500, or one for every 12,000, according to Mexican public intellectual Federico Reyes Heroles. Eighty-five percent of all Americans belong to five or more organizations; in Mexico 85% belong to no organization and, according to Reyes Heroles, the largest type, by far, is religious. In the United States, one out of every ten jobs is located in the so-called third sector (or civil society); in Mexico the equivalent figure is one out of every 210 jobs.[10] In polls taken in 2001, 2003, and 2005 on political culture in Mexico, a constant 82% of those surveyed stated they had never worked formally or informally with others to address their community's problems.[11] In another series of polls already quoted concerning Mexican and world values, a robust and inverse correlation was detected between Mexicans' happiness (which grew remarkably between 1990 and 2003) and their belonging to any type of organizations. In the words of the survey in question, "the more a Mexican joins an organization or belongs to any type of association, the lower the probability of his or her feeling happy. . . . Studies regarding values have constantly concluded that Mexican society is extremely difficult to organize."[12] As in all such surveys, correlation does not necessarily imply causality, but there is a reasonable possibility that the two attitudes—happiness and individualism—are linked, in one direction or another.

The situation is not dissimilar in politics. As long as Mexicans were denied a real and true right to vote (i.e., elections where the winner received the largest number of votes, and the loser received the smallest number of votes), that is, until 1989—and many would say until 1994—electoral turnout statistics were meaningless. But since then, they have remained dismally low, averaging in the low 60% range for presidential elections, and around 45% for midterm votes. It could be said that this is perfectly comparable to the United States, except that Americans did not begin to enjoy the right to vote for the first time in their history less than twenty years ago. And these numbers do not pass muster in the hemisphere, where nearly every country has equal or better figures, be they nations with long-standing democratic traditions like Uruguay, Costa Rica, and Chile (except under Augusto Pinochet), or countries just recently exposed to the joys and distress of democratic politics, like those that make up Central America, or Peru, Bolivia, Argentina, and Brazil. In all of these societies, turnout in presidential elections regularly rises above 70%, and often reaches 80%, regardless of whether voting is mandatory (Argentina), registration is mandatory (Chile), or both are simply voluntary (Brazil, Colombia).

A parallel situation prevails in what should be one of the most collective enterprises of any Mexican's life: religion. Polls have detected a certain return to spirituality during the last decade of the twentieth century, and the initial years of the present one. But this has not translated into a greater willingness to attend mass or any other church celebration. If anything, people are visiting their church less and less. All of this led pollsters to conclude that "the Mexican of the nineties and turn of the century returned to God individually, and not through his religious community. . . . This is an individualistic faith."[13] This was not always so, particularly when a majority of Mexicans inhabited their villages, nor for everybody. Women have traditionally been more assiduous in attending mass than men, and the sum of both could be seen as a collective whole. But today, in the cities, if going to church is a symptom of civil society organization, Mexico fails the test.

There are, of course, historical explanations for this peculiar trait of Mexico's civil society, which do not necessarily entail engaging in cultural speculation. Mexico was, during the colonial period from 1519 to 1821 (when freedom from Spain was actually achieved, although Independence Day is marked by the beginning of the struggle on September 16, 1810), the jewel in Spain's colonial crown. It was the largest Spanish viceroyalty of the hemisphere, extending from southern Oregon to what is today known as Panama. It was the most populated— and up to a point, together with contemporary Peru, Ecuador, southern Chile, and Bolivia in part, the only actual *mestizo* society with a preexisting population at least part of which survived. It was also the richest, despite the silver wealth of Upper Peru, as the region comprising the mines of Potosí and Oruro in today's Bolivia was then named. Mexico consequently possessed the strongest colonial structures in political, legal, military, religious, and administrative matters, this last point needing to be nuanced by the absence of any separation between Church and State in New Spain.

There was a real colonial administration in New Spain: that is, there was a state, albeit a ramshackle one, as independence would reveal. It then took much of the nineteenth century for Mexico to construct a semblance of government, even one that was authoritarian, corrupt, and, at least until the advent of the Porfirio Díaz dictatorship in 1876, unstable. But a state there was, if only because it fought three foreign wars (against Texas in 1836; against the United States in 1847; and against the French in 1862), and one civil war, between 1863, when the French left, and 1867, when the Habsburg emperor Maximilian was executed at Cerro de las Campanas, or Mount of the Bells, outside Querétaro, on orders of President Benito Juárez.

This state, in comparative terms, was a strong one in relation to others in Latin America, or to the one that emerged from the independence struggle, though it was certainly weak from an absolute perspective. Much strengthened by the Porfiriato, as the thirty-four-year authoritarian regime of Porfirio Díaz was later called, its structures were destroyed by the Mexican Revolution, which began as a political insurrection in late 1910, and rapidly morphed into a social and economic uprising. But if anything, the state that emerged from the Revolution, as crafted in the 1917 Constitution, and underpinned by the founding of the single party that would rule Mexico for seventy years after 1929, was further fortified. That state, political system, and party, which came to be known as a corporatist regime, because it "incorporated" everything and everyone in its bosom—the army, the unions, the business community, the press, even the opposition, and implicitly the Church and the United States—stultified and repressed civil society. Outside the state, from 1929 onward, there was very little; on occasion, nothing. But this was not a recent turn of events; it reached back at least to the Conquest, and in fact to the Aztec empire before, since a militaristic theocracy that oppressed and exploited neighboring peoples was obliged to construct a strong state with which to do so. The Aztec empire, because of its sophistication and violence, its theocracy and its domination of neighboring cultures/civilizations/tribes, was an equally powerful bedrock state, upon which the Spanish built their own empire.

So it should not be altogether surprising that today, after nearly five hundred years of a strong state, civil society should be weak. From this perspective, Mexicans are disorganized, except during exceptional circumstances (rescuing victims after an earthquake, for instance), because, tautologically, they are not organized, and they are not organized because a perennial, all-powerful, overwhelming state has crowded them out. This Hobbesian behemoth (unmistakable in colonial times, at least after the Bourbon Reforms of the late eighteenth century) has simply never allowed civil society to flourish, and absent an organized civil society, people fend for themselves. When they do that for centuries, they get used to it, and persist in their customs indefinitely, until something occurs that makes them change their mind. It hasn't in Mexico, and so the ways of the past continue. As we shall see further on, those ways—corruption, cronyism, disregard for the laws—persist and date back to those times.

Some scholars like Carlos Forment have argued that compared to other countries such as Peru, there was a more vibrant civil society in Mexico during the first half and in the last third of the nineteenth century. He provides interesting statistics about the number of civic and economic associations that were created in Mexico between 1826 and 1856, and then again in the second half of the century. One can wonder, however, whether the number, duration, and intensity of associative practices in civil and economic societies outweighed the overwhelming power of the state, and whether the Mexican disinclination to "practice democracy in political society" did not in fact extend to civil society also.[14]

We could complement this historical explanation with a current economic and political one. Whatever else one can say about conquest, *mestizaje,* and colonial rule elsewhere or in the abstract, in Mexico it both led to and perpetuated an extraordinary concentration of wealth and consequently of power. There were two forms of capital coveted by the Spanish when they disembarked in what they named Veracruz, in 1519: cultivable land and mines. These were soon controlled by the Crown, the Church, and large landowners who, through the *hacienda* system, kept the conquered alive and working, without rebelling, committing collective suicide, or needing to be replaced by slaves from Africa. The *conquistadores* and their heirs owned everything worth owning, a concentration of riches that in turn generated an equally awesome centralization of political, intellectual, and religious power. Independence eliminated the Crown, but the symbiosis of power, Church, and land remained intact and overwhelming, until the beginning of the separation of Church and State, with the 1857 movement under Juárez known as La Reforma (the reform), and until the breakup of some of the immense landed estates or *haciendas* during the Revolution. According to Sebastian Edwards, at the beginning of the twentieth century there were approximately twenty thousand banks in the United States; in Mexico there were only forty-two, "each with monopolistic power, earning huge profits, and offering a limited supply of credit." Worse still, "in 1910 only 2.4 percent of heads of households in rural Mexico owned land; approximately 19 percent of Argentinean rural households owned land in 1895. In contrast, in 1900 almost 75 percent of rural heads of household in the United States owned land."[15] So civil society could hardly emerge or flourish: it had no material base, no political context, no legal order on which to rest, grow, and thrive. There was no available avenue for collective action outside the state, in economic or political terms, either; civil society was, at best, flaccid and impotent; at worst, simply nonexistent.

But since everyone knew, at least intuitively, that this was the case, everyone proceeded accordingly. Mexicans, as they came into existence as a collective entity and as a nation, sought individual, family, community, or local solutions to collective, political, or national dilemmas.

It is true that a somewhat associative tradition lingers in the Mexican countryside, from the *tequio* in Oaxaca, Guerrero, and Puebla, mainly, to collective *ejidos* in some regions. But it never seemed to outweigh the individual attachment to the land we will describe below, and is vanishing anyway, like village life as a whole. Today, according to polls, nine out of every ten Mexicans believe that "if one does not take care of oneself, people will take advantage of you."[16] Some sought solutions by joining the state; others by leaving the country; still others, by retrenching into the past and the ways of that past. John Womack phrased it perhaps most brilliantly, when describing revolutionary hero Emiliano Zapata in his definitive biography: "This is a book about country people who did not want to move and therefore got into a revolution. They did not figure on so odd a fate. Come hell, high water, agitators from the outside, or reports of greener pastures elsewhere, they insisted only on staying in the villages and little towns where they had grown up, and where before them their ancestors for hundreds of years have lived and died—in the small state of Morelos, in south-central Mexico."[17] And, one might add, their movement was all about Zapata; without him, it was extinguished, since this was the movement of a leader, which is why he is still known as El Caudillo del Sur: the Southern Boss.

As Jorge Portilla, one of the country's few intellectuals who attempted to conceptualize his insights into the Mexican soul, wrote in the late 1940s: "Our history is that of a few remarkable individuals who emerge from time to time, above the quiet swamp of silent political infighting. It is the history of the actions of *caudillos* and their personal followers."[18] Most of Mexico's heroes reflect this trend, from which Portilla drew conclusions different from the ones sketched out here (he didn't believe in Mexican individualism). Although much has been made of the emergence of an indigenous people's movement throughout Latin America since 1992, and Evo Morales of Bolivia has invariably been referred to as the region's first "Indian" head of state, Mexicans since childhood know this to be untrue.

Benito Juárez was a Zapotec Indian from Oaxaca who became president in 1856, undertook La Reforma in 1857, led the struggle against the French and Maximilian in the 1860s, and remained in power until his death in 1872. But he was—with the arguable exception of his almost immediate successor, Porfirio Díaz, also dark-skinned and from

Oaxaca, but not a pure-blood Indian like Juárez—the only Mexican president to possess these archetypical Mexican traits, the only representative of indigenous peoples, then and ever since, to achieve such status. But his glory and accomplishments as a lowly peasant from one of Mexico's poorest regions were his and his alone, not the result of a broad collective movement that led his (indigenous) people to enfranchisement, pride, and empowerment. His goal was not to strengthen or extend the Indian identity, but to bring "Western Civilization" to Mexico. Thus Portilla's comment: "We Mexicans do not believe in liberalism as much as in Juárez, in order and progress as much as in Porfirio Díaz, in land reform and in the labor movement as much as in Zapata and Cárdenas; and liberalism, order and progress, democracy, land and labor reform do not exist if Juárez, Díaz, Francisco Madero, Emiliano Zapata and Lázaro Cárdenas do not exist. . . . In Mexico the adhesion to a *caudillo* is adhesion to a man, not a myth."[19] One of Portilla's predecessors, Samuel Ramos, in his classic *El perfil del hombre y la cultura en México* (*Profile of Man and Culture in Mexico*), traces the individualism all the way back to the Spanish, quoting Salvador de Madariaga: "The Spaniard inevitably rebels against any restriction imposed by collective life, and he is consequently an individualist. Indeed, individualism is the predominant note in all phases of Spanish history. The conquest of America, for example, was not actually the work of Spain as a nation, but the achievement of individual adventurers who operated on their own initiative. [And] the Spaniard in America was as individualistic as his European brother."[20]

It would not only be an overstatement but downright silly to imply that Mexicans perform poorly in team sports because of the Conquest, colonial rule, and the PRI. Similarly, there is little point in making too much of what is no more than an anecdote. We do well in equestrian competition and long-distance walking, and terribly in volleyball, but so what? If anything, the causality runs the other way. The PRI, colonial rule as it developed and lasted for nearly four centuries, and the Conquest itself (which might not have occurred had it not been for the division of the societies that greeted the Spaniards, and the political genius of Hernán Cortés), are more likely the result of an individual rejection of collective action. That rejection is deeply ingrained in the culture, almost, one would say, in the "DNA" or "chip" of the sophisticated, violent, and hierarchical civilizations present in what came to be

New Spain and later Mexico. And if one jumps from the most ancient Mexicans to the most modern, i.e., those who work and live in the United States, and who one way or another have to adapt to the mores of the most "modern" society in the world, that individualism is more pervasive than ever.

Mexicans in the U.S., no less than at home, fend for themselves. They relate to their families in the old country by telephoning regularly and by remitting savings; they rarely, if ever, engage in any type of collective action, outside of soccer games on weekends, or the so-called local clubs or *"clubes de oriundos"* that are attended by a tiny minority of the 12 to 13 million Mexican nationals inhabiting the United States. Family counts; group efforts don't. Nearly all of the collective efforts (the Program for Mexican Communities Abroad, the Institute of Mexicans Abroad, the Three for One Program) have failed or been plagued by divisions, infighting, and politicization. There are few self-help, mutualist associations, like those that sprang up in the United States during previous immigrant waves, legal or otherwise. There are even few gangster-type organizations, such as those that protected and exploited Italian, Jewish, Chinese, and other immigrant communities, sometimes under the worst conceivable circumstances, but that nonetheless became a breeding ground for labor unions and local political parties, as well as other collective efforts. Salvadorans have built the Mara Salvatrucha gang in Los Angeles and Washington, while Dominicans created their *bodega*-based protection schemes in New York City's Washington Heights. Some second-generation Mexican-Americans may even resort to gang organizations, but newly arrived Mexicans have nothing, except their incredible individual talent, perseverance, ingenuity, and ambition.

Again, however, like the crabs in the bucket, they usually prefer to reject the successful peer, rather than emulate and support him or her. Therein lies part of the explanation for an otherwise unfathomable feature of the Mexican immigrant community in the United States: its endless, acrimonious, self-flagellating divisions. Politically, legally, regionally, and socially, that community is fragmented, atomized, and polarized. Every time any type of election or unifying action is undertaken, it drifts off into recriminations, claims of cheating and tampering, new divisions and splinter groups, and unending complaints, regardless of who the organizers are. Few things have proved as frustrating to politicians in the new, democratic Mexico as campaigning among their expatriates north of the border. There is simply no way to bring them together, even when their families back home seem to have overcome local infighting.

This archetypical trait of Mexico's national character, confirmed also by data culled from surveys of all sorts over recent years, is counterintuitive. It does not stand alone, but it is constrained by other factors, and can be superficially contradictory with the country's prowess in multiple endeavors. The collective has traditionally occupied a singular and elevated platform in Mexico's iconography, or in the social imaginary Mexicans and foreigners have built in regard to the country and its people or roots. This platform ranges from the Casasola Photographic Archive, with its iconic pictures of heroic or everyday *individuals*, to Sergei Eisenstein's *Qué Viva México!*, from John Reed to César Chávez, from Diego Rivera and José Clemente Orozco's murals and easel works to Graham Greene's depictions of anticlerical or criminal actions, to Oscar Lewis's research and findings about Mexican families. The mass scenes from the Soviet director's time in Mexico, the descriptions of mass movements in Reed's initial journalistic adventures, and the manner in which Mexican muralists, from Detroit, Dartmouth, and the New York Museum of Modern Art to Rivera's original and destroyed mural in Rockefeller Center, all at least partly portray Mexican reality as one in which the collective figures strongly. The masses fill center stage. Even in Lou Dobbs's stereotypical and racist version of Mexican life, the masses are decisive: millions of Mexicans pouring over the border, bent on "destroying" American values and laws. Mexico is, in the conscious view of its portrayers, a country of many acting together. Mexicans themselves, and foreign observers of Mexican reality, tend to emphasize the collective in what they see, hear, believe, and understand about the country; this would seem to be the natural, intuitive, way of beholding a country where purportedly the masses are always central. Not just any masses: the "suffering" though "rebellious" masses.

And yet, even in the iconic celebration of Mexican history and culture, the individual always stands out, perhaps subconsciously. There is Prometheus in Orozco's Pomona, California, refectory; a long series of individual portraits of Mexican and international personalities in Orozco's New School mural; Rivera's cult of Trotsky and ultimately of Stalin; the architect Luis Barragán's masterpieces of Mexican homes, much more than in architecture for the community (no collectivist Le Corbusier was he, although architects like Mario Pani, Teodoro González de León, and Ricardo Legorreta did engage in "public works"), let alone the extraordinary talent of Mexico's musical and modern plastic artists. The individual is king. Mexico has no world-famous bands nor world-class orchestras, but its music has flooded Latin America and the United States like no other from abroad. Its stars are individuals, and always act that way. A collective concert of Mexican musicians—Juan Gabriel, the Tigres del Norte, Luis Miguel, Armando Manzanero, Selena in her own way, and long before, Los Panchos—like the Brazilian Woodstocks in Rio and Bahia against the military dictatorship in the seventies and early eighties is unthinkable.* A Mexican version of the Ravi Shankar–George Harrison event supporting the independence of Bangladesh in 1971, or Sir Bob Geldof's and Bono's concerts against poverty in Africa, or Peter Gabriel, Sting, and Bruce Springsteen's joint efforts for human rights or against AIDS, are simply inconceivable in Mexico. A watered-down remake takes place only when the television networks that "own" the musicians instruct them to perform for charity or what-not.[†]

It is also not surprising to discover that this individualism extends to all walks of life, even those involved in the shadows and unending violence of Mexico's biggest business, driven by what Hillary Clinton called Americans' "insatiable demand for drugs." Crime is an individual undertaking, almost always and everywhere; gangs of Italian origin in New York, drug cartels in Colombia, Salvadoran street gangs in Los

---

* In 2010 the Brazilian movie directors Renato Terra and Ricardo Calil made a film called *Uma noite em 67* (A Night in '67) about perhaps the most important and famous concert of that era. Among the participants were Chico Buarque and the MPB4, Caetano Veloso, Gilberto Gil and Os Mutantes, Edu Lobo, Roberto Carlos, and Sérgio Ricardo.

† In 2001 there were a couple of exceptions that consisted of Mexican rock concerts organized by the government supporting "peace in Chiapas." But this was much more a government operation than anything else. The only real exception was the Avándaro rock festival in 1971; most of the musicians were Mexican, and the bands that participated were Los Dug Dug's, El Epílogo, La División del Norte, Los Tequila, Peace and Love, El Ritual, Los Yaki, Bandido, Tinta Blanca, El Amor, and Three Souls in My Mind, and there was no political connotation to the event.

Angeles are all highly hierarchical structures, where loyalty to the top is paramount, and where only one person can occupy that top at a time. The fact that Mexican drug lords run their outfits this way is logical and predictable. But the Mexican *narcos'* passion for flaunting power, wealth, and individual prowess, with the obvious risk of detection and capture, as well as awakening resentment and treason among rivals, go beyond the pale. It represents the epitome of Mexican individualism: the possibility of making it "alone," becoming rich, powerful, and popular "alone," taking on the state and the Americans "alone," and facing and enthusiastically accepting death "alone." The legendary Mexican cartels, dating back to the 1980s, were all either individually run, or family-based; one of the most recent and violent ones calls itself, appropriately, La Familia. As we shall see a few pages from now, the *narcos* got it just right: Mexican individualism is an individualism of the family.

Even in wealth, the individual in Mexico reigns supreme. Every nation has its rich and famous, and they all enjoy an existence alien to the rest of society. There are a handful of extremely wealthy people everywhere who are inevitably separate and different from others. But nowhere, it seems, is the gap between the wealthiest individual and the other rich, let alone the poor, as wide as in Mexico. The country's most affluent individual is ten times wealthier than the next most prosperous magnate, as if the difference between Bill Gates or Warren Buffett and the Walton family were, precisely, ten to one. That individual has 50% more wealth, according to the 2010 *Forbes* list of the world's richest individuals, than the next eight Mexicans, and probably more than the twenty most affluent people in Mexico if they were tabulated in that list.[21] It's not that a few people in Mexico are rich; it's that one immensely successful businessman is much, much wealthier than all of his colleagues put together. That individual, as many know, is the world's first, second, or third richest individual, depending on the performance of the stock market on any given day, Carlos Slim.

He is unusual among Mexican magnates, as might be expected. Rarely ostentatious, almost always expressing with good taste the wealth he has acquired, devoted to his family (his wife died of kidney failure in 1999, and he has not remarried) made up of his children, sons-in-law, and grandchildren, rather progressive in his political views, Slim has achieved a curious stature in the country where he was born (he is of Lebanese ancestry) and made his fortune. He regularly courts and seduces intellectuals, but without any apparent self-interest, and he generally avoids the traditional tools used by Mexico's very rich—money and corruption—to win over the likes of writers, artists, and politicians. He dotes on the company of foreign leaders and celebrities, from Bill Clinton (with whom his main topic of conversation is baseball lore) to Gabriel García Márquez, from Spain's Felipe González to Carlos Fuentes, but he rarely "uses" them, that is, by asking favors that might compromise them. He is generous with his time, not always with his money, but is a disarmingly accessible, discreet, and good-natured tycoon.

But he is also fully aware of his position and power. Conversations with him are monologues, be they about his business, children's computers, the ice age, baseball, politics (domestic or international), or people. He pushes his views, on whatever subject, individually; any collective pursuit with him amounts to agreeing with his points of view, interests, and ambitions. With time, he has become more of a philanthropist than before, but he micromanages every detail of his various foundations' work. His only truly collective activity is his family. His children have taken over a semblance of day-to-day management of each one of his businesses, but he watches over them closely. Despite his enormous power in Mexico, and many parts of Latin America, where he owns the biggest or next-to-largest phone company in each country, he speaks, acts, and deals individually. Even in the midst of political or economic crises in nations where he enjoys immense sway, he prefers to work by himself: a lone wolf, in the great Mexican tradition. He is in no sense a postmodern Mexican, who places his impressive talents and power at the service of any type of collective action. The only possible and not exactly redeeming exception is a group of Latin American billionaires he convenes once a year in various settings across the hemisphere, together with their offspring, so the next generation can socialize and learn the tricks of the trade and prepare to carry the torch. Carlos Slim, regardless of his infinite wealth, power, and social capital, is as individualistic as the athletes, artists, politicians, and everyday Mexicans described in previous pages. While certainly not a robber baron in the American definition of the term, he is a product of the Mexican "system." Although he has fared well in Latin America, where the protection often granted monopolistic enterprises is similar to Mexico's, his ventures into the United States have been less successful.

## Housing the Family and Clinging to the Land

Perhaps another impressionistic example of this individualism lies in the picture of Mexico City from the air, in contrast with, say, Buenos Aires or São Paulo, two cities of roughly similar dimensions. All three sprawl and still have room to grow. But only the Argentinean and Brazilian metropoli feature countless residential—middle-class or even humble—high-rises. Many of them date back to the 1940s and 1950s, but a good number are more recent or even new. The view from the sky is that: apartment buildings reaching as far as the eye can see, housing hundreds of thousands of *porteños* or *paulistanos*. This is also the case in Havana, Caracas, and Rio de Janeiro, though these cities have much less room to expand. In the case of Buenos Aires and São Paulo, the European immigrant history may be part of the explanation; not so for Rio, Havana, or Caracas.

Mexico City is another story. Perhaps because it grew later, and on the basis of rural migration, not foreign immigration, it stretches out endlessly, largely because there are no high-rises (with recent exceptions in the northwestern outskirts, where the rich have begun to move in search of gated communities). It is a horizontal city, where its teeming millions live in one- or two-story homes, luxurious for a tiny few, modest or frankly decrepit for the vast majority, but in all cases highlighting the absence of apartment blocks. It is also a city where, even in midlevel individual buildings, the very notion of sharing a street front with a convenience store, a laundromat, a repair shop, or a diner is anathema. Similarly, every house is a decorative or architectural castle unto itself. There are no zoning or construction regulations regarding styles, heights, and so forth. Mexico City is a colorful and chaotic architectural piñata.

The first reason for this is the available space on the Mexican highlands, or altiplano. This is a high-risk seismic zone that has traditionally discouraged high-rises (although the city's, and until recently Latin America's, tallest skyscraper, the Torre Latinomericana, built in the early fifties, has survived at least five earthquakes, two of them devastating for the rest of the city). Further, with land until now relatively cheap, one- or two-story structures have been much more economical to build than twenty-story apartment buildings. Finally, as a matter of policy as well as because of frequent land tenure disputes, municipal property taxes have remained absurdly low. Mexico City is much older than São Paulo or Buenos Aires, and when vertical construction began in the late nineteenth century, the country's capital had already acquired much of its physiognomy.

There was a time when Mexico's urban planners or appointed mayors (the city only elected its first municipal executive in 1997) favored housing projects similar to those built in Chicago or Queens, New York, or those of the HLMs (Habitations à Loyer Modéré) in Paris or Madrid. At the time, they preferred these to American-style Levittowns. Officials tried to convince the capital's inhabitants that this was the most appropriate form of low- to lower-middle-income housing. Several *multifamiliares* were built in the city (some of these actually did collapse in the 1985 earthquake), but they never took. The people, particularly those recently arrived from the countryside during Mexico's gargantuan rural exodus of those mid-century decades, shunned them.* The old, landed aristocracy, transformed by the Revolution into a more modern, urban, industrial, or financial bourgeoisie, preferred mansions, not Fifth Avenue or Avenue Foch apartments. The emerging middle classes sought to emulate them, even in their proverbial racism: whites and *mestizos* live alone, thank you, not all bunched together.

An individually owned abode was a symbol of "real" property, unique and indivisible, a mark of social and economic ascent. The few projects quickly deteriorated, for many of the same reasons they did elsewhere, perhaps more acutely in Mexico because of the country's more acute traits in this regard. These were the absence of any civic culture or of "full-fledged citizens," as opposed to mere "individuals," or of what Mexicans call "*corporaciones,*" that is, more or less organized groups of employees, peasants, and workers instead of horizontally associated citizens. Resentment against the government, the powerful,

---

* And when they didn't, they reached extremes of individualism that defy the imagination: in a project known as Lomas de Plateros in the Mixcoac neighborhood of Mexico City, families would build metal cages in their parking spaces to make sure no one else would use them or even walk through them.

and the rich was always current, yet it translated not into political participation or collective action but into a form of aspiring middle-class retrenchment involving the primacy of individual possession and use: my house, my car. The neighbor was an enemy, to be placed at a distance as quickly and as radically as possible. At the same time, sporadic, though strong, urban movements (squatters, for municipal services, and so on) sprang up here and there, as in other large Third World cities. In part this explains the persistence of many popular "slum" neighborhoods, poor but well organized and tightly knit, one of the few exceptions to Mexican individualism, in part explainable by the strength of the Mexican extended family.

One explanation for this propensity for individual housing lies in the fact that the Mexican government, unlike those of Western Europe or Argentina after World War II, did not provide sufficient public housing of any sort. The scant dwellings that were built reached stratospheric prices and were rapidly devoured by the middle class. Squatting on land and building a tin-roofed hut, followed by campaigns for urban services and steady home self-improvements, consolidated this trend. In addition, until the 1950s, more than 75% of all housing in Mexico City was rented; but rent control and decay did away with much of the supply, and new construction was not for rent—thus the scarcity of apartment buildings.[22] For all these reasons, the supply of vertical low-income housing was minuscule, but there were also other motives of a deeper nature.

The Mexicans arriving from the countryside during the first half of the twentieth century initially settled in the famed *vecindades*, or horizontal tenements, where dozens of families lived in cramped quarters, with some common space in between, but where a peculiar characteristic of Mexico's individualism began to show its face—an endearing, close-knit, but ultimately archaic face that could not last. The Casa Blanca, where the Children of Sánchez, the subjects of Oscar Lewis's classic anthropological work, actually lived in downtown Mexico City, was not a collective housing project, or a community shared by occupants from multiple origins and walks of life. It was a family affair. Its 250 tenants sprang from four families, which perhaps explains the title of one of Lewis's other great works, *Five Families*. I remember the *vecindad* in the *barrio* of Actipan, an up-and-coming neighborhood of the Colonia del Valle, where my parents first moved in 1959 (the streets were unpaved, though we were located less than a hundred yards from one of the capital's two main thoroughfares, Insurgentes). In 1965, when we returned from an absence during which my father was posted abroad in a Foreign Service job, I befriended the very modest-living kids across the street, who all shared a single tenement. They came from three nuclear families, which in turn belonged to a single extended family, the three Sánchez brothers, with their respective wives and children—all told, perhaps fifteen individuals, residing in three "houses" of two rooms each. Forty-five years later, many of these children and grandchildren of the Sánchez brothers endure there, and every March, on the day of St. Thomas, the patron saint of the neighborhood, we get together to remember old times. But they still live in houses; not one of them that I know of has ever moved to an apartment.

There are many reasons for this rejection of housing patterns that thrived elsewhere, in rich and poor countries alike. One has to do with a well-studied Mexican penchant for a patrimonial attitude toward life and property: a house is mine, an apartment isn't, really. Another implies the possibility of expanding the nuclear family to the extended one. This can be accomplished in a tenement, but not easily in a project high-rise. A further reason, which reinforces the ideas previously sketched out in these pages, is the irredeemable nature of Mexican individualism. The people of the country do not like to share common spaces with others, which is exactly what an apartment building, high- or low-income, entails. They refuse to use the same elevator or stairwell, the same garbage chute or trash cans, the same front door or doorman, the same parking lot or garage, the same lawns or security arrangements. The rich and the poor, in this sense, possess a common approach to the collective imaginary. They prefer to be alone than to share anything with the "other."

This is well reflected in surveys on values in Mexico and elsewhere, where "mistrust of others" is quantified and compared with other countries. In 2003, only 10% of all Mexicans stated "one can trust most people," a decline from a high of 33% in 1990. This was not only much lower than in the United States—a highly individualistic country—where trust had fallen from a peak of more than 50% in the 1960s and 1970s to a low of 30% in the 1990s, but more importantly, well below any subsector of North American society, including Mexican-Americans, whose "interpersonal trust" level was double that of Mexicans in Mexico in 2003. Out of eighty-one countries studied in the World Values Survey, Mexico was number fifty-four, but this was with numbers from the 2000 poll. If one uses the 2003 statistics, Mexico found itself at the very bottom of the list, along with Brazil.[23]

The trend toward horizontal housing has persisted and grown more acute in recent years, even in the course of the new middle-class housing boom—the most spectacular Mexico has known—that began in the late 1990s and lasted through 2008. Over the last fifteen years, more than 5 million families obtained access to low-cost, new, and acceptable-quality abodes. Here are the numbers provided by the government. Out of a total of roughly 1 million homes delivered between 2004 and 2008, 800,000, or 97%, included one or two dwellings per plot, whereas only 32,000, or 3%, were vertical, multifamily homes, or in plain English, apartment buildings or "projects."[24] While the price per square foot was roughly the same, the cost of building high-rise housing, even where land and municipal taxes are modest, is much lower than home by home (which takes up much more space and thus more square feet), particularly in metropolitan areas and given the often shoddy nature of construction. What the ratio reveals is the ongoing manifestation of the persistent preference for individual dwellings, even by young couples born more than half a century after the moment when the initial families of the emerging Mexican middle class started enjoying access to proper housing in the 1940s.

Before moving on to the most emblematic illustration of this individualism—the Mexican peasant's ancestral, unconditional, perpetual, and passionate attachment to the tiny parcel of barren land he tills—the description of an initial constraint on this radical cult of the individual is in order. Indeed, this individualism faces multiple restrictions; it is not infinite. A first limitation involves its subject, which is not only the individual in the strict sense of the word, but often—almost always—the nuclear and, subsequently, the extended family. This is the core unit of Mexican individualism; it is an individualism of the family.* Within limits, of course: there are 7 million families or households that are headed by single mothers—25.2% of the total—so it's not that

---

* According to a long study carried out by MetLife in Mexico regarding the "Mexican dream," based on very detailed polling, " 'collective' in Mexico means sharing dreams and success among the members of the family." Deborah Holtz and Juan Carlos Mena, eds., *El sueño mexicano* (Mexico City: Trilce Ediciones, 2009), p. 176.

Mexicans are truly more attached to the traditional definition of the family than others.[25] Thus the typical, most frequently found family is, as elsewhere, the classic stereotype: a father, a mother, 2.1 children, a dog, and the Mexican equivalent of a white picket fence. Or, like Rita Macedo's in Luis Buñuel's *Los Olvidados* of 1950: a mother, two kids, and an intermittently present/absent stepfather who beats up and rapes the mother and/or the daughters. But whatever that family is—single mother–led or extended to several siblings or generations—it is the nucleus of the individualist traits described so far.

It is the family that works together in the informal economy, that eventually emigrates together, when it does; that hangs on to communal land tenure rights; that opens up a taco stand or a small diner, a repair shop, or a used clothing resale operation; that remains in the same city, neighborhood, and house or tenement forever; that obtains housing, health, pension, and other social security entitlements. This family-rooted individualism explains—as in a few other nations—why remittances from abroad are so high. The Mexican migrant travels abroad, and either returns to his family for half the year (at least until the mid-1990s, when the circular migratory movement between the United States and Mexico was interrupted), or fetches its members from Mexico, or saves at astounding rates in order to send money back home. Individualism of this sort is sturdier than a lonely, single-person obsession, but it is also condemned to fade and subsequently disappear, as it confronts the onslaught of modernity, in its positive and negative aspects. That family nucleus is breaking apart, as geographical and international mobility takes hold, as more and more women enter the workforce (nearly 40% of the laboring population are women today), and as individual solutions to collective problems become more difficult to explore and share with the rest of a family that continues to be, on occasion, quite extensive (although the average Mexican nuclear family numbers fewer than 4.1 individuals today).[26]

The same holds true for the most traditional expression of Mexican individualism, common to many countries, but longer-lasting and more stubborn in Mexico. The Mexican peasant's passionate attachment to the land, to barren, inaccessible, almost useless land, in a land tenure system that prizes collective property but guarantees individual use and possession, that keeps people on the land far longer than elsewhere, is proverbial. But it has not been sufficiently stressed as a manifestation of that ferocious individualism alluded to here. In Mexico today, agriculture generates approximately 4% of the nation's Gross Domestic Product, a figure that corresponds to that of other societies of an equivalent GDP per capita: Brazil, Chile, Uruguay, Venezuela.[27] But nearly 13% of all working Mexicans still live off the land—a number almost twice as high as the average of the above-mentioned countries, with the exception of Brazil, today one of the world's largest food-producing powerhouses.[28] In other words, agriculture in Mexico contributes more or less what it should to the economy, but Mexicans working on farms are many more than they should be. It is true that a large number of former occupants of rural Mexico no longer inhabit the countryside because they immigrated to the United States. But since in the absence of this safety valve some of them would have remained on the land, evidently something ties the Mexican peasantry to the land in ways that are not present in other societies, with similar income, education, and overall levels of development.

There are many explanations for this, of course, and they cannot all be boiled down to the extreme individualism of life in the Mexican *campo*. The Revolution, as well as some of the governments that sprang from it, gave land away massively to the peasantry: some good, some that was subsequently irrigated, and a lot that was lousy. But land it was, and it certainly facilitated retaining the peasants in the rural areas. Much of it was *ejido* land, subject to a peculiar, traditional, indigenous legal regime that bestowed inalienable *ownership* rights to the village community, and inalienable cultivation or *usage* rights to individual *ejidatarios*. However, until 1992 neither individuals nor the community could sell it. Moreover, the total land area allotted to each community was fixed, but the number of title holders of usage rights grew, along with the population, so that through inheritance and demographics, parcels became smaller and smaller. Even in recent years, the average size of each *ejido*, despite the rural exodus to the cities and the United States, has shrunk from 9 hectares in 1992 to 8.1 in 2001 to 7.5 hectares in 2007.[29] Plots in Mexico are getting tinier, as the remaining peasants cling to them desperately.

This system made for highly inefficient, labor-intensive, and uncompetitive agriculture on rain-fed land (in contrast to privately owned, capital-intensive, and efficient so-called small-property irrigated plots), but the setup helped slow Mexico's rural exodus. In Mexico it was much more difficult to expel peasants from the land than elsewhere, be it among the British yeomanry of centuries ago, or rural inhabitants in many other Latin American countries. In Mexico, those who stayed on the land suffered deprivation and oppression, but they spared their countrymen in the cities the overwhelming weight and distress produced by their flooding the urban areas.

Another explanation for these differences lies in colonial history. Along with Peru (which under Spain included Bolivia), Ecuador, and Guatemala, Mexico possessed a sizable, sedentary, hierarchical civilization, which was decimated but not totally annihilated by the Conquest. There was a settled, structured peasantry in Mexico before the Spanish arrived, and after much trial and error, as well as mass murder, collective suicide, and even attempts at slavery, the conquerors finally devised a system that provided both a labor force for agriculture and mining, as well as a means of subsistence for the peasantry that accepted, albeit under conditions of great coercive duress, indentured peonage. The *hacienda* system saved New Spain, as François Chevalier, in his classic *La Formation des grands domaines au Méxique,* demonstrated more than half a century ago, since it bound peasants to the land, but also cajoled them into working for the *hacendado*.[30]

This was a passable solution for everybody—the proof was in its lasting functionality—and it reinforced the previous attachment to the land. When the loans against wages from the company store proved insufficient (almost always), the peasants still had access to the land to grow their own food and maintain their frugal existence. Over time it became a salvation that everyone respected, approved, and even celebrated. Today 5.5 million plots survive, supporting more than 20 million inhabitants. The corollary is that 23.5% percent of Mexico's people live in communities of less than 2,500; that there are 500 counties (of a total of 2,500) just in the state of Oaxaca, together with Chiapas, the state with the highest percentage of indigenous people; and that not infrequently, the central government is forced to lay power lines as well as water pipes, and build schools, access roads, and health clinics for villages of not more than 50 townspeople.[31] In fairness to the national peasantry, in view of the universal distrust of government and its institutions, the possession of a plot of land is the ultimate defense or fallback in a predatory world.

This odd manifestation of rugged individualism—often nearly always self-sacrificial and self-destructive—also explains urban Mexico's cult of the peasantry and the land. Whenever a government in Mexico City takes on the peasantry and absorbs its land—to build a dam, an airport, a highway—or allows the formation of large estates and agroindustrial complexes, it runs into the brick wall not only of peasant resistance, but of an innate, intangible, and perhaps essentially nostalgic sympathy for the country dwellers' plight on the part of many city folks, in a fashion not unlike the French nostalgia and worship of the *terroir*. When in 2002 President Vicente Fox attempted to expropriate land on the outskirts of Mexico City to construct a new airport, he was defeated in his endeavor not only by fierce local resistance and his own indecision and mismanagement, but also support for the "peasants' " cause (they were actually university students and urban street vendors), and outrage over the apparently pitiful compensation Fox offered. Polls showed strong backing for the "valiant rural struggle," though it wasn't really a struggle, nor rural, nor valiant. Nevertheless 75% of all Mexicans thought that their government should let the "*campesinos*" demonstrate with their machetes in hand; three-quarters agreed with the cancellation of the airport project once it was clear the peasants opposed it, half of the opponents justified the suspension because that way the peasants were not affected, and two-thirds were convinced that the peasants were simply protecting their right to the land.[32] We could conclude that the Mexican peasantry acts collectively only when it seeks to conserve the past and bar the route to the future.

Mexican individualism and individual ties to the land (as well as the sympathy for the victim or underdog, about which more later) overpowered any rational sentiments on the part of those who would benefit most from the new airport: the urban, lower-middle-class inhabitants of Mexico City. This was not a new reaction. To the question of "What makes you feel most angry or indignant—a peasant exploited, a *peón* humiliated by his boss, an indifferent bureaucrat, a defenseless industrial worker, a polluting truck, an elderly beggar, a child shoe polisher, an arrogant bodyguard?"—all everyday examples of Mexican life—by far the two most mentioned outrages, in 1987 and 1995, were the peasant and the *peón*, together slightly more than 30%. Mexicans are as attached to the peasantry as the latter is to the land.[33]

Another example of this individualism lies in one of the most recent—and in many ways the most important—legal battles waged in Mexico with the purpose of reforming the legal code. Until 2010, there was no such thing as a class action suit in Mexican law; only individuals could file suit, and the premier instrument of protection in the face of abuses by the state against a citizen—the *amparo* (loosely translated as a writ of habeas corpus)—is by definition exclusively accessible and granted to individuals. In an effort to correct this anachronistic and absurd state of affairs, a group of legislators and legal experts attempted, in 2008, to reform both the Constitution and the criminal code. They justified their effort by arguing that the collective defense of rights and interests was far more advanced in other Latin American countries—such as Colombia, Brazil, Costa Rica, Uruguay, and Chile—not to mention the United States or Spain, than in Mexico, and that Mexican law emphasized the protection of individual rights over collective ones. What was especially noteworthy in this episode was that the main advocates of these changes were left-wing members of Congress and activists, who explicitly contrasted Mexican individualism with . . . U.S. protection of collective rights and interests. The supporters of these reforms claimed, correctly, that collective or class action rights were limited to consumer affairs and that, in fact, even in that highly restricted domain, during all the years of existence of the Consumer Affairs Prosecutor's Office, not a single lawsuit had been filed. They concluded, in their brief justifying the legal modifications they were seeking, that "the transformation of modern Mexican society into a mass society . . . has given birth to collective interests, of a group [class] or diffuse nature, that must be protected and regulated."[34] As a legal scholar put it, "The transformation of contemporary society into a mass society and of the liberal State into a social welfare State . . . [implies] a marked trend in comparative law toward the recognition of collective rights, through procedures such as the German *Massenverfahien*, the U.S. class action suit, the British relator action, and collective and diffuse actions in Brazil, Colombia and Spain. . . . Mexico experiences a notorious lag in the regulation of collective action procedures."[35] Perhaps the best proof of Mexico's obsessive individualism and its resistance to any change in this field lay in the tardiness of this reform effort. The constitutional amendments were ratified in mid-2010, but the implementing legislation was still pending in 2011.

### Marcos: A Postmodern Mexican?

Then there is possibly the most revealing example of all, the most relevant anecdote, the most telling drama and frustration. The Zapatista indigenous revolt in Chiapas, launched and aborted on January 1, 1994, could have become Mexico's signature, post-individualist political, social, and cultural experiment. Because it was based in the indigenous communities of the Chiapas highlands; because the religious component was both decisive and collective; because there seemed to be a conscious effort to diminish the role of the individual leader as a traditional Mexican hero (Marcos, the head of the insurrection, was known as a "subcommander" and permanently wore his famed ski mask or balaclava so as to remain faceless); and finally because of the unavoidable anonymity of the Indian faces and garbs millions of Mexicans and worldwide TV viewers awoke to on New Year's Day 1994, it seemed that herein lay the country's long-awaited entry into post-traditionalist, post-individualist life.

Alas, it was not to be. Marcos, the "*subcomandante*" of the erstwhile and largely fictitious insurrection, became a new version of the traditional Mexican hero: a politically correct rock star. He appeared on every TV show, flattered and infatuated every foreign correspondent and fellow traveler, and captured the imagination of thousands of Mexicans and tens of thousands of Europeans. He came to personify, more than ever before, a social fighter in a Mexico that, through the widespread identification of the struggle with its leader, remained perhaps more anachronistically individualist than ever before. Whether Marcos and his comrades sincerely tried to de-individualize the Chiapas rebellion and simply failed, or whether he was unable to resist the temptation to become an international celebrity is irrelevant from this perspective. The combination of worldwide stage lights, Mexico's persistent, congenital, individualist "chip," and his own predilection for glamour resulted in another typically Mexican complete identification of a movement with its *jefe*. Marcos was not "postmodern," revolutionary, or different, despite his talent for the coup de théâtre or the brilliant quip or stylish pose (always smoking a pipe through his disguise). He became, and probably was always destined to be, another failed and fallen Mexican idol, who wasted away his considerable political capital and talent, as he waded into the endless, esoteric, antiglobalization, "Another World Is Possible" discussions in the intellectual and student neighborhoods of southern Mexico City.

This was an unfortunate and paradoxical outcome. The Chiapas indigenous peoples' demands for autonomy and respect for their customs centered on terribly undemocratic, premodern, but nonetheless *collective* customs: public, group voting; habits and usages that included forms of subjugation of women not even the most rabid defenders of indigenous peoples could accept; so-called third-generation human rights purporting to defend collective aspirations and demands. With all its contradictions and confusion, the Zapatista movement in Chiapas could have represented a break with Mexico's individualistic past; it didn't. Marcos became much more than a charismatic chieftain. He transformed the movement he created into an archetypical, individualistic adventure whereby the fate of the person became indistinguishable from that of the movement. When he faded away into the sunset of the old-school Mexican, Latin American, and European radical left, his movement and the indigenous peoples of *los altos de Chiapas* did too.

It is not difficult to deduce from all of this that Mexicans today still are imbued with—and dominated by—a premodern individualism that is firmly rooted in the past. It reflects the real narrative of the nation, the traditions derived from the need to survive a conquest, colonization, a first century of independent chaos and violence, and a second century of relentless and ruthless social and economic change. That individualism manifests itself today in an almost categorical rejection of any form of collective endeavor, in a perpetual search for individual solutions for community problems and individual exits from collective dead ends, and, on the other side of the coin, in an endless and extraordinary source of creativity, tenderness, and simple good taste and manners. The poorest Mexican is a paragon of refinement, hospitality, and a full-fledged expression of the senses. He or she could not be this way in the absence of the extreme individualism we have described. It has virtues, such as leading many Mexico City inhabitants, for example, to accept abortion, gay marriage, and even drug legalization in the name of individual rights, in contrast to the rest of the country, but that's about it.

The limits are the family; the roots are the land; the adjustment to contemporary reality, impossible. This individualism has been hailed and lamented by novelists, decried and glorified by sociologists and planners, extolled by pundits and songwriters. It constitutes the bulwark of the country's defense of its identity, and simultaneously one of the main obstacles to its progress and modernity. For the country where that individualism still thrives today is no longer the nation of Zapata and Francisco Villa, of Paz and Fuentes, of Barragán and Orozco. It is far removed from the society hailed and depicted by Eisenstein and Reed, extolled by the muralists and Malcolm Lowry, glorified by the anthropologists and *zapa-tourists* visiting the insurgent villages in Chiapas. To the contrary, today's Mexico is rolling inexorably, and often recklessly, into a twenty-first century where the main traits of its national character, as described by the classics and the numbers, are radically dysfunctional. The individualism we have rapidly portrayed and criticized is just one of the multiple traits, though perhaps the most important one, that has become no longer just an obstacle, but an insurmountable hurdle to the country's progress, as well as the heart of its past glory and unending fascination for the foreign regard.

CHAPTER 2

# At Last: A Mexican Middle Class

Late in 2008, just before the financial crisis hit the world and Mexico, an intolerably large share of the country's population remained mired in poverty. Although extreme poverty (people living on less than one dollar per day) and plain-vanilla poverty (people living below two dollars per day) had dropped sharply over the previous decade, both persisted at unacceptably high levels. Between 1992 and 2008 extreme or so-called nutritional poverty (not enough to eat) fell from 21.4% to 18.2% of the total population; the broader category, also labeled in Mexico as patrimonial poverty (not enough to satisfy needs beyond food and shelter), dropped from 53.1% to 47.4%. More than 47 million people were still poor, and some 11.2 million lived in utter destitution.[1] Moreover, Mexico continued to be one of the most unequal countries in the most unequal region of the world. The concentration of wealth, income, and opportunities is enormous, and the gap between rich and poor is immense and has been denounced by national and foreign observers for at least two centuries now. But what these shameful figures hid was the number of Mexicans no longer sunk in poverty, that is, those who for one reason or another had emerged from below the poverty line, and changed into something else.* The something else was the new Mexican version of the traditional, North American middle class.†

---

* These numbers were worse than many in Latin America, but better than others. In the 2009 United Nations Human Development Index, Mexico ranked 53: higher than Brazil, lower than Chile, Uruguay, and others.

† Inequality in Latin America, surprisingly, has been declining since the year 2000. According to a 2010 study by Luis F. López-Calva and Nora Lustig, "of the seventeen countries for which comparable data are available, twelve experienced a decline in their

Mexico today has become finally a middle-class society. It is not definitively nor categorically one, having barely passed the bar where paradise begins, and being still highly vulnerable to a relapse, especially with the crisis of 2009. The nearly 7% contraction of the economy that year, plus a series of statistical quirks, led to a regression toward poverty of nearly 4 million people; the 2010 economic recovery, with growth of almost 5% and a slight improvement in income, implies that the situation in late 2010 was in all likelihood the same as just before the economic downturn. With the bursts of middle-class expansion between 1940 and 1982, then again from 1989 to 1994, and chiefly from 1996 to 2008, the country has reached the stage where a majority—albeit a slender one—of the population now matches virtually any definition of the term. At least since Independence, this is undoubtedly Mexico's greatest achievement to date, and if it lasts, one that will irreversibly transform the country. Over the course of three administrations—those of Ernesto Zedillo, Vicente Fox, and Felipe Calderón—Mexico has been transformed. The challenge for the nation rests in pursuing its economic growth and consequent expansion of the middle class, when the values, traits, and traditions of that middle class, particularly of its most recent members, retain their incompatibility with the modern world.*

## *What Is an Old Middle Class?*

There are multiple definitions of what a middle class is and is not, as well as of what constitutes a middle-class *society*. This is neither the time nor the place to explore this too deeply, other than to show that

Gini coefficient" (the Gini coefficient is the most widely used indicator of inequality). "In particular, inequality declined in the four countries analyzed here, beginning in 1994 in Mexico, 1997 in Brazil, 1992 in Peru and 2002 in Argentina. Income inequality . . . fell by 5.9% in Mexico, 5.4% in Argentina, 5% in Peru and 4.8% in Brazil." Luis F. López-Calva and Nora Lustig, *Declining Inequality in Latin America,* (New York and Washington, D.C.: United Nations Development Programme and Brooking Institution Press, 2010) p. 1 and 10.

* An example of the growing awareness of this fact can be found partly in essays, books and discussions about the issue in Mexico. See the May 2010 issue of the magazine *Nexos,* with a cover dossier titled "Clase medieros: una mayoría silenciosa"; the book *Clase mediero: Pobres no más, desarrollados aún no* by Luis de la Calle and Luis Rubio (Mexico City: CIDAC, 2010); the MetLife coffee table book *El sueño mexicano,* Deborah Holtz and Juan Carlos Mena, eds. (Mexico City: Trilce Ediciones, 2009); OECD, *Latin American Economic Outlook 2011. How Middle-Class Is Latin America?* (Paris, 2010).

whatever meaning one attributes to the term, Mexico today fits the bill. Indeed, it is worth noting that the diversity of definitions of the concept makes the country's access to this status all the more remarkable.

One old-fashioned way of approaching the middle-class conundrum is by occupation. From this perspective, the middle-class comprises people with certain types of jobs, which in Mexico excludes industrial workers and manual laborers, but incorporates independent professionals, public or private sector employees, teachers, administrative clerks, and small business owners, whose income is at least 50% above the national median. By this definition, roughly one-quarter of all Mexicans belong to the middle class. But by leaving out what used to be referred to as the industrial proletariat, in addition to other sectors, we overlook what forms the great bulk of the middle class in richer countries: the millions of industrial workers who at the end of the nineteenth century, and through most of the twentieth century, gradually achieved a living standard traditionally associated with the middle class.

The only advantage this occupational meaning possesses lies in its comparative value over time. This is the significance assigned to the term by the two earliest studies of the Mexican middle class, one by José Iturriaga in 1951, another by U.S. economist Howard Cline in 1961. Comparing their figures over the past half century, one can easily detect the rapid evolution of Mexican society. Iturriaga calculated that between 1895 and 1940, the Mexican "upper class" shrank, from 1.4% to 1.0% of the total; the lower class did the same, from 91% to 83% of all Mexicans; and the middle class doubled, growing from 8% of the total to 16%.[2] None of these numbers are especially well anchored in national accounts, nor are they fully reliable; they just happen to be the only ones available. According to Cline, who used an alternative methodology that included consumption, income, occupation, and language, the middle class continued to expand from 1940 through 1960, moving from 12.6% to 30%; the lower class fell from 84% to 65%; and the upper class decreased in size from 2.9% to 2.3%. American economic historians James Wilkie and Paul Wilkins, using a similar classification to Cline's, reached somewhat different conclusions, but detected the same trend for the 1960–70 period: the middle class increased from 22% to 29%.* Finally, Enrique Alduncín, a pollster who

---

* The lower class continued to shrink, from 74% to 65%.

generated the Values of Mexicans series we have already cited, estimated with other, comparable criteria, that between 1970 and 1987 the middle class jumped from 29% to 36% of the total Mexican population, whereas the lower class kept declining.[3]* In other words, by several definitions, in 1987, five years after the Mexican forty-year so-called economic miracle had come to an end, one-third of the population was middle class, two-thirds were not. This corresponded roughly to a typical, advanced "Third World" or developing country status, halfway between the poor countries of Africa and Asia and the industrialized nations of North America, Western Europe, and Japan. These figures will appear all the more remarkable when we analyze the current situation.

## Bogart's Tampico

The main reason why the definition that omits the industrial working class seems inadequate lies in its forsaking one of the oldest, perhaps most anachronistic, but still vibrant parts of the Mexican middle class: the public sector, protected, industrial, salaried workers who in Europe years ago might have been labeled a "labor aristocracy." This is the story, for example, of Ciudad Madero, in Mexico's northeastern state of Tamaulipas, just outside the steamy, seedy port of Tampico, from where Humphrey Bogart set forth to unearth the treasure of the Sierra Madre. The town was founded in 1924, when it split off from Tampico, already housing an oil refinery and several installations belonging to the then American-owned Compañía Petrolera El Águila and Pierce Oil Company; it received its current name in 1930. The old refineries and petrochemical centers were turned over to Petróleos Mexicanos, or PEMEX, the national oil company, in 1938, when El Águila and other foreign oil companies—essentially British and Dutch—were nationalized by President Lázaro Cárdenas.[4] Ciudad Madero is the epitome of a "company town."

Madero is the home of Local #1, the largest and strongest local in the National Oil Workers Union, itself the most powerful union in the country, together with the teachers guild. Madero is also the birthplace and retirement home of the legendary and fearsome former leader of

---

* The lower class kept falling, from 65% to 60%.

the union, Joaquín Hernández Galicia, also known as La Quina. Local #1 includes the four thousand workers who toil at the refinery, the main supplier of refined products for the entire Gulf of Mexico region.[5]* Through the sixties, seventies, and eighties, La Quina, for his part, became the symbol of the brutality and corruption of the labor movement, but also of the enormous social and economic progress its associates had achieved over the years.

Madero is a middle-class city of roughly 200,000 inhabitants.[6] Homes are individual, small but neat and well spaced, with a driveway, and at least one car parked in it. Practically every house has a dish antenna, a small garden in front, and, of course, all of the accoutrements of middle-class life: fridge, telephone, washing machine, microwave, bikes for the kids. These all go to school—elementary and middle school in Madero, high school and college in nearby Tampico, where a Jesuit institution educated a young man thirty years ago who then went by the name of Rafael Sebastián Guillén Vicente, and later became known to the world as Subcomandante Marcos, our man from the previous chapter. The public schools are unremarkable, though better than in other parts of the country, but the private upper-grade schools in the greater metropolitan area, made up of Madero, Tampico, and Altamira, are quite good. The overall number of years in school is ten and a half, nearly three years more than the national average (the U.S. national average is 11.5 years); there are approximately fifty thousand youngsters enrolled in school, from kindergarten to college: one out of every four inhabitants. In Madero, there are 110 nursery schools, 84 elementary schools, 33 middle schools, and 21 high schools of one type or another.[7]

The oil workers union has its own health care system, separate from the national Mexican Social Security Institute, for private sector workers, and the ISSSTE, for public sector employees, including teachers. Its hospitals, clinics, doctors, and nurses tend to be far superior to those of the other regimes, and union members pride themselves on the quality of the health care they receive. More than two-thirds of the city dwellers are entitled to public health care, slightly less than half of whom are covered by the oil workers' insurance. There are a bit more than fifty thousand homes in the town, of which 80% are privately

* The refinery processes 170,000 barrels per day.

owned;* the average number of dwellers per home is four; one in every three homes possesses a PC.[8] All of these exceptional benefits and standard of living are, as in company towns all over the world, hereditary. When a worker retires at any age between fifty-five and sixty-five, with a proper though not extravagant pension, his or her son or daughter inherits the job vacancy, and so it goes over the years.

The union takes care of its own, but nobody should even think of messing with the local or national leadership. Under La Quina, and even since his illegal imprisonment in 1989, it makes the Teamsters under Jimmy (not James) Hoffa look like a children's choir: opponents, dissidents, rivals and even simple misfits are beaten up by union thugs, jailed by the government, or eliminated by *sicarios* or paid assassins. La Quina's turn to be framed and thrown in jail for more than a decade came in 1989 when the recently installed administration of Carlos Salinas de Gortari wanted to consolidate its power through a spectacular gesture. He accepted his fate stoically, and his colleagues in the union leadership, as well as the rank and file, all resigned themselves to the loss of their leader. After all, they were not losing their perks, just their boss. The leadership today, two decades later, is less brutal, but just as corrupt.

The exclusion of towns like Madero from the above-cited definition of the middle class is one reason why the country's pollsters and market research experts reject that definition. They have adopted a series of guidelines, drawn up and laid out by the Asociación Mexicana de Agencias de Investigación de Mercado y Opinión Pública (Mexican Association of Market and Public Opinion Research Agencies) or AMAI, to determine standards for constructing polling samples. They established a battery of ten questions posed by their field surveyors, used to define six socioeconomic levels. The questions all have to do either with living standards or educational experience; none have to do with income, occupation, aspirations, or self-definitions. Pollsters and market researchers, in Mexico as elsewhere, distrust answers regarding income and occupation. Most people everywhere prefer to massage the truth, or simply lie about their revenue, for tax reasons and other equally noble and valid motives. The queries include number of rooms, bathrooms,

* And around 97% of the homes have the services mentioned above: drinking water, sewage, electricity, and TV sets.

showerheads, and lightbulbs in each dwelling visited by the pollster; they inquire into the type of floor the house has; the number of years of schooling the head of household claims; and, finally, how many (if any) TVs and DVDs, PCs, water heaters, toaster-ovens, vacuum cleaners, washing machines, microwave ovens, and automobiles the home features, and whether it has a stove. Although AMAI has updated some of its standards, adding some questions and deleting others, its methodology on occasion seems imperfect, or too dependent on rating firms.

A certain number of points are assigned to each question, and the total points scored are divided among six economic and social levels, ranging from A/B (the highest) to C+, C, D+, D, and E (the lowest). Most experts consider A/B to include upper-class citizens; C+ and C, middle-middle-class Mexicans; D+ to be lower-middle-class Mexicans; D those who are poor; and E those who find themselves in extreme poverty. The national averages for these numbers (which mask profound regional differences) are 3.8% for A/B, 10.5% for C+, 15% for C, 30% for D+, 20.3% for D, and 19.6% for E.[9] By this reckoning, approximately 60% of all Mexicans belong to segments of the population ranging from lower middle class to affluent, 20% are poor, and another 20% are destitute. As we shall see, these numbers, used by people who actually have to measure things—voting intentions, market size and share, audiences and advertising budgets—are very similar to those arrived at by other calculations, or by political grandstanding and barnstorming. It is through these measurements that we will find the new Mexican middle class.

The inhabitants of Ciudad Madero do not constitute, by any stretch of the imagination, this new Mexican middle class. They hark back to the so-called golden era of the country's development, between 1940 and 1982, when the economy grew at 6% per year, though the population also grew by more than 3%: an era during which import-substitution industrialization, or ISI, as it was known in the jargon of the time, fueled an initial burst of middle-class growth. The oil and electricity state-owned monopolies, the automobile industry, mining and consumer durables that began to be manufactured in Mexico (as well as elsewhere in Latin America), and the new factories, steel mills, refineries, power plants, dams, highways, and bank offices all employed low-wage labor that nonetheless granted its providers a series of fringe benefits and perks that even back then guaranteed a standard of living way above that of their parents. They also insured the survival of the political system. The cost to the country was enormous, since jobs in the protected industrial sector, in the state-owned area of the economy, or in the service industry created to cater to this emerging middle class were expensive, subsidized, and few in number, in relation to the overall exploding population. The social safety net they enjoyed—health care, pensions, nurseries—as precarious as it was, represented a positive trade-off for them, and a pernicious one for the immense informal sector of the economy and society that had nothing: no health insurance, no labor rights, no pension, no collective contracts, no access to public housing or to private mortgages. But despite the huge costs and undeniable disadvantages of this arrangement, it spawned a middle class.

A middle class of the past, however, whose growth ground to a halt in 1982, with the onset of the so-called debt crisis, and whose limits had already become apparent, in size, profession, consumption patterns, and even regional and ethnic composition. The 1980s came to be labeled, throughout Latin America, as the lost decade—a time when the middle class not only did not expand, but probably shrank, given the absence of economic growth, the high inflation, and the massive transfer of wealth from Mexico and the rest of the region to the rest of the world. The early 1990s brought about a change in this situation, but a short-lived one. Thanks to the trade opening and privatization policies of the Salinas de Gortari administration (1988–94), the economy grew somewhat during the initial years of the decade, but all of that, and more, was wiped out by the economic collapse of January 1995, no longer on Salinas's watch, but largely attributable to his excesses, mistakes, and refusal to adjust financial policies when they were clearly jeopardizing economic stability.

That year was a disastrous one for the Mexican middle class. What with inflation of over 100%, negative growth of more than 6%, and a spectacular spike in interest rates, it lost its savings, saw its newly acquired homes foreclosed, its cars repossessed, and its children thrown out of private schools.[10] The middle class finally rebelled, ejecting the ruling party from its perennial majority status in Congress and Mexico City in 1997, and from the presidency in 2000. It elected a president of its own that year, Partido Acción Nacional (PAN) candidate Vicente Fox, and again in 2006, with Felipe Calderón. But more importantly, that middle class began to suffer a dramatic metamorphosis, as its older cohorts survived, but ceased growing, and new sectors began to emerge over the following thirteen years of economic stability, of mediocre but consistent growth, and of policies tailored to its needs and desires. Its transformation was regional, professional, ethnic, and existential: a new middle class joined its forebears, and became a majority of the country. How this occurred will be now explained.

## What Is a New Middle Class?

Consumption patterns illustrate the evolution, though they do not necessarily define it. Perhaps the most striking example, anecdotal as it may be, can be found in a poll commissioned by a newly created low-cost airline, Volaris, in 2007. According to a survey of its early passengers, nearly half were first-time travelers—a feature undoubtedly due to the cut-rate prices it was charging for flights all across Mexico.[11] But one did not really need market research to figure this out. Just by observing the passengers, one could easily surmise that they were not the traditional airplane occupants of the previous era. They were construction workers and restaurant servers seeking jobs in Los Cabos, Puerto Vallarta, or Cancún, or potential migrants flying to Tijuana, where they would pursue their journey to the border and points north on foot, by bus, or in smugglers' pickup trucks. They were large families off to their first vacation by plane, with countless toddlers and youngsters, a sprinkling of in-laws and grandparents, as well as the young parents, all archetypically Mexican-looking: short in height, dark-skinned, beardless, and straight-haired; a bit of a paunch even in their twenties and thirties, and immensely happy with their new station in life.

These were the bus passengers of before, who now, because of lower prices, higher and more disposable incomes, were suddenly able to sit in the same transportation vehicle as, on one flight I took from Acapulco in 2008: the grandson of Mexico's wealthiest banker from the 1960s and 1970s; a former foreign minister and son of a foreign minister; the eighty-five-year-old owner of Mexico's largest radio network; and the great-granddaughter of one of the founding fathers of modern Mexico, Plutarco Elías Calles. They joined countless weekenders returning from their palatial homes in the new section of Acapulco, where Mexico City's upper middle class has bought nearly ten thousand rooms in condos over the past fifteen years.[12] The difference is that four or five decades ago, this new upper-crust neighborhood of Acapulco would have been totally segregated from where the lower classes flocked to during Holy Week and perhaps Independence Day: Caleta, Caletilla, Hornos. Today, next to the high-rises in Punta Diamante, behind them, or around them, there are lower-cost apartments, with less spectacular views, terraces, and pools, but with the same ocean in which to swim, the same sand on which their children play, and the same beach on which they ride horses, three-wheel motorcycles, Jet Skis and Delta planes, and buy clams, oysters, shrimp, and fish *quesadillas*. The beach is messy, noisy, crowded, and boisterous, but now, in deed and not only on paper, it belongs to everybody. Here one can see the new Mexican middle class in action.

Before describing it more fully and broadly, we have to return to the somewhat tedious technical discussion of what exactly a middle class is. Since the midpoint of the economic boom that began in the so-called emerging markets at the turn of the century (or several years before, in China and India), a whole cottage industry has sprung up to measure, classify, and hail the appearance of a "global middle class," mainly surging in the developing world. The World Bank, *The Economist*, Goldman Sachs, many authors, and newspapers or academic journals have taken note of the global trend of middle-class expansion, and have attempted to construct a taxonomy that is simultaneously universal, specific, precise, and operational.

How do all these experts and the various multilateral financial institutions define the global middle class? In terms of income, as well as consumption. According to the World Bank, the cross sections of this cohort of the earth's inhabitants "buy cars, engage in international tourism, demand world-class products and require international standards for higher education";* the bank cites economists who estimate

---

* At the turn of the century, the World Bank calculated that the developing countries' share of this segment of the globe's population comprised some 400 million people, a number that will more than double over the next twenty years. In 2000, 7.6% of the world's population belonged to this global middle class; by 2030 more than 16%, or twice that much, will be part of it.

that a good ballpark figure of incomes for this middle class is anywhere between the per capita income of Brazil ($4,000 U.S., in 2000 PPP dollars), and Italy ($16,700 U.S.), or approximately $12 to $50 a day.[13] The ample margin between the floor and ceiling figures is due to the fact that even when adjustments for purchasing power are made, being middle-class in India, China, Brazil, or even Mexico is very different from being middle-class in Germany, Canada, or Japan.

By these estimates, everyone in the developing world whose annual household income* lies above $72,000 is "rich," everyone whose annual household income falls below $16,800 is poor, and everyone else is middle-class.[14]† The British weekly *The Economist* translates this into more layman's terms, by estimating that middle-class status ranges, depending on the country, from $10 to $100 in income per person, per day. At least one-third of this income must be of a *discretionary* nature, that is, be devoted to nonessential food, clothing, housing, drinking water, and so forth.[15]

There are other definitions, some slightly older, others more recent, that attempt to address the difficulties and contradictions of these classifications. An initial distinction separates, as *The Economist* summarized in a special survey on the global middle class in early 2009, an absolute definition and a relative one, "as the middle income range of each country."[16] The most well known of these definitions would be MIT Management School director Lester Thurow's. He takes the median income of a country, adds 25% to that sum to establish the upper limit, and subtracts 25% from that median to determine the lower limit.‡ He subsequently calculates how many people fit in the range; they are middle-class. As *The Economist* says, however, this "relative" definition "changes from place to place," and for example in some countries of Africa it can become ultimately meaningless, because the absolute income levels it implies are minuscule. The objection to the

* For an average family of 4.1.
† In an oft-cited Goldman Sachs *Global Economics Paper* from 2008, two economists established a range for the "world middle class" of between $6,000 and $30,000 PPP, where the lower figure "corresponds approximately to the World Bank's current definition at which countries qualify to be upper middle income, and the higher figure is roughly equivalent to median incomes in the OECD group."
‡ The median is the income level at which there are the same number of people living above and below it. Thurow constructs a bracket extending from 75% to 125% of the median income.

absolute floor and ceiling classification is that it excludes literally billions of people in China and India, and perhaps in Indonesia and Brazil, who are lower-middle-class but do not make $12 per day. Perhaps the most appropriate synthesis of all of this lies with another World Bank economist, Martin Ravallion, who preferred to posit the existence of two middle classes in each developing country: the one that is so by international standards, and those who are middle-class by the standards of their own countries. He comes up with a range of $2 to $13 per day.[17]* This spectrum takes all the necessary substrata into account.

The World Bank, as well as many economists or other scholars charting these trends, foresee a constant and significant expansion of this slice of the world's demography over the next two decades. Today, approximately half of the "global middle class" resides in the developing world; by 2030, according to these calculations, that should reach 92%. The enlargement of the Chinese and Indian middle classes has a highly disproportionate impact on these statistics,[†] since the national performance and prosperity of just these two nations accounts for the welfare (or absence of it) of 40% of the globe's inhabitants.[18] What is important, however, is to understand that the impressive rise of the Mexican middle class over the past fifteen years is part of a worldwide trend, and that experts have advanced greatly in recent times in measuring and defining exactly what they are talking about.

If we apply all of these definitions and numbers to Mexico, in 2008 slightly over half the country's then 26.7 million households found themselves in this situation, according to the National Household Income-Expenditure Survey for 2008.[19] In fact, the data suggest that as much as 60% of the population now enjoys lower-middle-class to "rich" status, a figure not unlike the one pertaining to Brazil, Colombia, and Chile, with a similar 40% remaining in poverty. By the end of Felipe Calderón's term in 2012, the country will be roughly two-thirds middle-class, with everything this implies politically, economically, and socially, but perhaps not, quite unfortunately, in cultural terms.

According to the National Household Income-Expenditure Survey quoted above, the upper six deciles of the Mexican income scale all fall

---

* This range is in 2005 PPP prices. By choosing $2 per day, Ravallion makes his definition compatible with that of poverty, as we just saw, but also with "rich" country figures, since $13 per day in 2005 PPP prices is the U.S. poverty line today.
† In 2010 there were 6.8 billion people on earth.

roughly into the brackets we just outlined.* If we redo the calculations
by per capita income, the numbers spew out a GDP per capita for the
fifth decile of $8,440 U.S. in 2006 dollars,[†] more than twice the Brazil-
ian floor figure mentioned above. On the expenditure side, the first six
deciles of Mexico's population clearly assign more than 30% of their
income to such "luxuries" as cell phones, automobiles, private education and health care, vacations, or big-ticket consumer items. Going
back to the 2008 survey, the fifth decile spent approximately one-third
of its income on discretionary items such as "cars, vacations, parties,
accessories, education, personal effects, recreation, hotels, communications and other expenses."[20] And certainly within the fifth decile the
definition of "vacation" can vary; the figures must be viewed as indicative, not exact. The next five deciles on the way up the scale dedicated a
higher percentage of their income to these items. From the market
research perspective, the social and economic level labeled D+ (lower
middle class) destined 26% of its expenditures to so-called nonessential
items, and by 2008 the percentage in all likelihood had reached 28% to
29%, that is, virtually the 30% stipulated by *The Economist* as a necessary condition for middle-class status.[21]

Even the left-wing opposition corroborates this view. When
throughout the 2006 presidential election campaign—and ever
since—populist leader Andrés Manuel López Obrador obsessively
repeated that there were 40 million poor in Mexico, he was simply
restating the other side of the equation. In a nation of 112 million
inhabitants, that left 70 million individuals who were not poor; what
else could they be, but a broad, largely lower middle class of Mexicans,
and a few rich and famous?

All of this brings us back to our premise. Almost any way it is mea-
sured, Mexico today corresponds, like Brazil, to a country where the
middle class, defined by income levels, represents a majority of the
population. It may not be a carbon copy of the "Old World" middle

---

* Income deciles go from the first, the poorest tenth of the population, to the tenth, the
wealthiest. The least affluent of these six deciles, i.e., the fifth decile, received in 2006 a
daily income of roughly $7.3 (in 2000 PPP) per day, per person—less than the $12
quoted by some, very close to the $10 minimum quoted by others, and well above the $2
minimum established by Ravallion. By 2008, it fell back somewhat, to $6.8 per day.
† Or $10,487 U.S. in 2000 PPP, more than twice as much as the Brazilian floor figure
mentioned above. Again, needless to say, this is even more true for the higher five
deciles.

class, and it will certainly evolve in ways difficult to foresee. But it has become the bedrock of the nation, and it was nothing of the sort as recently as 1995, when we remained mired in the old middle class, comprising one-third of the population. Whether we compare the current data with 1994 or 1996, it is evident that since then Mexico has experienced the kind of middle-class expansion spurt that some economists have now come to consider typical. According to this perspective, the world's middle classes have grown in "bursts": a first one in the nineteenth century, in Western Europe and the United States, more or less between 1820 and 1890, thanks to the long cycle of industrialization, urbanization, and working-class organization; a second one, from 1950 through 1980 (during the period the French have called "*les trente glorieuses*"), in the same countries as before; and a new spurt, under way today, taking place chiefly in Asia and Latin America.*

Before moving on to the consumption-based discussion of how much of a middle-class society Mexico has become, it may be useful to evaluate the progress the country has made during the last decade and a half, from an income and expenditure point of view. We have to exclude 1995 from any comparison. That was the year of the so-called Tequila Crisis, when the Mexican economy collapsed and nearly one million layoffs took place; tens of thousands of people lost their homes, savings, and cars. It skews any comparison, so either we go to a year before or one after, depending on when the relevant surveys were carried out.

In 1994, the sixth decile of Mexican society received an average of $4 per day; under no circumstances did it even get close to the middle-class level.† The median income was $2,800, the "Thurow range" was

---

* "Latin America is becoming a middle-class continent. Consumer credit, which was previously nonexistent, is now plentiful. A third of the population has bank accounts, whereas ten years ago only 10% did." José Juan Ruíz, strategy director for Latin America, Santander Bank, in Maite Rico, "El fin del derrotismo," *El País* (Madrid), July 2, 2010.

† If we were to follow the Ravallion taxonomy of between $2 and $13 per day, per person, an even greater share of Mexican society has moved up the ladder; at least the fourth and perhaps even the third decile would fit the description. This may be taking things too far, since $3 or $4 a day, in Mexico, is stretching the definition of middle class a bit much. And yet were we to accept the Thurow theory of ±25% of median income as a marker, then, given a 2006 median income of $3,600 per year, and a range from $2,700 to $4,500, around 65% of all Mexicans would qualify. These numbers were obtained by converting total annual income for each year to household income and then to per capita income. This figure was calculated in 2000 pesos then converted to 2000 PPP dollars and finally to daily per capita income in 2000 PPP dollars.

$2,100 to $3,500, and only 45% of the Mexican population fit in that category. Per capita GDP was barely $2,500, just above the Brazilian floor. The discretionary income comparison is also revealing. Only the wealthiest three deciles* were able to spend more than 30% of their disposable income on nonessentials.[22] So by any of these aggregate, abstract measurements, the expansion of the Mexican middle class since 1994 has been simply spectacular, in the same way that the Brazilian middle class has also exploded. Just to provide one of the many examples given below, the number of cars in circulation rose from 11.3 million in 1994 to 29.1 million in 2009.[23] According to the Getulio Vargas Foundation, in 2008 Brazilians with household incomes from 1,000 to 4,500 reais per year (the "Thurow range") made up nearly 50% of the population, having risen from 38% in 2003, and 31% in 1993.[24]

But all of these statistics, which on occasion can numb the mind, are perhaps less illustrative and significant than the facts stemming from another type of definition—one that basically states that whoever consumes like the middle class, dresses like the middle class, travels like the middle class . . . belongs to the middle class. The huge difference since 1994, the enormous leap Mexico has achieved, lies mainly in the immense number of Mexicans who have gained access to a standard of living previously reserved to a much smaller group of the population and that is now open to these millions of aspiring middle-class members. This new middle class has ancestors and antecedents: Mexico had a middle class before 1996, and a relatively large one, roughly the size of Brazil's in relation to its total population. It's not that all of a sudden a country of as of then nearly 100 million people, where a tiny minority was immensely rich and everyone else was poor, sprouted a huge middle class that encompasses something like 65 million individuals. The *original* Mexican middle class was born in the 1940s and, while not thriving, is still around. It is the growth, the novelty, the geographic and professional distribution of the *new* one that is both startling and meaningful.

## *Lalo and Actipan*

The differences and sequences can perhaps best be illustrated by a quick chronicle of the lives of a family I have known well now for forty-

* The tenth, ninth, and eighth deciles.

five years and three generations. When my parents returned in 1965 from their stint as Mexico's ambassadors to Egypt, I had spent the previous quarter of my life without television. So my parents decided to preserve my younger sister's and my media virginity, and refused to buy a TV. I was nonetheless an avid sports fan, spending hours listening to Los Angeles Dodgers ball games on the U.S. Armed Forces Network (I heard Vin Scully's memorable broadcast of Sandy Koufax's perfect game in 1965), going often to the new Aztec soccer stadium inaugurated in 1966, and was dying to see Super Bowl I in 1967 and the 1966 soccer World Cup final played in Wembley, England. Since I could do none of this at home, and since most of my schoolmates lived on the other side of town, and because the kids across the street were more generous than I (but equally self-interested), I began to wangle invitations to watch sports at their home. That, playing sandlot soccer, and growing up was how I met the Sánchez Camacho family, and Lalo, my best friend ever since.

He, his older brother, and their parents, Raúl and Josefina, lived in two rooms in a tenement on Calle Tigre, in the heart of the *barrio* of Actipan. One was the "bedroom," i.e., a ten-by-ten-foot windowless room with a closet, a chest of drawers, and a bed where the parents slept; the other area was a combination kitchen, dining, and TV room, and bedroom for the kids, where we would eat, see the games, and watch Lalo's mother provide me with my adolescent introduction to the marvels of Mexican cuisine. His father was a garbage truck driver for the Mexico City municipal administration, and subsequently became a midlevel official of the garbage workers union he belonged to; he owned a 1947 Ford, was an archetypical Pedro Infante look-alike (except for his bald pate), a nondrinking, hardworking gentleman with an elementary school education, who loved his family but could not give them a better living at the time. This was urban semipoverty: two to a bed, two rooms to a house, a common bathroom for the three families in the tenement, running cold water, and a wood-chip-fired boiler that had to be lit each time someone wanted a hot shower. But Lalo's father had a job and health care, and his children were able to go to public school, the Secundaria 10 across Insurgentes Avenue in Mixcoac.

By the mid-seventies, the living he gave them had improved. Ten years before Don Raúl died in 1978, he had built a two-story house on the grounds the two rooms had previously occupied, together with an adjoining piece of land he bought from his cousins. The reason the family—Lalo and his older brother, Héctor—accomplished this improvement lay in the fact that the father was able to make more money in the same job, and probably received some help from his mother, a nurse, when she died. Héctor left home in 1977; the two brothers both went to middle school, high school, and college (Héctor graduated from the National University; Lalo enrolled but didn't finish), where they both studied to become CPAs. They joined a large accounting firm that had already hired some of the neighbors from the *barrio*, and by the time the brothers married and the parents passed away, in the late 1970s, they both enjoyed a proper middle-class situation: their own homes (having purchased an additional bit of property in the same ex-tenement, the two had individual dwellings), cars, TVs, decent jobs, and an adequate education for their children, who were all born in the early 1980s.

Lalo was not happy, however, in Mexico City, and he made much more money working for his accounting firm in Guadalajara, Mexico's second-largest city, to where he moved in 1985, and where his kids grew up. He rented a slightly larger house—nearly two thousand square feet; two years later, he and his wife, Tere, bought two cars. Raúl and Iván, their sons, both went to public elementary, middle, and high school; both attended the University of Guadalajara, the nation's second-largest public university, which unlike the National University requires a modest but not insignificant tuition. Raúl studied accounting; Iván, law.

The upward mobility experienced by at least parts of the urban poor but not destitute sectors of Mexican society of the fifties and sixties and through the mid-eighties, was undeniable, rapid, and substantial. Lalo and his brother enjoyed a much higher standard of living than their parents, and their children would enjoy, at least through the end of the twentieth century, a better life than they had at the same age. I met Lalo when he was fourteen; at that age, his two sons, Iván and Raúl, both fared far better than their father or their mother, who belonged to a numerous family, also from Actipan, that also lived in a family tenement, and who only finished middle school before marrying and subsequently getting a job as a poorly paid social worker at the National Social Security Institute.

But from the late eighties onward, Lalo and the Mexican middle class's climb up the scale began to stall. In June of 1993, he was still able to buy a new house: 2,500 square feet for $70,000 with an adjustable rate, twenty-year mortgage. But then the slower ascent dropped to a standstill in 1995, and reversed course as a result of that year's crisis. Lalo was unable to meet his mortgage payments after 1997, found himself forced to take a sharp cut (50%) in wages in 1998, and subsequently was let go from the accounting firm in 2000. The entire decade would be frustrating. The upward slope would only begin again in early 2001, when thanks to a friend he was able to land a job in the federal government's food stamp program, DICONSA, where he continues to work at this writing.

Iván, the younger son, still lives with his parents, drives his own car, and makes roughly $1,000 per month, before taxes. He received a master's degree in tax law at the University of Guadalajara and works in a law firm. Raúl and Sujeihri got married in 2006 and moved to a publicly financed home his mother gave them, measuring about 750 square feet, with two bedrooms; he works as a teacher and administrator at a public high school. His wife owns their second car and is also a CPA. They have both made several trips to Europe, Canada, and the United States; Iván has too. Lalo secured private health insurance for the family about fifteen years ago; they take fewer vacations than they would like, but Tere has traveled to New York and Vancouver; Lalo took Raúl to Disney World in 1982 and both kids to Disneyland in 1986, but other than those trips, and a Che Guevara–like journey in a VW minivan in 1973 across Latin America, he has rarely traveled abroad. Still, as he approaches sixty, he is a sophisticated, increasingly well-informed, well-off, politicized Mexican who has not only provided for his family but has seen, in real time, how he lived a better life than his parents, and his children are already living a better one than he.

### Cars, Plasmas, Vacations, and Housing, Once More

The aggregate numbers for the middle class that these children of Sánchez represent are as illustrative as their brief story. We can begin with cars, the quintessential middle-class, big-ticket item that has generated worldwide aspirations for a century now. Traditionally, like nearly everywhere in Latin America, Mexico possessed a protected, expensive, run-of-the-mill automobile industry that catered to a small domestic market, imported huge amounts of inputs for terminal assembly plants, and foisted old, expensive, and inefficient models on hapless consumers. A first transition occurred in the late sixties, when Volkswagen opened its plant in Puebla and began producing Beetles for the "old middle class." Matters started to change further in the late eighties, as American, German, and Japanese automakers began to shift their manufacturing units to low-wage countries, no longer just to supply torpid local markets, but to reexport back home or across the world, taking advantage of Mexico's—and others'—high productivity, proximity to the U.S. market, and miserable salaries. Brand-new plants were built throughout the 1990s in Hermosillo, Chihuahua, Saltillo, Silao, and Aguascalientes, and old factories in Mexico City, Toluca, and Durango were shut down. Mexico began producing spanking-new, top-of-the-line models, but not for Mexican consumers: all for American, Brazilian, and Asian buyers—the cars sold in Mexico remained costly, and still not very efficient or modern. When the North American Free Trade Agreement came into law on January 1, 1994, it set a long waiting period for new-car imports from the United States into Mexico (until 2002) and an even longer delay for used cars (until 2008). Given these constraints, as well as the perennially constricted purchasing power of the previous Mexican middle class, it was only in 2003 that domestic sales of all vehicles recovered the level they had attained in 1992, the best year of the entire decade, or 1981, the best year ever until then.[25]*

But cars really moved into high gear in the early years of the twenty-first century. First, as tariffs on imports were finally phased out, local prices plunged, and it became possible to buy a new compact for around $10,000, something unheard of in Mexico barely a few years before, with the exception of VWs. Second, as inflation was flushed from the economy, interest rates began to drop and credit began to flow, in volumes not only higher than before the 1995 crash, but than at any time in recent memory. With monthly payments of as little as $100, Mexican customers could buy a Chevy, a Spark or Matiz, a Tsuru, a French Clio, or a modern-day version of the VW Bug. And most important, for better or worse, as the long-awaited opening of the country to used car imports approached, the government moved up the date, and in August 2005 permitted the unlimited entry of cars from

* In 2003, domestic sales of all vehicles were 650,000. The total of vehicles sold in 1981 was 535,000.

the United States, on the condition they be at least ten years old and that purchasers pay a modest duty on each vehicle. This was not exactly the greenest idea (old models burn more fuel, pollute more, and are less safe), and was deeply unpopular with the national automobile industry, but was widely applauded by consumers. They didn't just applaud. Thousands flocked to border towns, mainly to Matamoros, across the river from Brownsville, which rapidly became the used car capital of the country, if not of the entire world. Among the more folkloric consequences of these events was one of the strangest sights ever seen on Mexican highways: five to ten cars in a queue, tied together with chains or ropes and hauled by a single pickup truck to save gas, on the way to central or southern Mexico, or even to Central America. The price of used cars fell precipitously in Mexico, and demand exploded.

While comparisons are difficult in this realm—before the 2005 opening, used cars were also imported, but illegally—in 2006 anywhere between 1.2 and 1.5 million ten-year-old used cars were lawfully brought into the country. New-vehicle sales that year reached 1.15 million, so around 2.5 million* units were added to the stock of Mexican cars. In 2009, to provide some perspective on this total, Americans purchased 10.6 million vehicles—it was a terrible year, of course—with a U.S. population almost three times larger than Mexico's.[26] In per capita terms, a bad U.S. year and a great Mexican year were not that far apart, with the undoubted caveat that the southern sales constituted an environmental nightmare, and the northern ones simply a bad dream. The overall stock of motor vehicles in Mexico in 2009 reached roughly 29.1 million; the yearly increase in recent times amounted to nearly 15%.[27]† The most significant aspect of these statistics lies in the dramatic expansion of the number of people owning automobiles, to the tune of close to a couple of million heads of households per year, allowing for renewals and two-car families. Given the number of households in Mexico, the magnitude of this car boom becomes even more striking.‡

The Mexican middle class's fascination with plasma (and LCD or LED) television sets is no less remarkable. Mexico came of age, television-wise, in the mid-sixties; at the beginning of that decade, only one-tenth

---

* In 2006, 2007, and 2008 between 2.3 and 2.6 million units were sold yearly.
† The actual percentage is between 12% and 15%.
‡ The total number of households in Mexico in 2010 was 27.8 million. The percentage of families with automobile loans—leasing does not yet really exist in Mexico—reached an average of 4%. "National Survey," GAUSSC, Mexico City, July 2010.

of all households owned a TV set. As early as 1970, more than 90% of all homes had one, and the virtual monopoly held by the largest network, Televisa, allowed it to become one of the most powerful corporations and political actors in the nation. Its contribution to world culture, i.e., the "*telenovela*" or Mexican soap opera, may be of dubious artistic value, but its business impact was monumental. Although Mexico's level of cable penetration is significantly lower than other Latin American countries (in 2001 only 13.5% of all homes had cable; by 2010 the number had doubled, an impressive rise, but still a low percentage), open and free TV has been a fixture of national life for decades now. It is not reserved for the middle class, since precisely what made it big business was the extension of an open signal all over the land, and the availability of low-price sets, bought on credit, for the broad masses of the Mexican poor. Just about every Mexican household owns a television and, of course, has built an extraordinary love affair with *telenovelas*. So strong is this passion that Mexicans claim, with some basis, that color TV was born in their country, thanks to inventor Guillermo González Camarena.[28]*

Over the last ten or so years, Mexicans, like consumers the world over, have switched to plasma or LCD-LED, wide-screen, flat TVs, and a whole replenishment of the television universe has taken place. Plasmas are, of course, far more expensive than old TVs; despite their being mainly manufactured in Mexico, they are more costly than their predecessors, and they require more gadgets to go with them. Despite all of this, the numbers are impressive. In 2008, just before the financial crisis hit, more than 2 million units were sold in the country, an increase of 40% over the previous year,† when they represented a bit less than a third of all TV sales.[29] The explanation: prices have been tumbling, as more competitors enter the market; more Mexicans hook up to cable and enjoy a wider range of TV entertainment; and their incomes are rising. Between 2000 and 2010, when the status symbol hit the streets, nearly 12 million Mexican families had acquired them.‡

A similar, and perhaps more notable, process has occurred with

---

* By 2010, 27.2% of all homes had cable. The exact percentage of Mexican households with a television is 95%. According to a GAUSSC poll taken in July 2010, the number of homes with cable is actually higher, that is, 36% of any kind of paid TV system.

† In 2007, 1.7 million flat-screen TVs were snapped up by consumers.

‡ The exact number is difficult to determine because of the confusion in Mexican statistics between digitalized televisions and regular flat screens.

credit cards. Again, this is not a new phenomenon in Mexico. Millions of low-income individuals with plastic were stung when recurrent bubbles in the financial markets popped: 1976, 1982, 1987, and finally 1995. Banks were irresponsible in handing them out like hotcakes, consumers were irresponsible in accepting them and running up huge liabilities, and regulatory authorities were incredibly irresponsible in allowing all of this to happen. Holders would use one card to pay off another (like in the U.S.), and would rapidly sink into unpayable debts. But once again, unlike television but similar to automobiles, this occurred on a relatively small scale, which was swept away by the evolution of the middle class. In 2003, 5.8 million new cards were issued; in 2004, the number reached 8.5 million,* and exploded to 22.6 in 2006, falling off somewhat in 2007 and much more severely in 2008, the first year of the crisis, to 9.8 million.[30] (These are figures for newly issued cards, not reissued ones.) By the end of 2008, there were 75 million credit cards of all sorts (banks, department stores, supermarkets, appliance outlets) in circulation, deposited in the often otherwise empty wallets of more than 50 million holders.[31] Granted, many of these cards were "passive," that is, virtually unused; in the 2009–10 crisis, many of their holders lost their cards or their shirts, and many of them should never have owned a card in the first place. Still, at the onset of the recession-depression, one out of every two Mexicans had a credit card; while it is hard to restrict middle-class status to this generalized feature of the rich world's everyday life, it is equally hard to imagine the middle class, by whatever definition, without credit cards of one sort or another.[†]

But perhaps the most extraordinary facet of middle-class expansion during the thirteen years starting in 1996 and the recovery from the Tequila Crisis, through 2008 and the onslaught of the new, U.S.-originated disaster, was in a domain directly linked to credit, though not to credit cards. For the first time in recent memory, inflation was sufficiently contained for a long enough period of time for interest rates to tumble to levels unknown in Mexico since the early seventies. This, plus major reforms in the tax code, the federal housing agencies (INFONAVIT and FOVISSSTE), and the financial system, led to a

---

* In 2005, the number of credit cards was 10.7 million.
[†] Mexico remains an underbanked society. For example, only 25% of all Mexicans have a savings account, while for example 61% of all Brazilians have one. "National Survey," GAUSSC, Mexico City, July 2010.

housing boom the country had never experienced before. Low-income individual homes finally became available to enormous numbers of people, as the gigantic national housing deficit began to be soaked up by what was essentially a public-private partnership.

Instead of building houses, the government began simply extending or guaranteeing mortgages, and providing bridge financing for private developers, thus insuring that the construction of downscale housing became both profitable and feasible. The fixed percentage of their salary government agencies charged private or public sector employees for a mortgage rose from 18% to 25%; private banks began extending fixed rate, long-term mortgages in pesos to middle-income borrowers. All of this at relatively low prices, not excessively far from workplaces, and, of course, as we saw in the previous chapter, with full respect for the Mexican penchant for horizontal construction. Houses of between six hundred and seven hundred square feet were priced between $20,000 and $30,000; given a fifteen- or twenty-year mortgage, the monthly payments were quite affordable. Moving upscale, the government institutes (rough equivalents of Fannie Mae and Freddie Mac) also supplied financing for larger, one-thousand-square-foot abodes, at around $80,000 to $100,000 each. Eighty percent of the homes cost between $20,000 and $60,000.[32] The largest agency—INFONAVIT—financed 101,000 homes in 1996, just after the crash of 1995; it decreased to 96,000 in 1997, and then took off, jumping from 104,000 in 1998 to 191,000 in 1999, and 242,000 in 2000, Ernesto Zedillo's last year in office.[33]* We mention this to underline the continuity involved in the process. The spectacular growth began with the last PRI president, expanded dramatically under the first PAN president, and continued under the second PAN chief executive. By 2005, Vicente Fox's last year in office, INFONAVIT financed 371,000 families with credits to buy new homes, and the total in 2010, Felipe Calderón's fourth year as president, rose to 796,000 credits.[34]† For the

---

* The exact amount in 1996 was $101,215 of loans to buy a new house. In 1997 the exact amount was $96,974 loans to buy a new house.

† In 2005 the exact number of granted credits was 371,706. In 2008 the estimated number was 476,001 credits. It must be mentioned that the existing differences between delivered new houses and the total of credits granted for buying houses is because since 2005 the credits could be used, also, to buy preexisting houses (10% of the credits). And by 2010, 70% of the credits were utilized for buying new houses, and the other 30% was for the acquisition of preexisting ones.

fifteen years in question, the total reached 4,630,168 credits, benefiting some 15 million people, far more than the institute had provided during the first quarter century of its existence. These are all credits for new dwellings, not for refurbishment or touch-ups of existing ones.

But this was not all. The FOVISSSTE—which among other beneficiaries includes Mexico's 1.2 million elementary and middle school teachers—financed a total of 457,000 new homes during this period, and the private banking system financed another million and a half.[35] So all in all, more than 6 million new homes, housing more than 25 million people, were placed—with deeds, electric power, sewage, running water, pavement—in the hands of Mexicans who heretofore lived in tin-roofed shacks, shantytowns, and cardboard-walled slum dwellings. A six-hundred-square-foot house is not a mansion for two adults and two children, but it is a sight better than anything the country had witnessed before. This is lower-middle-class status: property, cement walls and floors, appliances, bathrooms, and at least two bedrooms. Lalo and Héctor Sánchez do not have to sleep in the same room where they also cook, eat, and receive intrusive guests to watch ball games on television.

Our next three indicators are also impressive, and not devoid of contradictions. Many scholars, perhaps beginning with C. K. Prahalad in his now classic *The Fortune at the Bottom of the Pyramid* (BOP), have argued that cell phones are not necessarily a symbol nor a symptom of middle-class status, but rather of the poor's growing access to certain consumer goods whose price has plummeted, and whose manufacturers and/or distributors have found it good business to seek out BOP customers. It is also true that in many emerging economies, not all handheld phones are equal. On any given day, more than half of those in circulation may be "passive," that is, units with no credit, that can receive but not generate calls. And finally, many people in the developing world purchase phone cards for use only when they absolutely need to call, but most of the time turn the phone off to avoid charges. Still, in 1991, when cell phones began to be merchandised in Mexico, there were 150,000 units in use; by 1994, just two years after the privatization of the main fixed line company, which was allowed access to the mobile network, the total had jumped to 560,000. At the turn of the century, the number of users had skyrocketed to 14 million, and by 2010, the figure had reached an astounding 89 million. If we consider that the total of homes with landlines increased "only" from 9.4 million in 2001 to 13.9 million in 2010, it seems quite obvious that Mexico, like so many other Third World nations, simply skipped the fixed line stage and leapt directly to the mobile phone era.[36]* This does not imply that all 80 million users were the equivalent of landline customers in the United States in the 1950s, but it does mean that compared to countries like France, Italy, and Spain, for example, where as late as the mid-seventies a private landline was a luxury, Mexico hurdled the traditional, reduced middle-class phase and went on to the future. Perhaps a similar phenomenon is occurring with computers: in 1994 there were only 2.1 million PCs, almost all desktops, in Mexico; by 2006, there were 15 million, mostly small laptops, and by 2010, estimates surpassed 25 million, suggesting the possibility that the spurt phenomenon referred to above was at work in this domain too. As also happened with access to and use of the Internet. In 2001, there were 7 million users; in 2010, 34.8 million.[37]† More important perhaps are the changes taking place among young people. In a telephone poll carried out by the *Reforma* newspaper, among Mexicans between sixteen and twenty-five years of age the percentage of Internet users jumped from 55% in 2001 to 86% in 2010; the percentage using e-mail went from 43% to 81%, and Facebook from 0% to 53%.[38]

Three further examples warrant a brief comment: private health insurance, vacations, and private school education. Health care is a simple enough affair. Although all Mexicans with formal jobs are covered by one of the governmental health care plans, the middle class is increasingly seeking private coverage, for reasons similar to those that led government ministries (Foreign Affairs, Treasury) and the National University to purchase private plans for their employees: public care leaves much to be desired. In 1994 only 1.4 million individuals held private health insurance; by 2009, the number reached more than 6 million.[39]‡

Private education is even more conclusive—and controversial—than phones or plasma TVs. Traditionally, Mexico, like most of Europe

---

* Mexico has one cell phone for every 0.75 Mexicans. According to a poll taken in July 2010 by GAUSSC, the number of households in Mexico with a landline had reached 56%.
† According to the GAUSSC poll quoted above, 31% of all households had at least one computer at home and 27% had Internet access at home.
‡ The exact number is 6.3 million.

and Latin America, was a public education country, at all levels. It was
thanks to the tremendous literacy effort of the fifties and sixties that
illiteracy was mostly eliminated. And thanks to the excellence of the
National University in Mexico City as far back as the twenties, the
country could count on world-class lawyers, doctors, engineers, and
architects with which to build, run, and keep itself healthy. All of this
changed in the seventies, as higher education rolls exploded, and elementary education stagnated in quality and also ballooned quantita-
tively because of the demographic boom of a decade or two before.
Public expenditures on education swelled, but inevitably quality suffered as pesos spent per student sank. Then, after the recurrent crises of
1982, 1987, and 1995, spending also was cut, and quality as well as
capacity compared to demand dropped accordingly.

It was no surprise then, that after 1995, the split between public and
private education began to shift, chiefly in higher education. The elementary, middle school, and high school shares remain more or the
same as before, that is, 90% public.[40]* But the higher one went up the
scale, the more public and private shares of enrollment were transformed. In addition, outside of the National University in the capital,
tuition fees began to be levied in public colleges all across the country.
And logically enough, parents who had to pay for their youngsters'
education persuaded themselves that private schooling was superior to
the one available at public institutions. The numbers did not always
bear out this conviction, particularly at some of the newer, fly-by-night
"universities" that sprang up after 1995 and received governmental certification even if they did not deserve it. Nonetheless, many of the
quality private institutions were superior to the public ones, and most
of the time (with the exception of the medical, engineering, and law
schools of the National University), the market corroborated this.
Graduates from the private schools got better jobs than those from
public ones. And private education became a symbol of middle-class
status, not one of the poor making a special effort to move their children into the middle class.

In the 1991–92 school year, there were roughly 1 million students
enrolled in Mexican higher education, all included (universities, tech-

* Around 8% to 10% attended private schools.

nological institutes, college, and graduate level), of which 18% belonged
to private institutions.* By 2007–8, the overall total had reached 2.6
million,[†] an enormous increase in fifteen years, of which 33%, or nearly
double the share of a decade and a half before, belonged to private institutions.[41‡] This balance is about the same as Brazil's, and is a far cry
from the all-public, all-lay (many of the private schools are confes-
sional), all-free education that Mexico prided itself upon.

The situation with tourism or vacations is analogous. It is more difficult to calculate, but at least indirectly, there are several indicators that
suggest a huge jump in domestic and international travel by Mexicans.
In 1994, the number of passengers on international flights originating
in Mexico amounted to 10.7 million; in 2009, the total had reached
22.5 million; the expansion of the number of foreign tourists visiting
the country was far smaller. For the same initial year, there were 18 million purely domestic passengers; by 2009 the number approached 24
million.[42§] And the most spectacular rise consisted of regional charter
flights, since they are probably more linked to tourism than regularly
scheduled ones.[43‖]

Anecdotal evidence confirms these trends. In 2006, the number of
Mexican soccer fans estimated to have accompanied their team to the
World Cup finals in Germany was 35,000: this to cheer on a team
doomed to fail. And today, the beaches, archaeological ruins, national
parks, and colonial towns of Mexico are often jam-packed with domestic tourists who obviously are undertaking their first trip. One can see it
in the wondrous look in their eyes, in the pride with which they gaze
upon Mexico's marvels, and in their garb, habits, phenotype, and inno-
cence. They are beginning to know and understand their own country,
and they certainly know and understand what they want, even if they
may remain confused about who they are. In a poll commissioned in
2001 that asked Mexicans how they viewed themselves by social class,
1% said "rich," 16% replied "poor," and an astonishing 82% stated that

* The exact number of students enrolled in higher education was 1,091,324.
† This is an increase of 150%.
‡ And 67% belonged to public institutions.
§ For 1994, the exact number of international flights was 10,737,422. For 2009, the exact
number of international flights was 22,540,000. For 1994, the exact number of domestic
passengers was 18,393,897.
‖ More than 1.5 million (1,631,000) in 1994, and more than 9 million in 2009.

they belonged to the middle class (4% upper middle class, 44% middle middle class, and 34% lower middle class).[44] This is a clearly "aspirational" reaction. We know that 82% of Mexicans are not middle class; at most 60% are, so at least 25% of the respondents are mistaken, but their expectations are not. They want to be middle-class and believe that this status is just around the corner. But as Federico Reyes Heroles explains in an essay reflecting this poll, they see themselves as much better off than their parents (like Lalo Sánchez) and their very poor compatriots.[45]

## *So How Did This Happen?*

Where does this new middle class come from? Is there that much social mobility in Mexico that one can easily detect the upward trend from the poorer* to the middle-class deciles,† as the middle class receives over time a greater share of the national income, and the very rich realize a smaller slice of the pie? Or has the pie grown so rapidly over the past fifteen years that everyone is sharing the same proportion of a bigger pie, or, mixing metaphors, the rising tide has lifted all boats? Probably all of the above, but other factors also explain this notable expansion.

Mobility is not the full answer. A study carried out in 2008 by ESRU, a Mexico City think tank, found that those who belonged to the two bottom deciles were doomed to stay there forever, and those that were part of the upper 20 percent of the population, income-wise, would remain so, more or less permanently. The study discovered that the possibilities of Mexicans from different income or educational levels intermarrying were almost nil, unlike during the initial years of the post-Revolutionary period. Any churning took place exclusively in the middle of the income spectrum.[46]‡ But the real answer is probably to be found in a convergence of explanations, which we can only rapidly enumerate here. First, the economic stability and the undeniable though mediocre growth of 1996–2008 were biased in favor of the

---

* Let's say first, second, and third.
† Deciles forth through ninth.
‡ The three deciles below the middle and above it.

poor: because of effective antipoverty programs, remittances from rela-
tives in the United States, formal and informal employment (most of
the increase in jobs in the last decade and a half occurred in low-wage,
low-skill jobs), and well-contained inflation, the people in the bottom
three to four deciles, but also those in the next two or three, clearly saw
their lot improve, and significantly so.[47]

Second, price stability, government policy, and social programs
allowed many of those at the top of the pyramid of the poor, or at the
bottom of the pyramid of the middle class, to have access to previously
unavailable credit, which led to the housing and automobile boom, as
well as to a series of consumer durables and middle-class services. These
goods and services were heretofore only accessible to the old middle
class;* suddenly the new middle class† enjoyed the same privilege. And
finally, as is best exemplified by the cell phone explosion, the price of
middle-class goods and services literally collapsed in many realms of
society and the economy. These factors allowed people who were
slightly better off, and who enjoyed access to credit at reasonable
(though far from cheap) rates, to acquire accoutrements that traditionally were beyond their grasp. In Mexico twenty years ago, a landline
telephone was a luxury. The waiting period was eternal, the line and
installation cost over a thousand dollars, and one needed all sorts of
papers, deeds, titles, etc., in order to purchase a phone. Today any
teenager with some spare change can buy a cell phone at the corner.

The fall in prices of these new, virtual necessities was due, in turn, to
many trends. One was the privatization of some of the providers of
goods and services. A case in point was Telmex, the state-owned
telecommunications company, spun off to Carlos Slim in 1992. Another
was enhanced domestic competition: low-cost airlines, for example,
that from 2006 onward cut airfares to the bone, lost a lot of money, but
forced the main carriers to proceed likewise. The trade opening that
began in 1987 and culminated with NAFTA and its phased-in tariff
cuts—for used cars, for example, or plasma TVs—was another ingredient, as it both provided consumers with cheaper items from abroad, but
also forced domestic producers to slash their prices. And finally, but perhaps most importantly, technological progress simply brought down

---

* In the sixth through ninth deciles.
† The next three deciles.

the cost of producing computers, cell phones, plasmas TVs, automobiles, and even homes for the lower middle class. The latter's income may only have grown slightly, but it went a lot further in 2008 than in 1994, as was the case during the early years of industrialization in nineteenth-century Europe. And so by consumption, as well as by income and habits, the upper-scale poor became lower-scale middle class, and the country was dramatically transformed, immensely for the better.

There are many examples of this metamorphosis, but one might be especially revealing because of its combination of an old-middle-class town and a new-middle-class community. Moreover, it is in Sinaloa, one of the more dynamic and prosperous states of Mexico, without belonging to the atypical "north" along the border. Los Mochis was a sleepy, sugarcane-producing midsize city that included old, American-owned *cañaverales* and a large mill, founded in 1903, around which the town grew, and which led to the fortune of some of Mexico's wealthiest traditional families, like the Redos (Ronald Reagan's best friends in Mexico). Today it is a city of 230,000 inhabitants, and Mexico's breadbasket.[48] It is smack in the middle of a large irrigation district,* fed by dams and reservoirs built in the thirties and forties, where subsequently the country's bountiful exports of winter fruits and vegetables took hold. Now it also produces soybeans, wheat, and corn, with two crops per year and yields on occasion higher than those of Kansas, Nebraska, Brazil, and Central Europe.[49] It is linked to another agricultural community, the equally prosperous town of Guasave, and to the Pacific deepwater port of Topolobampo. And just east of Los Mochis, as the fields rise toward the western Sierra Madre, can be found many of Mexico's traditionally most productive drug zones. Since World War II and even before, peasants have grown poppy for heroin and—at least until California's boom—the highest-quality marijuana in the world. Close by, in southern Sonora, lies Etchohuaquila, which, as every Los Angeles Dodgers fan remembers, is Fernando Valenzuela's hometown.

Mochis, as it is known, claims social statistics that the rest of Mexico would die for. More than three-quarters of its people have health care; the average number of school years is 10.2, nearly 50% above the national figure; and two-thirds of its homes have more than two bed-

---

* More than 150,000 hectares.

rooms. Practically every dwelling possesses a television set, and almost 30% feature personal computers.* It's a clean, safe, thriving town, where people go crazy about baseball and look down on soccer; where migration is not a synonym for departure to the north, but rather for the arrival of farmhands from Oaxaca, Chiapas, and Central America to harvest the summer crops; and where the Sinaloa drug culture (this is where the [in]famous *narcocorridos* were born) not only does not get in the way of capital-intensive, competitive, world-class agriculture, but complements it. People are tall. Its most famous businessman and most popular mayor and politician was elected state governor in 2010, despite charges of being gay, linked to drugs, or both. If one day all of Mexico resembles Los Mochis, many of the country's travails will have concluded.

So why is this middle-class nature of Mexican society incompatible with the exacerbated individualism of the Mexican character? Essentially for two reasons. The first is the most obvious. In a middle-class society, whatever its members may think or desire, the majority of the people—an overwhelming majority as in Japan, or an exiguous one like in Brazil—are, essentially, all alike. Americans prefer to disbelieve this truth, and convince themselves that it does not apply to them; Swedes, on the other hand, brood over it, acknowledge it, and loathe it. People may seek and on occasion find ways of emphasizing their differences, be they political, religious, ideological, fashion-based, or rooted in popular culture. But ultimately, anywhere from 60% to 90% of the inhabitants in a given land will work the same hours, make roughly the same money, consume the same goods, send their children to the same schools and live in the same homes, dress the same way and go to the same movies and rock concerts, experience a similar sexuality and vote for the same parties and leaders, and be subject to the same rules.

Marx and Lenin's classless society has yet to emerge, and maybe never will, but the closest we will probably come to it can be found in the modern middle-class societies as we know them of the North Atlantic and Pacific regions. It is not a just society (the income and wealth gap between a laid-off GM worker in Michigan and a Goldman Sachs director, and the equivalent abyss in other countries, dwarfs the imagination). And it is a society where, with minor and fortunate exceptions, there will always be an excluded underprivileged sector: the

* Some 98% of dwellings possess a television set.

poor, either homegrown or imported, the minorities discriminated against, and the immigrants, the impoverished region, or the unattended-to elderly, the crack babies and the Beurs, the homeless and the junkies, the imprisoned population and those who simply do not fit in. It is not anywhere near as mobile a society as its apologists claim: the GM hourly worker's son will probably also be an hourly laborer, and the Wall Street banker or broker's offspring will also probably end up working on Wall Street.

But it is a society where regardless of the specific intensity of one country or another's individualism, the collective is ultimately king. These middle-class societies cannot function any other way. Americans will reject public transportation more than the French, Germans and Italians will reject speed limits more than Americans, Canadians could not live without their cherished and imperfect National Health Care, and Americans may never accept not "choosing" their own doctor. And each society will select its favorite forms of collective action: the British like labor unions, the French their Maisons des Jeunes et de la Culture, the Americans their faith-based solidarity and self-help vocation. But they all play by the same rules, and abide by them, or face the consequences of breaking them.

Mexico's individualism is a different story. We do not want to be "all" the same, we do not think we are "all" the same, and we simply do not accept the consequences of being "all" the same. So we refuse to pay taxes (Mexico has one of the lowest tax takes over GDP in the world, and the smallest one in the OECD), we don't vote or join unions or civic organizations, or take the subway if we have a car, or accept the inviolability of laws and rules, or turn down individual solutions (bribes, exit from Mexico, or monopolies) to collective challenges. If we continued to be a country comprised of a few fabulously wealthy (which we still have) and an immense poor majority (which we don't), perhaps we might still function with the ingrained individualism that allowed Mexico to emerge and survive as a people and as a nation under adverse circumstances. But the norms that regulate a society of equals are alien to Mexico, undoubtedly because for centuries it was not a society of equals: neither of citizens nor of middle-class members. Unfortunately, today its society cannot function without those norms, habits, customs, practices, and basic agreements that its archaic individualism cannot countenance.

Second, and more concretely, the incompatibility involves public policy. It is virtually impossible to govern the country appropriately and simultaneously pay tribute to its individualism, given the mass society it has rapidly become. The policies that accommodate the former are totally unsuited to the latter. No Mexican government dares go up against the ingrained individualism springing from the past, yet practically no public policy is desirable or feasible if it does not accept the premise of the nation's middle-class nature. Two examples illustrate this point clearly.

In the previous chapter, we mentioned the country's preference for individual, horizontal housing. We attempted to show that there were material, topographical reasons for this choice, in addition to cultural ones. Those reasons are wearing thin, and wearing out. Land is still bountiful and cheap in most of Mexico's large metropolitan areas, but the urban transportation and almost unlimited time required to live tens of miles away from city centers is not. The only way to provide individual housing is to increasingly reposition it away from workplaces and far from the heart of urban agglomerations. That means taking water, electricity, roads, schools, transportation, and security to zones farther and farther removed from where all of these amenities are currently available. The obvious solution, which the federal government and most state and municipal authorities are correctly seeking, is to gradually or even abruptly shift to vertical housing. Whatever its drawbacks—and anyone who has visited projects in the Bronx or HLMs in the Paris *banlieues* is aware of them—at least it reduces costs and travel times. But officials and developers are skeptical. They quite rightly fear that the Mexican home "consumer" will not conform and react rationally to incentives and arguments in favor of high-rises. But otherwise, the nation's urban sprawl, already chaotic and nearly unmanageable, will soon become a nightmare.

A second, related, illustration resides in the Mexico City middle class's adamant refusal to use public transportation. Everything has been tried in the country's capital to reduce traffic congestion: second-story freeways, rapid transit arteries cutting through old neighborhoods, banning cars one day per week, and so forth. Nothing has worked, among other reasons because of the automobile explosion referred to earlier. Many cities in the world have more cars per capita than Mexico, but not its traffic or pollution. Why? Because, with the obvious exceptions of Los Angeles and Dallas, for example, the middle classes of New York and Berlin, of Paris and Madrid, of London and Tokyo, even if they own several vehicles per family, use mass transportation to go to and from work—anything else is unimaginable. Prices of gas, parking, insurance, tolls, and automobile taxes, plus the time wasted in traffic, are just too onerous to be affordable. So despite the love affair with the car, they dispense with it on weekdays, at least during working hours.

But not *chilangos,* as the rest of the country refers to the capital's inhabitants. It is true that the subway system was—rightly—built forty years ago to serve the poorer neighborhoods, and that none of the incentives are aligned properly to push middle-class commuters toward buses and the subway. It is equally true that the conditions of subways, buses, and so-called collective taxis are not easily amenable to the middle class. The crowds, the time, the heat, and the social churning, petty crime, and sexual harassment (despite separate subway cars for men and women during rush hours) cannot be easily assimilated by that cohort of society. But the cultural baggage is at least as weighty as these undeniable material considerations. Even in the—much older— Buenos Aires *subte* or the—far newer—São Paulo and Santiago *metros,* one can see loads of middle-class passengers riding off to work in the morning and returning in the evening, not for lack of an automobile, but rather of the time to waste, or of the individualism to offend.

Middle-class societies can be individualistic and function adequately. The United States is far less individualistic than it thinks, but more so than other rich countries. In the last analysis, though, self-awareness or consciousness of one's real station in life is less important than the material conditions in which it takes place. Mexican individualism, as described in the previous chapter, is utterly dysfunctional to the middle-class nature of the nation's society.

CHAPTER 3

# Victims and Enemies of Conflict and Competition

There is an iron law of Mexican pop anthropology, with a corollary in Mexico's politics. It states that Mexicans love to see themselves as victims, and that they also love victims. This is a good starting point for the next venture into the national character, again with all the caveats laid out at the beginning of this book. Here we deal with this cultural or character trait, as such, while in the next chapter we show how it clashes with Mexico's current reality.

Mexico as a country of victims, and politics as a sport where the pole position, so to speak, is the status of the victim, is perhaps the best-known and most stereotypical trait associated with the Mexican soul, and with Mexican politics. It is not entirely false. In the writings of the classics—e.g., Manuel Gamio, Samuel Ramos, and Octavio Paz—victimization is portrayed diversely as an "inferiority complex" of all Mexicans (Ramos, though D. H. Lawrence may have detected this first, in *The Plumed Serpent*); as the sorry and threatened lot of the "Indian" (Gamio), who is "timid, lacks energy and ambition, and lives in fear of the abuse and exactions of the 'enlightened ones,' of the whites. His forehead still bears the scar of the Spanish *conquistador's* iron boot."[1] And of course, Octavio Paz, more than anyone:

> In his harsh solitude, which is both barbed and courteous, every-thing serves him as a defense: silence and words, politeness and disdain, irony and resignation. . . . He passes through life like a

man who has been flayed; everything can hurt him, including words and the very suspicion of words. . . . Stoicism is the most exalted of our military and political attributes. . . . We are taught from childhood to accept defeat with dignity. . . . Resignation is one of our most popular virtues. We admire fortitude in the face of adversity more than the most brilliant triumph.[2]

There are endless explanations for this penchant for suffering, feeling victimized, and bearing it stoically, as well as cheering on those who are thrust, or able to place themselves, in this eminently desirable political slot. As always, many of the explanations date back to the Conquest, and the initial rape it entailed. As so many of the classics and semiclassics have endlessly repeated, the Spanish did not come to settle but to conquer; that meant they came without women and, being *hidalgos* and squires, were certainly not destined for manual labor in the fields and in the mines. So they needed local women to satisfy their masculine needs, and local men to satisfy their economic ones; the two satisfactions were not entirely compatible objectives. The consequence is easy to imagine. In this narrative (which is certainly not a totally accurate rendition), the women were raped, and the men were enslaved. In order for the two tragedies to occur simultaneously, both men and women had to be credibly threatened with death, and the correlation of forces (as Lenin might have put it) necessarily had to corroborate the threat, materializing it often enough to be believable, but infrequently enough to allow the survival of both sex and forced labor. Given this view of the perceived circumstances, no wonder the first Mexicans considered themselves victims, and may continue to view themselves as such until kingdom come; no wonder that they instantly, almost automatically, empathize with victims in general and with those running for office or seeking power as underdogs.

The narrative continues, and remains virtually consensual among the classics, both with regard to independent life as it evolved after 1821, and at least through the end of the Revolution. The "people" (almost always identified, until very recently, with the indigenous population, or, as Gamio repeatedly formulates it, with those of "mixed blood where the dominant strain is Indian") were subsequently and successively exploited and oppressed by the newly emancipated *criollos,* the Texans and Americans, the French invaders in 1862 and their conservative acolytes, the Porfirian dictatorship and the new American imperialists, and, finally, no longer in the language of the classics but rather, in the social imaginary of their successors, by the victors of the betrayed revolutionary epic. In a nutshell, the Mexican people, even before they were Mexican, have always been screwed by others (in Ramos's lament, "Up to now, Mexicans have known only how to die"), and therein lies the nature of their masks (Paz), inferiority complex (Ramos, Ramírez, and Uranga), of being a "poor and pained race" (Gamio), and of the infinite anecdotes told about the intuitive Mexican association with "*los vencidos*" (the defeated), not "*los vencedores*" (the victors).[3]

The following story has been told so many times that it defies repetition, but here goes anyway. There are numerous effigies of Spanish *conquistador* Francisco Pizarro in Lima and throughout Peru, though the one in the country's capital has its own, wonderful history. It was removed in the twenties from the central square, because, having been originally intended as a statue of Hernán Cortés created by an American sculptor, Ramsay MacDonald, it was first offered as a monument to the conqueror of Mexico, whose government promptly rejected it, since it "offended its history," and because it decided it didn't really look like Cortés anyway. So the artist took the sculpture back with him to Virginia, but when he died in 1935, his widow decided to donate it to the Lima municipal authorities, who received it and placed in the atrium of the Cathedral. Since then it has been moved around many times and is currently placed in the Parque de la Muralla. In Cuba, the home of conqueror Diego Velázquez de Cuéllar is conserved in Santiago de Oriente; in Puerto Rico there is a statue of Ponce de León in the central square of San Juan, and he is buried in the Cathedral; in Guatemala there is a city named after Pedro de Alvarado; and in Chile, there is not only a statue of Pedro de Valdivia in the central plaza of the capital, but one of the country's main cities carries his moniker.

There is no statue of Cortés anywhere in Mexico, and he remains buried in the desolate and uncared-for, rarely visited Church of Jesus of Nazareth in a neglected neighborhood of downtown Mexico City. The Incas in Peru were as brutally treated as the Aztecs in Mexico; Pizarro and his colleagues were as bloodthirsty and cruel as Cortés and his minions; still, one country acknowledges its heritage, the other does not. Or rather, does and doesn't at the same time. Peru had no revolution (at least not until 1968) and the whites who wrote its history remained in charge until recently and identified with Pizarro, while perhaps its Indians did so with Tupac Amaru.

## Indians and Mestizos

Which actually makes sense only if the country does not (or did not) really subscribe to the myth of *mestizaje*, and ultimately recognize that its identity is not the result of an imposed melting pot, but of an Indian defeat and a Spanish—that is, foreign—triumph. This vision may actually track history closer than others, but it contradicts the ethos of Mexico, the *mestizo* nation par excellence. Mexico abides by the maxim inscribed in the (in)famous Three Cultures Square of Tlatelolco in Mexico City, inaugurated in the mid-sixties when a then new Foreign Ministry was constructed, and where the three cultures of Mexico were thus present: the pre-Columbian through the Aztec ruins of Tlatelolco, the colonial because of a Catholic convent on the grounds, and the modern one thanks to the ministry and a new housing project constructed in the area. The inscription reads: "On August 13th, 1521, Tlatelolco fell to Hernán Cortés, after having been heroically defended by Cuauhtémoc. This was neither a victory nor a defeat, but rather the painful birth of the *mestizo* people that is Mexico today."

It is difficult to determine which came first: Mexicans' embrace of themselves as victims, from which the anthropologists, historians, and poets drew their conclusions, or the scholars' work and laments, which over the years were thrust upon a people that did not necessarily adhere to that view. This last conclusion is clearly the one modern anthropologists, such as Roger Bartra, insistently cling to. No one has developed this notion or defended it with as much intelligence and eloquence as Bartra. He and some of his colleagues, like Claudio Lomnitz of Columbia University, believe that the entire notion of a Mexican character or soul is an ideological or cultural construct, derived much more from the classics' imagination than from the actual psyche of the masses. Furthermore, the classics were not acting (or writing, as the case may be) with naïveté or altruism, but rather, they crafted this notion with a purpose: enabling Mexico's only two lasting political regimes since Independence, the Porfiriato and the one that emerged from the Revolution after 1917, to clothe their elitist, authoritarian, and pro-American domination in a nationalistic, popular, and consensual robe. Herein lies the explanation, according to Bartra and others, of the exceptional longevity of both regimes: thirty-five years for Porfirio Díaz, and seven decades for the PRI. The very notion of a national character is a product—spontaneous or deliberate—of a cultural, political, and social endeavor. But it cannot be produced just any old way: it must "fit" the reality it both reflects and acts upon.[4]

Between a preexistent "national character" discovered by the anthropologists and poets, and an ideological structure imposed by the dominant elites, there is probably an intermediate interpretation. It suggests that as long as Mexicans perceived themselves—and were perceived—as Indians, the ingrained notion of the victim was unavoidable, and was both easily forced upon them and reflected their existing sentiments. It was only when the trick was finally turned and the country proudly and justly saw itself, mainly in the mirror of its "official history," truly as a *mestizo* society, with a rapidly shrinking indigenous minority, that it could begin to separate most of its feelings from the intellectuals' description of them, and start to change both the scholars' views, and its own.* But the momentum was too strong to curtail immediately, and so in the Mexican cosmology of the twentieth century, if the Indian was the perennial victim of the Conquest, and the *mestizo* was simply a reflection of the Indian, then the *mestizo* was ipso facto a victim too and, more importantly, was quite justified in resorting to many of the same defense mechanisms for survival that the Indian had adopted since 1521. To a large extent, the classics and their disciples or critics were right, as we shall see below with specific numbers: Mexico only became a *mestizo* nation in the first third or so of the twentieth century, and for much of the first half of that century the traits attributed to the "Mexican soul" were those generally attached, falsely or accurately, to the indigenous peoples.[†]

---

* At least for educational purposes, Mexico's official history was born probably in 1905 when Justo Sierra was appointed minister of education by Porfirio Díaz, and promptly transformed two of his own works, *Historia patria* and *Historia general,* into official textbooks for elementary school and high school.
† I am particularly indebted to Héctor Aguilar Camín for sharing his reflections on these issues with me before publishing them in several of his outstanding historical essays and books.

The transformation from a largely Indian society to a *mestizo* one got under way—and can be loosely associated—with the Revolution of 1910. It is most closely and intellectually identified with Andrés Molina Enríquez, and his so-called *mestizo-filia*, as well as with José Vasconcelos, the Revolution's first education minister, best known for having invited Diego Rivera and José Clemente Orozco to paint their murals in several government buildings in the early 1920s. Vasconcelos's *raza cósmica* (cosmic race) vision of *mestizo* Mexico is both remarkable for its optimism and pride, and somewhat absurd in view of the claims it formulates.

According to Vasconcelos, who ran for president in 1929 and shifted to the extreme right in his later years, unlike in the United States and Britain, which he believed excluded most people from their melting pot, in Mexico the *mestizo* ethnic blend was inclusive and certain to be successful, since it brought everything and everyone together. First, it was generous: "They [the Anglo-Saxons] . . . committed the sin of destroying previous races, whereas we assimilated them, and this gives us new rights and the hope of an unprecedented mission in history." But it was also superior: "What will emerge [from Latin America] is the definitive race, the synthesis of all races or the integral race, constructed with the genius and blood of all peoples, and thus, more capable of true fraternity and of a truly universal vision."[5]

The central point about *mestizaje*, though, does not involve its origins as an ideological construct, but the fact that until very recently and, in a few specific ways even today—including the identification with and predilection for the victim—the *mestizo* in Mexico was associated with the Indian. As Emilio Uranga phrased it:

Most recently, Mexicans have accidentally chosen the Indian essence. . . . When the European sees the *mestizo*, he walks right past him; he crosses the ford and only halts before the Indian, who fascinates him. The *mestizo*, in turn, grasps this, and figures things out: he will advance toward the European showing his Indian facet, in order to be saved by the accident of that facet. The *mestizo* is an Indian's accident, a bit of nothingness adhered to the Indian essence, which when loved or justified by the European or American is also justified. . . . When Indian relics are displaced and fascinate Americans, the *mestizo* feels justified; he

would want everything to be transformed into an Indian product, for his entire life to become a compact block of the Indian
vision of the world. Every revolution is carried out on behalf of
the Indian . . . [because] only that which is Indian acquires a
universal brand; the *mestizo* culture has not transcended our
regional boundaries.[6]

The American and the European had their say in this whole affair,
as Guillermo Sheridan has shown.* There was a modern demand for
indigenist exoticism in Europe and the United States during the
twenties and thirties, in arts and letters, which co-generated an
idealized, falsified, exportable, and rebellious "Indian" for foreign
consumption.

There are solid demographic, historical reasons for admitting this
association of the *mestizo* reality with the indigenous one. As long as
Mexico was still an overwhelmingly rural country, that is, at least until
the mid-1950s, where was the *mestizaje* supposed to take place, after its
initial emergence in the *haciendas* of the colonial period and of the
nineteenth century? In the country's first full-fledged census, carried
out in 1895, 89% of the population was rural; the majority only became
urban in 1960. Strangely, though, in 1910 only 11% of Mexico was tabulated as indigenous, barely twice the proportion of today, and 10%
was deemed European.[7] The numbers just don't pan out; they imply
that roughly 75% of Mexico's population at the turn of the last century
was already *mestizo*, given that there could hardly have been many
indigenous inhabitants in the nation's cities. Hence, many have questioned these figures, among them the authors of a study carried out by
the National University in 2005, partly based on census data from the
nineteenth century. They estimate that in 1885, 43% of the country's
population was *mestizo*, and 38% was Indian, that is, statistically, the
two sectors were almost identical; only until by 1921 did the ratio reach
two to one in favor of the *mestizo* cohort.[8] While the point can be
argued that a *mestizo* can be a full-blooded Indian who has changed his
or her way of life, the definition used then tended to be limited to
bloodlines, language, and living in community villages.

* Guillermo Sheridan, "México en 1932: la polémica nacionalista," in *Vida y pensamiento
de México,* (Mexico City: Fondo de Cultura Económica, 1999).

Is the 1910 census figure credible when it classifies only 11% of the country's population as indigenous? Were the majority of the Mexican countryside's inhabitants that overwhelmingly *mestizo* on the eve of the Revolution? Had such a churning of ethnic groups taken place exclusively in the countryside over the previous four centuries? Some devoted and occasionally fanatical defenders of Mexico's indigenous roots don't think so. Guillermo Bonfil, perhaps the most eloquent and most strident example of Mexico's current *indigenismo,* says so openly: "The masses that fought [in the Revolution] were, to a large majority, Indian peasants."[9] Similarly, Manuel Gamio, writing in 1917, emphasized the fact that the "majority [of the population] was made up of people racially and culturally Indian"; and like Bonfil, he also insisted, but writing at that time, that the majority "of the rebels belonged to the indigenous race."[10] More realistically, wasn't the countryside, at least through the thirties and the beginning of industrialization in 1940, essentially a large sea of heterogeneous indigenous populations and cultures, never all the same, living chiefly in the kind of villages where Zapata was born, where devout Catholicism was still mixed with some pre-Columbian rituals, where Spanish was understood but rarely spoken, and where perhaps some physical traits could suggest a strictly biological *mestizaje,* but certainly not a cultural, social, or political one? If language was the main defining attribute for the census takers, isn't it likely that an affirmative response to the question "Do you speak Spanish" actually meant "Yes, I possess a rudimentary knowledge of utilitarian Spanish, which I use in the marketplace, in church, and in the army." According to the 1910 census, four-fifths of Mexico's inhabitants spoke Spanish, but this was the Spanish they spoke.[11] Probably as many as two-thirds of those 15 million spoke indigenous tongues among themselves. It is true that in those villages, like in modern-day Guatemala, for instance, distinctions within indigenous communities are drawn between groups on the basis of tiny doses of *mestizaje.* Those who possess them are subsequently considered not "fully" Indian, even though to the outsider they may appear so. Mexico has never really come up with a good answer to the question "What does being Indian mean?" The definitions of the term stretch from use of a non-Spanish language to a way of life, and include as we shall see in Chapter 6 the terribly racist and derogatory connotation generally implied by the words "*pinche indio,*" one of the

worst insults Mexicans, including indigenous people, use to insult . . .
Mexicans.*

Porfirio Díaz, in a famous interview he granted to an American
journalist in 1908, after having ruled the country for nearly thirty years,
and knowing it probably better than anybody else, thought along these
lines: "The Indians [are] more than half of our population."[12] In 1951,
José Iturriaga stated, basing himself on the work of Gonzalo Aguirre
Beltrán, that when the Independence wars began, back in 1810, Indians
outnumbered *mestizos* two to one.[13] Andrés Molina Enríquez, in his
1909 classic *Los grandes problemas nacionales*, which became an ode to
the country's *mestizaje*, identified "*mestizos*" with "middle class," which
at that time could not have represented more than 10% of the population. And as late as 1934, Samuel Ramos proclaimed that the Mexican
peasant "almost always belongs to the indigenous race," and in 1930,
82% of the population was still rural.[14] Moreover, the *mestizo* population was nowhere near a unified core.† As British historian Alan Knight
put it: "There has been no definable *mestizo* society—or social personality—only *mestizo campesinos*, *mestizo* workers, *mestizo* priests, politicians and businessmen, their shared *mestizaje* relevant only in that it
collectively differentiated them from the Indian."[15] Perhaps for this
reason, today the Census Bureau does not classify Mexicans by "white
or Caucasian" or "*mestizos*," including only "indigenous languages."
Only after 1921 did the numbers become somewhat more reliable and
consistent, though still approximate; in that year "*mestizo*" was still
used as a category. In that year's census, 60% of the population was
*mestizo*, 30% Indian.[16]

If on the eve of the revolt, *mestizos* represented a minority of the
population, and indigenous peoples a majority, were not the stereotyp-

---

* A similar phenomenon can be observed at a more anecdotal but perhaps deeper level.
Since the 1950s, Mexican TV, movie, and magazine advertisements for cosmetics, beer,
and many other consumer staples have used blond, white-skinned, blue-eyed models,
which obviously have very little to do with the appearance of the immense majority of
Mexicans. The reason has always been evident: the aspirational nature of advertisement
in Mexico. Perhaps the most famous example was for a mid-quality beer—Superior—
that featured dazzling and scantily clad blond bombshells in the sixties and seventies,
claiming that its beer, a light-colored one, was "*la rubia superior que todos quieren*" ("the
superior blond that everybody wants").
† This also I owe to long conversations with Héctor Aguilar Camín.

ical virtues and vices attributed to the Indians since time immemorial conceptually transferred to the urban *mestizos*? The majority of the traits generally ascribed to *mestizos* were almost certainly those seemingly detected—but in fact elaborated on—by the writers (and probably even the artists), as they "saw" them in the indigenous populations of the territory named Mexico. And one of them was the identification with victims, and its corollary: an extraordinary panoply of defense mechanisms developed over nearly four centuries of oppression (colonial and postcolonial). The jewel in the crown, the fundamental defense mechanism behind Octavio Paz's enigmatic masks and Carlos Fuentes's remarkable ruminations about Mexican identity, is the avoidance of conflict, the flight from confrontation, the perpetual quest for euphemisms and quasi-sacred forms of courtesy and gentleness, which can, or cannot, coexist with outbursts of violence, insults, and anger. In psychoanalyst Santiago Ramírez's words: "The trauma imposed by the Conquest on the Indian was so great that his possibilities of struggle under the new culture were annulled; his only defense mechanism and strength was to accept what he had, to mistrust everything that the Spaniard, the *criollo* or the *mestizo ladino* could offer. . . . The Indian eludes conflict with the cultural elements found above him, be they friendly or aggressive."[17]

### Never Put Up a Fight You Can Avoid

In many ways, the Indian, and thus the *mestizo*, and seemingly every Mexican, was right. Confrontation had always been a bad deal for them, from Moctezuma and Cortés all the way to the heroes of the Revolution, each and every one having been assassinated: Francisco Madero, Emiliano Zapata, Francisco Villa, Venustiano Carranza, and Álvaro Obregón (who were either all white or whitish *mestizo*, except for Zapata, who was a strongly Indian *mestizo*). Their elaborate defense mechanisms were fully and blatantly justified, if not always effective or easy to comprehend. As the German geographer Alexander von Humboldt put it, as early as 1805, "Mexicans love to envelop their most insignificant acts in mystery."[18] Carlos Fuentes in particular has written brilliantly about the Mexican flight to euphemisms and excessive courtesy, as instruments of self-defense, if not of conflict aversion:

The extraordinarily elaborate formulae of verbal courtesy in Mexico, the use of the subjunctive, the constant appeal to the diminutive, all are defenses against verbal abuse and its violent sequels. People say "This is your home" in order to ensure that the guest respects it as if it were his or hers; the formula encloses a fear of the "other," of the thief, the vandal, the rapist; Mexican homes are hidden behind enormous walls topped with broken glass. People say "If you were so kind as to lend me . . ." because if they simply, dryly said "Lend me this or that" the answer would be "Why don't you lend me your sister?"[19]

The key is not so much to defend oneself against aggression, as Fuentes eloquently suggests, but rather to avoid conflict, verbal or otherwise. Conversely, one of the worst offenses a Mexican can experience is to be spoken to "*golpeado*," or brusquely or abruptly: countless workers, domestic employees, girlfriends, and administrative personnel prefer to lose their jobs than to put up with it. When asked why they left, the answer invariably is: "*Es que me habló golpeado.*" Which basically means that the boss, the boyfriend, the owner, or the woman of the house addressed the victim in direct, explicit, harsh, though not necessarily insulting terms. Those terms generated a feeling of unpleasantness, discomfort and awkwardness that became simply unbearable, even if the consequences were losing a job, a partner, or friend. Confrontation is intrinsically deplorable, to be avoided at all cost, regardless of the causes or the outcome. It is inherently undesirable and pernicious.

I remember a scene in the town of Tepoztlán, southeast of Mexico City, known for the beauty of its mountainous setting and folk cults that for years have charmed and intrigued visitors from around the world. A preferred site for foreign residents and tourists, as well as for anthropologists, this is where Oscar Lewis wrote one of his key works on the Mexican peasantry, and to which Anita Brenner devoted her classic *Idols Behind Altars* in the 1930s. Its inhabitants are known for their fierce pride (and resentment), for their attachment to traditional ways, and for letting matters get out of control on weekends when everyone (*tepoztecos*, as the locals are called, and *tepoztisos*, or "fake ones") has a bit too much to drink, even by Mexican standards. It was in 1989, just after the massively tampered with presidential elections of the year before, when PRI candidate Carlos Salinas de Gortari edged out or lost out to rival Cuauhtémoc Cárdenas. The defeated son of the iconic president who nationalized Mexico's oil in 1938 decided to build a political party and contest elections at all levels throughout Mexico: in towns, cities, states, local congresses, and nationally. His followers ran slates, watched over polling sites on election day, and were especially attentive to the vote-counting mechanism: how votes were counted and registered on tally sheets. But since Cárdenas knew his people well, he was fully aware of his supporters' reluctance to pick fights with local PRI hacks, so he attempted to send aides or sympathizers from the capital to watch over the over-watchers. This was how I accompanied one of those aides, Jorge Martínez, El Chale, to several polling booths in Tepoztlán on election day, and how we witnessed the beginning of a quarrel in the early evening.

We insisted that the local *cardenistas* put up a fight, and not accept or co-sign the tally sheets, given the obvious tampering that had taken place in the vote-counting process. They were not enthusiastic about this, and gave us all sorts of explanations, but finally one of the *tepoztecos* spit out the real one: "If we protest, the PRI guys will get upset." Which was undeniably true, and entirely the point: to stop the old ruling party gangsters from stealing another election, even if they were ultimately unhappy about it. Our side backed down, though we probably could have taken the debate and the fight. The PRI won fraudulently, and it would require several more years for the opposition to conquer the town, electorally speaking. We were bewildered at their behavior, but then upon reflection, we realized that, in their own way, they may have been right. The next day, we would return to Mexico City; they would be forced to continue dealing with and resisting the PRI's abuses and insults. Cárdenas had a million things to attend to; they had only one: living their lives in Tepoztlán pretty much the way they had over the past four centuries. Confrontations in the past (the Rubén Jaramillo movement nearby, in the early 1960s, and the cradle of Zapata's uprising in Anenecuilco, just miles away, in 1911) had led nowhere, except to death and destruction.

This trend and tradition is borne out by contemporary comparative polling. In a Latinobarómetro poll undertaken in 2008, citizens from eighteen Latin American nations were asked to give their opinion as to whether street marches, protests, and demonstrations were "normal in a democracy," "necessary in order for demands to be heard," a "way of allowing young people to acquire a stake in the political process," or "only produce chaos and destruction." Mexicans chose the last option more than any other country, except for Ecuadorans and Salvadorans. It is worth remembering that Ecuador had seen its previous five presidents overthrown by "the street," and El Salvador experienced a bloody civil war from 1979 through 1992. A resounding 65% of all Mexicans agreed with the last statement in the questionnaire, though this figure may have been distorted by the recent memory of highly disruptive street marches in Mexico City in protest over the 2006 presidential election.[20]

### The Whys of Conflict Aversion: Violence, Irreparable Futility, and the Excluded Middle

There are four generally accepted explanations for the national predilection for conflict aversion, supposing one acknowledges that it's real, widespread, and long-lasting. As Jesús Silva-Herzog Márquez summarized it:

> the First Fight we have to wage is in favor of the principle of conflict. Mexico's imagination is dominated by the fear of the precipice and the condemnation of antagonism. To be cautious is to reject conflict, to see it as the worst of all evils. Perhaps it is the deep revolutionary heritage that bestows on every political faction the drama of imminent chaos. We think that conflict will immediately throw us into an ungovernable jungle. . . . We have to begin trusting in the fertility of conflict.[21]

The first explanation emphasizes a sort of built-in, automatic self-containment mechanism that a supposedly archviolent society, since time immemorial, has acquired and developed as a way of insuring that the brutal atavisms of what is often referred to as *"el México bronco,"* the "rough-and-ready Mexico," not get out of control. The accent is here placed on the consequence of violence, not on the avoidance of confrontation, and it is linked with the hyper-stereotypical Mexican indifference in the face of death. Nothing has fascinated the literary and sociological soul-searchers more than the Mexican attitude toward death, exemplified by the late-nineteenth-century "cartoons" of José Guadalupe Posada, the celebrations of the Day of the Dead (November 2), and the endless commentaries of foreigners from all walks of life regarding the country's resignation and often humorous attitude as death approaches or arrives.

The proof would seem to be in the pudding. Mexico was deemed to have undergone some of the most violent episodes in history anywhere, from the Conquest, when the "Black Legend" tells of how a large part of the indigenous population then inhabiting what came to be known as New Spain was decimated; the Revolution of 1910–17, which took a million lives; the student movement of 1968, when during a single afternoon more than five hundred students were massacred; and most recently, the drug wars, which by 2011 had taken more than 35,000 deaths directly related to trafficking, gangland warfare, and abuses by the military and police. If one adds to these "facts" the anecdotal evidence of Mexican violence and brutality, as described by Mexicans and foreigners alike (D. H. Lawrence and Evelyn Waugh, mainly, as well as Graham Greene in *Lawless Roads*, Malcolm Lowry in *Under the Volcano*, Eisenstein in *Qué Viva México!*, Paz, Fuentes, and Rulfo), as well as the endless stories of shootouts, police torture, revenge wrought by landowners against peasants, industrialists against workers, and so on, one sees a rather well drawn portrait of a land so intrinsically plagued by violence and blood, and so frequently on the verge of drifting out of control, that it is only understandable that people should be averse to confrontation. They know where it leads, and have suffered its consequences too many times.

Except that the massacre of 1968 produced "only" sixty-eight victims with names, and there will never be, and never were, any more; the fallen in actual combat during the Revolution could not have exceeded thirty or forty thousand (a different statistic is the number of deaths brought about by the economic and social chaos generated by civil strife, and the 1918 Spanish flu epidemic, but that is not a reflection of violence). And Mexico, even in the midst of its self-induced drug disgrace, has fewer homicides per hundred thousand inhabitants than most countries in Latin America. According to the Pan American Health Organization, in 2007, Mexico experienced 11 homicides per 100,000 inhabitants, while El Salvador led Latin America with 43, followed by Colombia with 38, Venezuela with 34, and Brazil with 31.

Canada averaged around 1.8 in 2006, and the United States 6.1 in 2007; Western Europe topped 5 in 2004. In 2006, Russia averaged 20 homicides per 100,000 inhabitants, and South Africa, 49.5.[22]

This assessment became counterintuitive after 2010, when the gruesome nature of drug-related slayings as well as the number, the dispersion, and the publicity of "regular" homicides generated the impression of Mexico as a country at war. News reports, statistics, and private evaluations all concurred: violence in Mexico seemed to be totally out of control. In fact, the numbers continued largely to bear out the previous appreciation, despite the apparent inconsistency, though by late 2010 they had grown quite dramatically.

The reasons for this paradox are well known. Until the late 1980s, violence in Mexico, while not alien to large cities, remained a throwback to the rural past; it was concentrated in, and fed by, fights over land, water, roads, and privileges in the countryside, and among village communities. As recently as 1995, in Aguas Blancas, Guerrero, and Acteal, Chiapas, over Christmas 1997, two significant massacres took place in rural areas over land and water and community rights. This violence was hidden, swept under the table, far from the lights and sound bites of foreign correspondents, human rights activists, and diplomats. It was there, corrosive and tragic, but far from what the eye could see.

No longer. Since 2008, beheadings, mutilations, torture, and destruction are urban, often close to the United States, reported on and taking place in broad daylight, even if they are rarely investigated and punished. This violence is strident, scandalous, and intolerable for modern minds and middle-class souls. But it is far less widespread than before, though far noisier. It is just one more of Mexico's paradoxes of modernity.*

These comparative statistics are notoriously imprecise and difficult to use, since the sources, the years, and accounting procedures are far from uniform. Thus they should not be viewed as exact figures, but they nevertheless serve as indicators of relative degrees of violence. Similarly, according to a Latinobarómetro poll from 2008, comparing levels of violence among neighbors, gangs, families, and schools, among eighteen countries in the region, Mexico placed tenth; it was less

---

* These reflections were taken partially from Joaquín Villalobos, "Doce mitos de la guerra contra el narcotráfico," *Nexos,* [Mexico City] no. 385 (January 2010); "La guerra de México," *Nexos,* no. 392 (August 2010); and from Fernando Escalante Gonzalbo, "Homicidios 1997–2007," *Nexos,* no. 381 (September 2009).

violent in each one of these categories than Brazil (number one), Guatemala, Panama, the Dominican Republic, Venezuela, Honduras, Nicaragua, Peru, and El Salvador; Chile was one of the least violent.[23] Mexico, then, is nowhere near to being the most violent society in Latin America today, although it does rank well above the industrialized nations. Brazil's music is undoubtedly more mellow and less apologetic of death and violence (one can hardly imagine, even in Antonio Carlos Jobim's world-renowned melancholy score for *Black Orpheus* from the 1950s, a phrase like the proverbial Mexican "*La vida no vale nada*"—Life is worthless—from José Alfredo Jiménez), but the South American giant and home of the bossa nova is a more violent place than Mexico, mariachis and all.

Even the Black Legend of the Conquest has been greatly exaggerated, according to many historians. Between 1521 and the end of the sixteenth century it is nowhere near obvious, as many have always claimed, that the population of New Spain was almost destroyed by the "invaders." The initiators of the "legend," Sherburne Cook and Woodrow Borah, came up in 1950 with the conventional numbers: the Mexican highlands' population went from 25 million in 1519 (just before Cortés arrived) to 17 million in 1532, and a dramatic 1.9 million in 1580.[24] Already in 1960, Spanish historian Nicolás Sánchez-Albornoz warned that while the population *had* shrunk drastically, two caveats were in order. First, the baseline was very difficult to ascertain, since the Aztecs did not really have a serious head count; secondly, most of the decimation was due to epidemics and illness in general, not necessarily to direct violence.[25] According to Mexican historians Andrés Lira and Luis Moro, a demographic catastrophe hit New Spain in 1576, lasting until 1579, and perhaps even two years later. During that time, an epidemic of astounding intensity provoked the deaths of 2 million Indians, leading to labor scarcities and rationing.[26] This, we should note, took place more than half a century after the Conquest, and generated significant economic difficulties for the conquerors. Even the Church wanted its converts alive, not dead.

Thus, as an Argentine revisionist historian phrased it more recently:

The truth is that Spain neither planned nor executed a genocidal plan; the collapse of the indigenous population was not linked to military confrontation with the conquerors, but rather to a variety of causes among which the most important was microbial contagion. The truth is that intentional homicide as an explanation for the demographic disaster does not resist serious historical research by authors like Sánchez-Albornoz, José Luis Moreno, Rolando Mellafe. The fact is that the Indians of America, as Pierre Chaunu said, "did not succumb to the blows of Toledo steel swords, but to viral and microbial shock. The truth is numbers are bandied about irresponsibly, without any qualitative analysis, or any serious historical-statistical discipline. No one denies that indigenous demography suffered a circumstantial reduction. But we are denying that it was caused by a genocidal plan."[27]

In short, there is an undeniable degree of violence in Mexican society, but the ideological surplus and the effects it generates are a social construct, not a simple fact of life. Mexican thinkers from Manuel Gamio, generally referred to as the country's first anthropologist, to Paz himself, generally subscribe to this view. Gamio wrote in 1917 that if Mexico had been conquered by the French, for example, instead of the Spanish, it would subsequently have been taken over by "American pioneers, who were much more radical than the Spanish, pursuing and persecuting Indians until they extinguished them."[28] (The truth may of course be more contradictory.) Paz makes a simple and oft repeated point: during the Conquest itself, "smallpox accounted for more Aztec lives than the Spanish harquebus"; the poet goes as far as stating that the vulnerability of the New World civilizations to disease was a consequence of their own isolated, insular nature, implying that any contact with the rest of the globe would have produced the same consequences: "America was a continent removed from world history during thousands of years and this immense solitude explains the originality of its creativeness, as well as its fatal and most damaging limitation: the first contact with the outside world annihilated those societies. Lacking biological defenses, the Mesoamerican indigenous populations fell easily victim to European and Asian viruses."[29]

In relation to the casualties of the Revolution, the National Statistics Institute states that the country's population went from 15.1 million in the 1910 census, on the eve of the turmoil, to 14.5 million in 1921. *The Cambridge History of Latin America* offers an explanation: "War, emigration and flu [meaning the 1918 worldwide epidemic of Spanish influenza]" were the main factors.[30] According to a historian of the Revolution, a reporter from a Mexico City paper was able to piece together the following statistics: "[there were] around 436,000 deaths from Spanish flu in 1918–19, more than the 300,000 deaths attributed to the Revolution itself. The demographic fracture that appears in the study of the 1910 and 1921 census is much more due to epidemics than to revolutionary violence."[31] In the same vein, the Franco-Mexican historian Jean Meyer has concluded: "between 1914 and 1919 one million Mexicans died, about one-quarter of them on the battlefields, or facing firing squads, and about three-quarters from epidemics and famine."[32] The Revolution was of course a violent event, but only up to a point. In December 1914, for example, when Villa's troops from the north and Zapata's from the south captured and occupied Mexico City for a few brief weeks, often remembered by the "chattering classes" of the capital as their worst nightmare, what actually took place was a somewhat more subtle and subdued affair. According to the least inaccurate calculations, some two hundred inhabitants of the city were assassinated that month, many of them as a result of drunken brawls and inadequate policing, rather than systematic violence.

In fact, there are excellent reasons for thinking that the overvaluation of the deaths springing from the Conquest, the Revolution, and the 1968 student movement (obviously of dramatically different dimensions) have served a direct, if not deliberate or conscious, purpose: to forestall other revolts against authority, or another revolution, or another student movement. For decades the Mexican people were led to believe that given the violent country that was theirs, and the violent soul that they shared, along with the absence of legal or cultural restraints on that violence, any attempt to overturn the status quo would lead to . . . what the previous attempt had led to. That attempt had been "justified" since matters before 1910 were so terrible that everyone could understand why the peasants, workers, and middle classes rose up against the Porfirian dictatorship; it was even worthwhile in spite of the proverbial million fatalities, in view of the benefits the perpetrators of the Revolution received. Nonetheless, no other similar intent against the new order could ever be warranted in the light of the terrible cost in lives the country would once again have to pay. This hardly veiled threat worked, and in its success lies part of the secret of the Mexican authoritarian regime's notable staying power.

The student movements of the sixties suffered a similar fate. The students, their parents and friends, as well as journalists, politicians, and academics in Mexico and the world over were shocked when Oriana Fallaci, as she lay bleeding on the pre-Columbian stones of Tlatelolco Square, described the hundreds of bodies around her.[33] They were, according to her dispatch, victims of indiscriminate shooting by the Mexican army into the packed crowd, on orders given to them by a cruel and cynical president, Gustavo Díaz Ordaz, determined at all costs to suppress the protests before the Olympic Games in Mexico City ten days later. Except that the hundreds of bodies, the indiscriminate shots, and the rivers of blood never existed after 1968, and another massacre in June 1971, and for the following twenty years. For the next twenty years, and indeed, in a fashion until today, most Mexicans believe that the governments of back then, and even of now, are quite capable of mass-murdering countless students. The old PRI regime scared the daylights out of its opponents, and this largely contributed to the disappearance of student movements for two decades, and their reemergence only as single-issue, narrowly based struggles in the late eighties and nineties. On the other hand, since the government in fact did *not* assassinate six hundred youngsters, it did *not* pay the political, international, or even legal price for having done so. The myth of Mexican violence was a splendid business for the political system.* Mexicans may be averse to confrontation partly because they fear violence, but part of the violence they fear is a product of someone else's imagination, or of cynical disinformation. With the exception of the Cristero War of 1926–29, where thousands of Catholic peasants rose up against Calle's anticlerical regime, there have been no other significant insurrections over the past one hundred years.

This strange quid pro quo—where students and governments, victims and executioners all tacitly accept a lie that is politically expedient for both sides—had another consequence, which bears out the Mexican fear of violence, although it also illustrates where that fear stems from: a distortion of truth. Ever since 1968, governments of all stripes have proved reluctant to resort to the use of force, regardless of the cir-

---

* I am particularly grateful to the many conversations on this matter that I have had over the past thirty years with Joel Ortega, who was part of the 1968 student movement, and who shares this view.

cumstances or its justification. There were of course exceptions, as in 1971, when President Luis Echeverría sent out paramilitary goons to beat up students, and later when he ordered the military to wipe out several leftist guerrilla groups, without much regard for human rights or due process. But after that it became almost unfeasible to proceed in this fashion, and polls today show why. Given the question in 2009: "Under what circumstances do you consider justified the use of force by the government?," 28%, the largest contingent, replied "Under no circumstances," and only 24% responded "in violent confrontation with the police."[34] For practical purposes, this makes government use of the police or the military virtually impossible, except when directed at "others," or "noncitizens": drug traffickers and organized crime. Even when Mexican society believed—wrongly—that it was being attacked by an armed indigenous insurrection in Chiapas in January 1994, a majority disapproved of the use of force against it, and ultimately pressured Carlos Salinas de Gortari to declare a cease-fire, open talks with the Zapatista militants, and allow the Chiapas revolt to fester for another eight years. Even during the country's most recent "war" on drugs and organized crime, Mexicans favored by more than 10 points "respect for human rights and everyone's freedoms, even if this makes crime-fighting less effective," over "using raids, check points, or curfews to better combat crime, even if this violates human rights."[35] In short, perhaps Mexico has only a distant—though deep—memory of violence, which dates well back to before the Spanish arrived. As Santiago Ramírez originally wrote, and Paz suggested years later, "[During the pre-Columbian era] social differences and hierarchies between one social class and another, and in particular between the people and the religious and military aristocracy, were so great that they constituted fertile ground for conflict and drama."[36] Herein may lie, then, the purpose behind widespread ritual execution at the time.

The second broad explanation generally provided for the insistence on avoiding clashes, fights, verbal exchanges devoid of euphemisms or explicit expostulations, is the irreparable nature of such behavior, or the impossibility of putting the toothpaste back in the tube. In the Mexican mind, there is no solution after confrontation; there is no walking back from a fight. In an altercation, things are said or done that cannot be silenced or undone; after a quarrel, the wounds or damages cannot be healed or dismissed. So it is best to avoid confrontation whenever possible, especially if one identifies with the weaker party, which, as we said before, is what Mexicans tend systematically to do. The only benefit possibly derived from direct confrontation is for someone to win and someone to lose, and almost all of the time, the loser will seem more "Mexican" or "popular" than the winner. This is perceived as true in politics, in social strife, and in interpersonal relationships. A simple symptom of this lies in the different natures of Mexican and Anglo-Saxon rhetorical education. Americans and the British belong to debate clubs or societies where they confront each other verbally on given issues. Mexicans from early on in elementary school participate in public-speaking contests (known in Mexico as *concursos de oratoria*) where children, all alone, show off their speaking skills, blustering on any topic they or their teacher chooses. There is by definition no confrontation.

The way the Mexican political system functioned for years was on the basis of perpetual negotiation. So much so that, on occasion, conflicts were artificially created in order to be later subjected to a negotiated settlement. Everything was the subject of bargaining, although the parties to each negotiation were far from equal. Workers, through their unions, bargained for wages and rights, but avoided, whenever possible, strikes or factory takeovers. These were not part of the pattern, and when they occurred, as with railroad employees in 1958–59, or university professors and administrative workers in 1977, they ended badly: with leaders imprisoned, the installations taken over by the army, a bitter campaign in the press against the "rabble-rousers," and so on.

The same was true for the peasantry in the countryside. After the Revolution, the 1926–29 religious revolt known as the Cristero War, and a few uprisings in the mid-1930s during the Cárdenas years, Mexico's rural areas became the silent, barren desert depicted by Juan Rulfo. The promises of the Revolution were betrayed, then forgotten. Peasants without land, or with only small parcels of uncultivable land, bargained for subsidies, price supports, handouts, and small increases in the size of their plots, but they rarely resorted to direct confrontation. Instead of fighting, they preferred to flee . . . to the United States. And in politics too the opposition recurrently favored any type of deal over any type of struggle; one of Mexico's favorite sayings—in a country where popular wisdom is kept alive by elegant elliptical sayings—is *"Más vale un mal arreglo que un buen pleito"* ("It is better to reach a bad deal than to have a good fight"). In a poll taken in 1993 on Mexican values by Enrique Ald**u**ncín, when asked which of two sayings—beat the steel when it is hot, or he who waits gets what he waits for—was preferable, 25% chose the first one (i.e., direct, immediate action) and 75% opted for the second (be patient and let things happen).[37]

Similarly, when pollsters inquired whether better results were achieved through cooperation or competition, 84% preferred the former, and 16% the latter.[38] Open, unfettered competition is perhaps the most frowned-upon and distasteful type of substantive strife in the Mexican state of mind. It is one thing to drag the proverbial crabs back into the bucket surreptitiously, or to practice the most ruthless forms of bureaucratic business, political, or academic infighting; it is quite another to do so transparently, in the light of day. That type of competition is unseemly, unworthy, and ultimately futile. The bigger, stronger, richer, wilier competitor will always win: why bother to compete with him or her, if the outcome is preordained and more can be achieved by cutting a deal than picking a fight? And yet few things hurt Mexico today more than the absence of competition in its economy, political arena, labor movement, or media.

There are an infinite amount of Mexican (not just Spanish-language) sayings that mean the same thing, more or less. Here is a brief sampling: *"Es mejor decir aqui corrió, que aqui murió"* ("Better to say from here he ran away, than here he lies"); *"Es de pendejos jugarse el pellejo"* ("Only jerks risk their hide"); *"A enemigo que huye, puente de plata"* ("For an enemy who flees, a silver escape way"); *"Aunque veas pleito ganado vete con cuidado"* ("Even if you see a fight that's been won, proceed with caution").

On at least two occasions over the past twenty-five years, a powerful but ultimately defeated opposition preferred to back off from conflict, largely because its *leaders* knew, in the first case, that their followers would not jump off a cliff with them; and in the second, once *their supporters* felt themselves too close to the cliff, they deserted their leaders. In 1988, left-wing candidate Cuauhtémoc Cárdenas, his advocates, and a huge swath of Mexicans were convinced, with much reason, that the presidential election had been stolen from him. In the days and weeks after the July 6 vote, massive rallies took place in Mexico City; not since the 1968 student movement had so many people dared to concentrate in the Zócalo main square to protest against the government.

There was no room for negotiation this time; nominal winner Carlos Salinas de Gortari tried to find common ground and cut a deal with the *cardenistas*, to no avail. Hundreds of thousands of demonstrators clamored for electoral justice, for the official results to be overturned, and for Cárdenas to be declared the winner. The final showdown came in early August, when Cárdenas addressed his followers in front of the presidential palace, which, rumor had and has it, was jammed with armed troops ready to fire if the crowd attempted to break in and install Cárdenas as president by force. But the leader's wisdom and "Mexicanness" prevailed; he maintained his stance that the election had been stolen, that there would be no accommodation or deal with the enemy, but he called on his supporters to go home, build a political party, avoid confrontation, and return to fight another day. They have returned many times, and continued to fight, but many of them feel their struggle has not triumphed.

Cárdenas was probably right in backing down; nothing would have been gained by bloodshed or destroying the famed stability of the Mexican political system. When I asked him three years later, in regard to a midterm election his new party was thrashed in, why he did not at least boycott the Congress (in 1988 his legislative caucus constituted a large minority), he replied that his allies would not have gone along with him. It was one thing to demonstrate in the streets, shouting slogans and carrying incendiary banners; it was altogether something else to give up a congressional seat in protest over electoral fraud.

A vivid counterfactual example took place in the 2006 presidential election, when the left anew felt the election had been stolen from it, in our view at least, with far less grounds for its claim than on the previous occasion. It came in second, by less than one percent, and once again took to the streets in protest. This time its leader, the former Mexico City mayor and Cárdenas's successor, Andrés Manuel López Obrador, decided not to back down. He called on his followers to permanently occupy the city's central square and to shut down its main artery, Paseo de la Reforma, which they did for over a month. He denounced the winner, conservative candidate Felipe Calderón, and the outgoing president, Vicente Fox, as criminals, usurpers, and thugs, and he pressed matters as hard as he could, all the way through Calderón's inauguration, on December 1, when the left in Congress attempted to stop Calderón by force from being sworn in.

López Obrador failed, just as Cárdenas had, and for the same reasons. They both lost because of the unwillingness of their supporters to go all the way, Cárdenas understanding this in time, López Obrador paying the price for hoping—at least on the surface of things—to overcome the age-old reluctance to fight. But both also proved their supporters right: there was no return after confrontation, no road to walk back on, no reconciliation with the enemy after the war. Neither Cárdenas nor López Obrador was to normalize his relations with the government and the other parties; this may explain why to this date, a country that should logically be governed from the center-left has been ruled from the center-right.

The third and next explanation offered for the Mexican dislike of direct controversy is simultaneously the most elementary and fundamental one. It basically boils down to the fact that confrontation is useless, particularly when one feels, is, or identifies with the weaker party in the conflict. Nothing useful, in the Mexican social imagination, has ever been gained by fighting, except the nobility of death and failure. All of Mexico's heroes, with the sole exception of Benito Juárez, have died in conflict: from Cuauhtémoc in 1521 to guerrilla leader Lucio Cabañas in 1972. Picking a fight with a neighbor, a relative, a husband or wife, a son or father, confronting a rival or friend with evidence of betrayal or animosity, is simply useless. If the sought-after goal is to amend matters, bringing them out into the open and making them explicit will not help; if the objective lies in making a point, knowing full well that nothing else will be accomplished, why bother? And if the aim consists of defeating the adversary, avenging the grievance, or correcting the slight, the best recourse for this purpose resides in the other party not even noticing what happened. As a wise and profoundly Mexican politician and friend once advised me: "If you want to destroy an enemy, you have to thrust your sword through his body without his even feeling it or realizing what has occurred."

Personal altercations are considered both rude and idle: why be ill-mannered and give someone—a police officer shaking you down, a wife-beating husband, a treacherous friend, a duplicitous politician, a plagiarizing academic—a piece of your mind if nothing will come of it, except the affected party's displeasure, and the discreet disapproval of third parties? Myth has it that Mexicans put up with all sorts of abuse endlessly, until they don't: one day they explode. But in fact, they haven't. With the exception of Independence—largely achieved by the Spanish-oriented, *criollo* elites—and the war against the French, the Revolution, and the very localized Cristero War in the mid-twenties, where the masses did rise up, there is scant proportion between the dimensions of the abuse and the frequency or intensity of the violent response.

A fourth and final explanation for conflict aversion stems from a broader feature of the Mexican psyche, which is all the more difficult to convey as it is clearly intangible and less well described by the classics. It is an almost magical pursuit of the negation of the Law or Principle of the Excluded Middle, of a way to avoid not only confrontation, but binary or polar choices. The principle of mutually incompatible terms (*a* and non-*a*) not being able to coexist in time and space is as old as Aristotle. It is a logical, natural, and philosophical tenet, whereby, given two contradictory propositions, one is true and one is false; or, similarly, if two propositions are contradictory, the truth or falseness of one implies the truth or falseness of the other, respectively. As Aristotle put it, "there is any mean between a contradiction; but there is a necessity either of asserting or denying any one thing whatsoever of one."[39]

It is also a political tenet, although many politicians would argue that the whole point of politics is to make the mutually incompatible seem possible. Legal, contractual, mathematical, and ethical systems are partly based on this principle. One cannot be guilty and innocent at the same time; one cannot sign a contract and break it at the same time; one cannot establish a syllogism, a proof, or a theorem where one term and its opposite are both true. The same holds for ethics and morals: it is difficult, if not impossible, for mutually incompatible aspirations, desires, ambitions, or hopes to coincide. This is of course not valid for the subconscious, or even for conscious passions, desires, and impulses. If Freud discovered anything it was that the mind and the psyche contain contradictory drives. What becomes complicated is when the normal and even frequent emergence of incompatibility among polar goals in the mind and the heart are transferred to everyday life, to the geopolitical, economic, political, and social realms. Most of the time, in these fields materialist reality trumps psychological or cultural passions.

Just as Mexicans are terribly averse to conflict, they also abhor having to choose between polar, binary opposites. In everyday language, they persistently, ferociously, want to have their tortilla and eat it too.

Everything that is binary repels them: elections, the law, the market, competition, choosing sides in practically any area of national or human endeavor. To choose is to take sides; to pick sides is to make someone happy and someone else angry; and anger is to be avoided whenever possible. Indeed, psychoanalysts like Federico San Román believe that many Mexicans resort to word games and the consecration of language as a substitute for the violent response that aggression would normally provoke. A certain discourse—identified but not limited to *albures,* a sexually connoted word game—allows the coexistence of two different messages. The first carries an apparently innocuous, playful type; the second conveys information that if freely and explicitly expanded would result in being offensive. This becomes an instrument for compensation through language for the tensions, insecurities, and dangers of everyday life; since acts are forbidden because of their consequences, all that is left is the imagination. That is where every desire is realized, where magical powers are conferred on words, and where the impossible is finally achieved: victory, control, and even revenge. In this magic world the fear of defeat and the underlying insecurity that explains it are vanished; there is nothing left to be afraid of.

### Cantinflas and Pedro Infante

The Mexican aversion to confrontation, then, stems from a combination of these four factors—fear that any type of confrontation leads directly to violence, in a supposedly violence-prone society; the notion that after controversy, there is no reconciliation; the conviction that altercation is fruitless; and the rejection of binary propositions and of the Principle of the Excluded Middle. It is a direct consequence of the identification with the victim of violation. The most extraordinary example of the Mexican's flight from conflict, both because he reflected indubitable national traits and because he has been held up on infinite occasions as a "typical" Mexican is, of course, Cantinflas. The immensely talented comedian and movie actor of the 1940s and 1950s, whose incursions into the Hollywood genre (*Around the World in Eighty Days*, as David Niven's valet Passepartout, and with Tony Curtis and Debbie Reynolds in an Acapulco-set, racist bomb titled *Pepe*), is unique in many ways. He created a word—*cantinflear*—that was included in the *Diccionario de la lengua española* of the Royal Spanish Academy (the equivalent of the Oxford English Dictionary) in 1992. The definition states: "To speak in an outlandish and incongruous manner, without saying anything; or to act in the same manner."[40]

This is exactly what we have been referring to. *Cantinflear* or being *cantinflesco* signifies avoiding a direct expression, or taking a stance, avoiding any definition or conflict, and in Cantinflas's films of the 1940s, being extraordinarily funny and endearing by doing so. Cantinflas managed to wiggle himself out of any conflict, talk himself out of any contradiction, finagle his way into wherever he wanted to enter, all by double-talk and double-entendres, euphemisms, implicit and/or incomprehensible sentences and gestures. He lost much of his popularity in the 1980s and before his death in 1993 because of his conservative political views and poor movies, but remains an icon of Mexican mid-century urban life, and a monument to this aversion for confrontation. As Santiago Ramírez phrased it: "With his ingenuity and elusive language, Cantinflas once again evades difficult contact with the authorities; his way of speaking is a way of not getting caught: mistrustful and fearful, he systematically avoids contact."[41] The Egyptian-born, Italo-Mexican poet Fabio Morábito puts it more lyrically: "Here I came to live in this largest city, which never heals; here the tongue hides itself under so many wounds that speaking hurts; where he who speaks best, hurts most, and hides best."[42]

The aversion to conflict is easier to measure in the political sphere, since polls are generally more directed at political motivations. Still, in a survey on discord carried out in 2009, when people were asked if they agreed or disagreed with the behavior of certain political groups, the answers were highly illustrative. Marches and sit-downs received a 73% disapproval rating; hunger strikes, 78% against; taking the floor by force in the legislative chambers, 80% disapproval; shutting down highways, toll both plazas and bridges, 84% against. More convincingly, even regarding *verbal* aggressions between groups, 96% of those polled stated they opposed them; physical confrontation with the police or the military was rejected by 97%. Lastly, when asked about physical aggression among groups, 98% stated they opposed it. It is hard to imagine similar statistics in other democracies.[43] Some pollsters believe that one of the reasons for this reluctance to use force stems from a broader interpretation of the innate sympathy for the Mexican peasantry we describe in Chapter 1. According to this view, if their cause is just, any form of struggle to achieve it is also just and justified, and consequently any repression of that struggle is unwarranted.

The temptation to quote Emilio Uranga again is irresistible. He says what most of the classics thought but were not always courageous or irreverent enough to state out loud. Uranga explains the reluctance to engage in conflict through weakness and fragility, and does it eloquently, if not graciously:

> The Mexican feels weak inside himself, fragile. He has learned since childhood that his inner soul is vulnerable and precarious, and this is where all the techniques of self-preservation and self-protection that Mexicans have built up around themselves to insure that the impact of the outside world not reach them or wound them, actually stem from. This is also the origin of his delicateness, his refinement in dealing with others, his constant avoidance of abruptness or foul-mouthed expressions. But it is also the source of his constant concern or search to slip away, to go by inadvertently, and subsequent impression that Mexicans convey to others of evasion and prevarication, of not making themselves noted.[44]

Beyond the psychobabble—this text was written and published in 1949—Uranga detected then what the polls show now. There is a Mexican conflict-aversion trait, and somehow and somewhere in the depths of our soul, it explains many features of Mexican behavior, and is explained by many facts of Mexican history.

All of this brings us back to the predilection for victims in general, and for victims in politics in particular. It allows us to understand why most Mexican heroes are victims—Cuauhtémoc, Miguel Hidalgo, José María Morelos, and the other fathers of Independence, who all died for their cause; the children who saved the Mexican flag from being captured by American invaders in 1847, plunging to their death from the heights of Chapultepec Castle; Villa, Zapata, and in more recent years, guerrilla leaders Genaro Vázquez, Lucio Cabañas and Subcomandante Marcos, and López Obrador. Only the last two have not died for their ideas. Mexicans tend to empathize with victims, because the latter are not the product of accidents of history or natural causes: they are the defeated ones. And Mexicans identify with defeat because in our historiography it has constituted the recurrent theme, and because it is the direct consequence of conflict under unfavorable circumstances.

One of Mexico's greatest film icons, on and off the screen, has been Pedro Infante's fabled character, Pepe el Toro, who was unjustly jailed in the 1948 black-and-white classics *Nosotros los pobres* and *Ustedes los ricos.* He was falsely charged—or framed—for the murder of a love affair rival, fled from prison to visit his mother on her deathbed, then returned to jail to find the real murderer, who eventually confesses, freeing Pedro Infante as his friends and neighbors welcome him back to freedom, shouting *"Pepe el Toro es inocente."* He is the victim par excellence, who takes his fate with dignity and stoicism, and he is also par excellence the Mexican hero, played by Infante, who died in a plane crash in 1956 and was accompanied to his final resting place by hundreds of thousands of fans and worshippers. Pepe el Toro fights back, but also is largely resigned to his fate, as the films' titles suggest: We (Are) the Poor, You (Are) the Rich. They are still watched on television in Mexico by a third or fourth generation of devoted fans.

Resignation is the better part of conflict, many Mexicans would admit. As the twelve religious elders of Tenochtitlán begged, together with the main indigenous lords in 1524, three years after the fall of the city to Cortés, "Since our gods have died, just let us now die, let us now perish." Whether at home, in the face of domestic violence, or in foreign policy; either in the neighborhood or the Congress; be it in the streets or within the intellectual and academic community, direct confrontation and competition possess an inevitably negative connotation. There are times when they cannot be avoided; passions get out of control, drinks and resentment get out of hand, political goals and national interests bring altercations that break the rules and, more importantly, deviate from the national "standard operating procedure." But this is never a desirable outcome; it is always a second-best choice. Ideally, negotiation, compromise, submission, or imposition are always preferable to their opposites. On occasion, the second-best choice becomes unavoidable, and aggression or conflict emerge and lead to violence, often of a brutal nature. Far from us to believe that Mexican society is totally devoid of the violent traits it has so frequently been cast as possessing. But this is a last resort, springing from the failure of the default option: avoiding conflict. The various intermittent episodes of violence in Mexican history, from the Chichimeca uprisings in the sixteenth century and Jacinto Canek's rebellion in 1761, all the way to the Caste Wars and the Speaking Cross Rebellion in the land of the Mayas in the nineteenth century, and the Catholic Cristero War in the 1920s are examples of this default option: sporadic, ephemeral, doomed from the outset, and futile.

## Perpetuating Power*

Perhaps the best transition to our upcoming analysis of democracy in Mexico today, and how this national dislike for debate and disagreement is totally dysfunctional to that democracy, lie in the way presidents were chosen until the year 2000. The country never had it easy with the transfer of power. From Independence in 1821 through the Porfirian era beginning in 1876, Mexico veered from coups, insurrections, dictatorships, foreign invasions, and local complicities to civil wars and leaders heroic in war but incompetent in peacetime. Finally it came to terms with its inability to establish, at a minimum, peaceful and regular successions by finding itself a dictator who solved the problem by remaining in power for more than thirty years. This, of course, led to revolution—almost a decade's worth—and the rebirth of the same dilemma: how to transfer power in at least an orderly and nonviolent fashion, however undemocratic the long-sought system might seem.

The first step was taken in 1929, a year after the last revolutionary leader, Álvaro Obregón, who had been president from 1920 to 1924, was gunned down in Mexico City, just past his election to a fresh term as president. A political party was created by his colleagues, successors, rivals, and perhaps even assassins, within which every major decision would be taken, and mainly the main one: who would be president. A single six-year term was established, without reelection; the incumbent would be omnipotent, and reach the pinnacle of his power when he handpicked his successor—almost like a Roman emperor, but instead of making his heir his son, making his son his heir—who would be nominally elected but in fact single-handedly chosen by the incumbent. All of his rivals and adversaries would unquestioningly accept the chosen one's designation and

* Much of this material stems from my book *La herencia: Arqueología de la sucesión presidencial en México* (Mexico City: Alfaguara, 1999), published in an abridged form in the United States with the title *Perpetuating Power* (New York: The New Press, 2000).

"electoral victory"; the outgoing leader would, for his part, abstain from any further involvement in politics. The new mechanism functioned fully for the first time in 1940, when Lázaro Cárdenas relinquished the opportunity to succeed himself, picked an heir, handed power over to him, and forsook the chance to push forward his progressive agenda.

The system was based on several premises, but the chief one consisted in the irrevocable nature of the incumbent's choice: it could not be appealed. Every one of the contenders for his favor accepted his decision; nobody bolted the party or contested the victor's triumph, and the winner abstained from severely punishing any of his vanquished rivals. The quasi-magical mechanism worked to perfection until 1994, i.e., for almost half a century. Every six years, like clockwork, Mexico availed itself peacefully of a new president, leaving behind more than a century of the previous mess. This was, of course, anything but a democratic procedure; nonetheless, it was considered successful, and even admirable, by locals and foreigners, left and right, winners and losers, the elites, and, at least tacitly, the masses. It was an archetypically Mexican solution to the problem. Controversy, confrontation, open competition, and conflict were set aside; everything was carried out in secret; no candidate ever declared his intention of being a candidate until the outgoing president made his final choice, and in the memorable words of Mexico's perennial labor leader Fidel Velázquez, "Whoever moves doesn't come out in the picture."

The key, however, resided in the losers' attitude: accepting their defeat gracefully, hoping to fight another day, or at least receive a cabinet appointment in the winner's new government, but never, under any circumstances, questioning the decision. Remarkably, but predictably, given how well rooted this device was in the conflict-aversion attitude of the Mexican people and its politicians, it worked. In 1940 there was a real split in the party—logically enough, since this was the first time the mechanism became completely operational—and the election had to be brazenly stolen from the dissident rival of the official candidate, insuring that everyone understood. The incumbent's decision could not be appealed, anywhere, at any time. By 1946 and 1952, the disenchanted rivals' rearguard rejections of "*el dedazo*"—the "finger"—as it came to be known, had become ludicrous, pro forma responses; from 1958 through 1988, there was not a single fracture or split, and every fallen aspirant accepted his fate like a Roman gladiator.

Every loser preferred peace and fortune to bucking the system; all of their supporters were brought back into the fold, and their loyalties were rapidly transferred to the anointed one. Everything was negotiated in smoke-filled rooms; nothing was fought out in the open.

Of course—and herein lay the weakness of the system as well as the congenital defect of conflict aversion as a way of life—the clashing interests represented one way or another by the candidates vying for the incumbent's favor were very real, and did not evaporate when the final verdict was handed down. The post-Conquest indigenous peoples may have resignedly accepted their fate; the peasants deprived of their land during the Porfiriato may have taken more than thirty years to fight back, accepting their defeat a decade later without much of a quarrel; students and other opposition movements may have all preferred negotiation to confrontation; but the divisions and cleavages in Mexican society did not vanish. The succession system essentially worked because it swept those contradictions under the single-party carpet, but not because it addressed them, let alone solved them.

Logically enough, as the system tired and the country changed, this last weakness came to the fore. In 1988, the government was forced once again to flagrantly cheat in the election, since a split did occur, and Cuauhtémoc Cárdenas, son of the system's true founder, refused to play the old game. He rebelled and, indeed, may have won more votes than the sanctified candidate, Carlos Salinas de Gortari. The 1994 loser, Mexico City mayor Manuel Camacho, tried to put up a fight, subsequently backed down, but was then saved from disgrace or political ostracism by probably unrelated events, like the Chiapas uprising on New Year's Day, that overturned the proverbial applecart, and the assassination of the chosen candidate, Luis Donaldo Colosio, in March of that year. That year, the PRI was still able to retain control of the vote, but has not won a presidential election since, and if it ever does, it will not be thanks to the old system. That system, like its roots in the Mexican psyche, was able to defer, contain, and defuse conflict, but never to suppress its causes or consequences. "It" didn't really believe in Freud and the "return of the repressed" in the ever-present "work" of the subconscious, in other words, in the underlying origins of political conflict (in our examples), or of the personal, social, cultural, ethnic, and economic confrontations in every walk of life.

In the modern, racist, class-conscious, tacit zeitgeist of the Mexican middle class, there is a repugnant expression that unfortunately captures the spirit of the country's aversion to controversy: "*Se fue como las chachas*" ("He or she quit his or her job like the 'help' "). It generally refers to domestic employees, but in fact is implicitly addressed at those who are considered to be unjustifiably and incorrectly acting like them, that is, quitting without providing or demanding an explanation, or attempting to fix whatever problem may have surfaced in their working environment, without even fighting for their severance or back pay. They left surreptitiously, on the sly, the way the most looked-down-upon category of Mexican paid workers (generally associated with an indigenous background) are said and thought to behave. It is a derogatory, disrespectful, and hateful expression and notion, but it says much more about how Mexicans view ourselves than about how we view a particularly downtrodden sector of society.

## CHAPTER 4

# Finally, Mexican Democracy

Mexico today is a representative democracy, albeit an imperfect one. But as previously suggested, the national character trait of conflict aversion is totally dysfunctional to this budding democracy, and stifles it. Something will have to give: either the old ways and institutions, or any further progress in building a functioning democracy. This chapter is devoted to describing how Mexican democracy works, and doesn't work.

For the first time in its history, excepting a couple of freakish and unique exceptions (Juárez in 1868, Madero in 1911), the country has managed to build and sustain a political system where power is won, kept, and lost at the ballot box. Not only are there regularly scheduled elections; they are fundamentally clean, free, and fair at the federal, state, and local level. As we shall see, blanket statements such as the above leave much to be desired in terms of the details of truth and justice, but at a certain level of abstraction and in broad terms they are accurate. The country seems to have definitively entered the era of democratic rule, a tidier and deeper one than in some countries in Latin America, rowdier and more chaotic than in others, with some Mexicans more committed to it than others. Not a minor affair for a nation that is late to experience democracy, unlike many of its hemispheric partners, where at least limited suffrage or democracy for contending elites without masses has been practiced since the end of the nineteenth century.

This democracy is meant to function for the same purposes and in the same way as other democracies, since Athens, have all operated.

Their logic is not to erase social, ideological, political, or even ethnic cleavages, but rather to allow those inevitable and often desirable disagreements and clashing interests to be thrashed out peacefully. Democracy does not eliminate conflicts among various groups in society; it does not really reflect Rousseau's *volonté générale,* but rather the divergent interests in society; it simply channels all of them into a pacific, orderly, legal, and generally efficient process of resolution. And even the latter term is not absolute. Most of these differences are never resolved; they are simply managed or administered, in the least costly and damaging fashion for society at large. This is accomplished essentially through a combination of majority rule and minority rights. No one ever wins everything, and no one ever loses all. Majorities change, and govern within limits; minorities are respected and express their frustration or ambitions within those same confines. But that expression of interests, the fact of engaging in full-scale debate and contradiction, including all of its manifestations—with the exception of those that are clearly outside the law—is part and parcel of the democratic package. Democracies are not meant to bring people together. Their raison d'être is to allow people who remain apart to live more prosperously, peacefully, and compatibly.

### The Justice System, Drugs, and U.S. Aid

This is the tricky part for Mexico. If the national trait we described and discussed in the previous chapter implies anything, it is that Mexican political culture, because of its deeply rooted rejection of confrontation, competition, and controversy, remains ill equipped for democracy. It is indeed dysfunctional to an effective, freewheeling, socially accepted democracy. The defects of Mexican democracy, which are real, do not only stem from its novelty, its incomplete nature, and the country's obstinacy in conserving the same institutions it availed itself of during the authoritarian period. They spring, above all, from this fundamental flaw: democracy implies bringing altercation out into the open, letting, as Mao said in relation to a totally different matter, "a hundred flowers bloom," thriving on dissent and disagreement, instead of sublimating all strife in sight.

Mexico's anachronistic institutions were, at least subconsciously, a reflection of the previously depicted atavism of the national character: conflict aversion. Perhaps one of the most illustrative examples of the peculiar institutions Mexico constructed during its so-called perfect dictatorship (in Mario Vargas Llosa's brilliant quip) was the system of written administration of justice inherited from the Spanish, but brought to perfection in Mexico. As in most of Latin America, Mexico has no jury system, and specialists can argue endlessly about the relative merits and disadvantages of juries or verdict- and sentence-rendering judges. But neither are there generalized oral trials, in criminal or civil justice; they only recently began in a couple of states and will be extended across Mexico by 2016. In a nation where until half a century ago the majority of the population could not read or write, everything in court is done in writing.

As a matter of fact, it is not even done in court. Written arguments, depositions, documents, testimony, and so forth are all presented to a judge's *office*, where they are reviewed, and where verdicts and sentences are delivered. Actually, most of the time, it is not even a judge who judges, but rather a lowly, overexploited, and underpaid clerk (known as a court secretary, or *secretario de juzgado*), who does the work. No wonder, then, that according to a survey carried out in 2009 by the Mexico City daily *Reforma*, 92% of all criminal court hearings are held without the presence of a judge, and 80% of Mexicans arrested by the police never speak to a judge. One consequence is that 40% of the prison population has never been sentenced and is held in pretrial detention on occasion for years, leading to prison overpopulation and intermingling of sentenced prisoners and those awaiting judgment.[1] There is no adversarial process, no oral arguments or testimony, no courtroom, no judge, and neither in civil nor criminal cases do victims and perpetrators, prosecutors, and potential criminals ever confront each other.

This started to change toward the middle of this century's first decade, as some states, chiefly Nuevo León in the north, adopted oral trials in criminal cases. The Calderón administration submitted a judicial reform proposal to Congress seeking to replace written justice with oral process at a federal and criminal level. This was a welcome transformation, since the advantages of the oral system, which most countries in Latin America adopted years ago, are significant: greater transparency, a more expeditious and lower-cost justice system, adversarial procedures, the presence of a judge, and the possibility of saving money—and time—through out-of-court settlements before everything is engraved in writing, if not in stone.

It was no coincidence that Mexico was the last country in the region to abandon this vestige of Spanish rule, that it did so only grudgingly and slowly, and that many lawyers, judges, and scholars decried the change, complaining that it represented the beginning of a slippery slope toward the "American" style of "Perry Mason" justice, where rhetoric, courtroom antics, money, and jury tampering become more important than the truth. But as matters stand, only seven out of every hundred crimes are reported to the police in Mexico anyway, largely because no one believes in the justice system, which represents a direct reflection of the penchant for avoiding confrontation. More than two-thirds of Mexicans polled in 2009 mistrusted the police or state prosecutors, 61% did not trust judges, and 50% had no confidence in the Supreme Court.[2] In the end, the rule of law in Mexico consists in wielding political power or influence, which is subsequently reflected in judicial *rulings,* not justice.

These strange features of the judicial branch were also expressed in the legislative and executive branches and in the relationship between them. As long as Mexico lived—and for a time, flourished—under an authoritarian political regime, the flaws in the overall institutional design were invisible and irrelevant. The issue of whether the executive branch enjoyed a majority in the legislative branch that enabled it to govern did not arise because members of Congress were not really elected; they were de facto presidential appointees. Since the mid-1930s, the sitting president chose the ruling party's candidates, and they always won. So the head of state and government was assured an automatic majority in both the House and Senate. The first opposition senators were elected in 1988: four out of sixty-four. The PRI only lost its majority in the House in 1997, and in the Senate in 2000. It was unimportant that there is no consecutive reelection in Mexico and that there is not a two-party system as in the United States nor a first-past-the-post, winner-take-all arrangement as in Britain nor a hybrid structure as in France. All of these constructs ensure the emergence of a majority, whether it is the prime minister's (as in Britain), the president's (as in the United States or most of the time in France), or the legislative opposition's (again, as in the United States). How to assemble a majority, though, was not a concern for the Mexican president, since he always had one; how to deal with large minorities in Congress, or how a minority president could perform successfully were also inconsequential. Those hypotheses never materialized.

More broadly, the reality and the consequences of confrontational debates in Congress, the media, unions, churches, or town hall meetings did not need to be addressed because they were nonexistent. Altercations in the political arena—and there were multiple examples—took place mostly in the streets, on university campuses, in a few isolated factories, and, in the sixties and seventies, mainly through land seizures. It should be no surprise that as late as 2010, there were still no prime-time, major TV network political or news discussion shows on television in Mexico: no *Meet the Press*, no *Nightline*, no *60 Minutes*. Anchors and in-house commentators appear on both principal networks during programs that start well past midnight; the nickel-and-dime cable networks have their nickel-and-dime talk shows. All of these are watched exclusively by news junkies and night watchmen; Mexico's men and women in the street are still alien to the process.

Similarly, the country did not need to figure out how to change its laws and Constitution, or ratify international treaties and covenants, if the president lacked a legislative majority, because he never did. Until 1997, the 1917 Constitution had been amended 489 times, and one article in particular, #73 regarding the powers of Congress, had been modified *sixty* times.[3]* Most of the modifications were sops to different sectors whose demands could not be accepted, but had to be placated; the Mexican solution was to include their desires in the Constitution, transforming the foundational document into a Christmas list of good intentions and national aspirations.

Likewise, when the president decided it was in the best interest of the country to sign any number of treaties—from the United Nations and Organization of American States charters to the North American Free Trade Agreement—he just did, and instructed his employees in Congress to approve them. There was never any major debate regarding their pros and cons, much less their implications, which was why

* "The exact number of constitutional amendments can vary depending on how one actually counts them: whether one is counting articles, fractions, or subchapters of each article, or issues and decrees that can imply reforming many articles simultaneously." Sergio García Ramírez, "Las reformas a la constitución vigente," *Vigencia de la Constitución de 1917, LXXX aniversario,* Secretaría de Gobernación (Mexico City: Archivo General de la Nación, 1997), p. 255

disagreements, for example on NAFTA, were thrashed out elsewhere. The very notion that, as in the United States or Canada or the European Union, *society* had to deliberate and decide directly, by referendum, on matters of such magnitude was alien to Mexico. The country assumed far-ranging foreign commitments without debate and, thus, without division—not because it was united on the issues, but rather because it approached with great distaste the notion of debate, confrontation, and division. No wonder it didn't craft the instruments to address these matters; it didn't need them, and it didn't want them.

Today that is no longer possible, and the proverbial chickens have come home to roost. An interesting example of the conundrum involved in proceeding in predemocratic fashion in a working democracy lies in the country's drug enforcement cooperation with Washington, and the human rights imbroglio it generated. On taking office in December 2006, Felipe Calderón promptly declared a war on drugs. He ordered the military onto the streets and highways of Mexico, and sought U.S. support for his efforts. This was certainly not the first time a Mexican president attempted to control a drug trade that was perceived to have gone beyond the traditionally accepted bounds of business as usual. And it was not the first time Mexico requested American backing. As recently as 1995 the country had received more than seventy Vietnam vintage Huey helicopters for drug enforcement purposes, which were subsequently returned to the U.S. because they were too old, too battered, consumed way too much fuel, and had too many conditions attached to their use.

When Calderón asked George W. Bush for software, hardware, money, and training, at a meeting in Mérida, Yucatán, in February 2007, the American president was forthcoming, but ambivalent. His aides explained that the amount in question (approximately $1.4 billion over three years) was above what the State Department or the Drug Enforcement Agency could disburse; only the Department of Defense could provide them. But Defense Department resources had to pass through a lengthy, complicated, and thorny legislative process. One of its main components, and the most menacing one for Mexico, comprised the human rights provisions attached to U.S. arms sales abroad, often violated in the breach but always nominally included in any assistance program since the 1970s.

Calderón wanted the money and the backing right away, and he accepted the agreement worked out by U.S. Senate committees, the

Bush administration, and nongovernmental human rights organizations (NGOs), chiefly Human Rights Watch. The deal stipulated that part of the package would be subject every year to the State Department "certifying" that Mexico was complying with several specific human rights commitments, and that the Senate accept this certification as well founded.*

Thus Mexico had solicited aid, received it according to existing and well-known American conditions, and had been an active witness and tacit participant in the negotiations where the assistance laws were drafted. But predictably, when the time came for "certification," problems arose. Sending an unprepared army to fulfill police work in Mexican cities and villages had generated a human-rights violations storm of significant dimensions. It wasn't so much that the military was guilty of egregious, widespread human rights violations; the ones committed tended to be isolated, sporadic, and more or less par for the course. But domestic and foreign human rights groups were watching closely, and so was the U.S. Senate; the Obama administration found itself in trouble with the NGOs involved in this field, and the process became excruciating for Mexico and its armed forces.

The political elite, intellectuals, the press, and the military itself rebelled against "American" meddling, demanding to know by "what right" did the perpetrators of Abu Ghraib and Guantánamo sit in judgment over Mexico's military and its "valiant" efforts to combat organized crime. Behind the absurd complaints and laments lay a fundamental problem. When Mexico entered into the so-called Mérida Initiative, it lacked any mechanism in Congress, the media, or civil society with which to debate the advantages and drawbacks of such a deal with Washington, once its terms had been fully publicized and fleshed out in the political arena.

The ensuing confrontation between supporters of the drug war, with human rights conditionality, and its opponents, on grounds of

* This was not a unilateral, heavy-handed American ploy to impose its views on another country, in a way that many believed the much loathed Drug Enforcement Cooperation Law of 1975 had functioned until its repeal in 2002. Under that law, the U.S. executive certified which countries were "cooperating" with Washington on drug enforcement matters, and which were not. Every year, a number of nations—among them, Mexico—would be threatened with "decertification" and were forced to jump through a number of hoops in order to avoid it. In the case of Calderón and the Bush and Obama administrations, however, the issue was totally different: Calderón asked for support and accepted the conditions it entailed.

infringed-upon national sovereignty, could not be assimilated by either the Mexican institutional framework or the country's cultural mindset. Such a confrontation, with a decision made after a major debate, on a matter of singular import, by a small majority, was simply not in the Mexican DNA. The best way to manage the matter was to ignore it. Neither the Calderón government, nor the PRI or PRD opposition (Partido de la Revolución Democrática or Party of the Democratic Revolution), felt it necessary to utilize existing mechanisms to resolve this issue and others like it, or, in the absence of such mechanisms, to invent them. The conflict would continue to poison U.S.-Mexican relations and ties between Obama and Calderón.

## Do Mexicans Like Democracy? If So, Why?

The issue is not that because all of these disconnects between existing Mexican institutions—and the requirements of democratic rule—Mexicans aren't deeply attached to their democracy, or that they truly miss the old authoritarian ways (though on occasion they say they do). The broad democratic coalition of recent years is not intact but remains latent. It is made up of local and social opposition activists, intellectuals, national political leaders, and parts of the international community. It eventually brought proper elections, a free press, multiple political parties, and at least the beginnings of a separation of powers. No one wishes to go back to the authoritarian system symbolized by the PRI, though many still vote for it. Yet Mexicans seem unwilling to devise a political regime compatible with representative democracy. More dangerously, they are terribly reluctant to be weaned from their traditional rejection of controversy, bluntness, and direct confrontation, a sine qua non for democracy to function.

Even as late as 2008, after the conflictive presidential elections of 2006 (in a poll taken that year, 66% of all Mexicans did not agree that elections were clean; only 16% thought they were), and the beginning of Mexico's disenchantment with representative democracy, the nation ranked smack in the middle when LAPOP (Latin American Public Opinion Project) put the classical Churchillian formulation—democracy may have problems, but it is preferable to all other forms of government—to citizens in twenty Latin American countries. A strong 68% of its nationals responded affirmatively. Similarly, in 2008, 55%

agreed that "democracy was the best form of government," whereas 20% did not think so; 61% thought "it is better to have a democratic government than an authoritarian one."[4] In 1996, two years after the country's first more or less democratic elections, seven out of every ten Mexicans thought it was a good or "very good" thing for their country to possess a democratic political system; by the year 2000, the share had grown to 73%, and by 2005, to 80%. In that same year, 84% of all Mexicans considered that it was important or very important to live in a country with a democratic government.[5] All of these percentages compare favorably with the rest of Latin America, and even with Western Europe or the United States and Canada. Moreover, when questioned in 2003 if they would willingly surrender their freedom of expression in exchange for living without economic constraints, 61% of all Mexicans refused, and just 34% replied they would.[6] This was a notable statistic, in a country where freedom of expression had hardly existed until the late eighties or early nineties, and where attachment to it has been, at best, irregular and lukewarm, and where 40% of the people live in poverty. It is true that toward the end of the century's first decade, Mexican devotion to democracy began to decline in comparison with other Latin American nations (perhaps as a result of the 2009 recession, which affected it more than any country in the region). On the Churchillian question, approval dropped to 42%, well below the Latin American average of 59%; only 44% thought democratic governments were better equipped to deal with the economic crisis; the average for the region was 54%.[7]

The issue, then, is not Mexico's commitment to democracy, or Mexicans' overall, fair-to-middling satisfaction with the imperfect democracy they enjoy. The problems arise when one starts seeking the reasons for this dissatisfaction and realizes that they almost always reflect unhappiness with how democracy has not led to agreements among politicians or to a consensus on the country's direction, and it has not put an end to divisions and disagreements among Mexicans.* Here we reencounter our familiar rejection of dissent and conflict.

---

* The dissatisfaction with government may also have an origin in the past. Since governments were not democratic before, Mexicans didn't like them. And since many continued to consider them undemocratic, they still don't like them. They then transfer their discontent from government to democracy. This has a lot to do with the infant nature of Mexican democracy, unlike, for example, Chile's or Colombia's.

Most Mexicans believe that the main purpose of democracy resides in allowing and promoting convergence among political forces, not in guaranteeing that inevitable divergences will remain within the realm of peaceful resolution. Mexican lack of faith in democracy is expanding, and one reason lies in this confusion about its aims. In 2001, 50% of all Mexicans thought their country was "living in democracy"; in 2003 the figure had dropped to 37%, and it fell to 31% in 2005. There is a clear income gap in these convictions: among people making more than seven times the minimum wage (clearly middle-class status); about 65% thought the country was a democracy; among the poor and very poor, the number was approximately 45%. But most distressingly, in 2008, after nearly fifteen years of democratic rule, and of paralyzing gridlock between branches of government, 75% identified living in a democracy with a high degree of willingness by members of Congress to reach agreements with their colleagues from different parties.[8] This is most Mexicans' Kumbaya definition of democracy. It is wrong.

Democracy is not about civility between government and opposition during Question Time debates in the House of Commons; it is about insuring that the strident, sarcastic, on occasion nasty exchanges remain just that: rhetorical flourishes, reflecting real differences of opinion and conflicting interests. This is Mexico's challenge today, particularly as so many supposedly consensual principles that were taken for granted for much of the authoritarian period are now either obsolete, counterproductive, or contrary to the beliefs and convictions of large chunks of the population, who were never consulted before.

A good example of this paradox, whereby Mexicans are attached to democracy but for the wrong reasons, resides in a technical, budgetary point that few experts have spotted. Between 2000 and 2009, that is, during the nine years of PAN presence in the presidential palace, the government enjoyed a budgetary windfall; 1.5% of GDP during the Fox years, and 2.2% for the first three Calderón years, over and above what was estimated.[9] The origin of the surplus lay, on the one hand, in lower than expected outlays,* and on the other, in greater than expected revenues, essentially thanks to higher oil prices. This amounted to an overall bonanza of roughly 17% of GDP over nine

---

* Due to a smaller interest bill on the public debt, because of prepayments abroad and lower inflation and interest rates at home.

years, a substantial sum. Simultaneously, the Mexican economy averaged 2.5% yearly growth for this period, a mediocre performance by any standard.[10] Why? Or more specifically, where did all the money go?

The answer lies in the political system. Since 2000, the PAN government, lacking a majority in Congress, has not wanted to depend on either of the two opposition parties to get its budget passed. So it cut deals with both, essentially by promising PRI and PRD state governors, who tended to "own" their congressional delegations in Mexico City, a huge transfer of federal funds to their unaccountable coffers, in exchange for unanimous backing for the budget. The governors delivered the votes (practically every federal budget since 2000 has been approved by consensus), and took their pound of flesh: vast sums of unearmarked, unsupervised resources, spent partly on nonsense, from expensive cars and trips, to showy but needless public works programs. The PAN governments, like their PRI predecessors, preferred unanimity to confrontation, and they were able to buy it. The price was significant, though. A sizable portion of the 17% that was wasted on states, towns, or federal pork for the governors could have been invested in growth-generating areas of the economy.

The crucial decision that Mexico has not made, and essentially for the types of cultural reasons we have been arguing, lies squarely in the refusal to truly consummate a break with the authoritarian past. When the PRI lost the presidency in the year 2000, two schools of thought competed for the new president's favor and for the support of those segments of the elites that were not completely bound to the outgoing ancien régime. One, the ultimately victorious faction, held that Mexico's institutions, at least on paper—its Constitution, laws, political parties, Congress, media, labor unions, and so on—could perform perfectly well under the new, democratic circumstances. There was no need, according to this view, to pursue a clean separation from the past and to investigate or dwell upon it nor to assemble a new institutional arrangement for the novel environment. The existing structures could be easily adapted to a different set of conditions.

In addition to this conceptual rationale for continuity, there was a strictly "business" argument for it. Mexico had to stop plunging itself into a major financial and economic crisis every six years (as in 1976, 1982, 1987–88, 1994–95), and this was more than ever indispensable in 2000, since for the first time the reins of the state had passed into inevitably inexperienced hands. So for both sets of motivations, this school was in favor of letting sleeping dogs lie.

The other school maintained that the country's standing institutions—the all-powerful presidency, a rubber-stamp Congress, a controlled media, a judicial system based more on corruption than on justice, a highly competent bureaucracy totally separated from society and from a corrupt, incompetent, and ill-prepared political class— were woefully inadequate for modern democracy. They could not prosper or even survive in the new era. A different institutional setup was necessary, and a split with the past was the only way to assure its birth and acceptance.*

This school of thought lost, and its defeat has persisted. The result of which is that Mexico has lived since 1997 in a full-fledged representative democracy, with the same set of institutions it developed during its authoritarian epoch, and which are completely dysfunctional, as the nation's paralysis amply demonstrates. Three presidents of totally different backgrounds—a Ph.D. economist, a businessman, and a lawyer– professional politician—have all tried to get things done on several fronts, and have all failed, since 1997, when the PRI lost its majority.

Two main democratic challenges defy Mexico's imagination, perseverance, and national character; they are at least partly the product of this national character. The first is an unmanageable three-party system; the second is a direct consequence of the aversion to conflict: how to impose democratic political confrontation and full-fledged economic competition on a society that fears them and mistrusts them like the plague, in order to allow democratic, transparent political compromise, economic growth, and social justice.

## The Worst of All Worlds: A Three-Party System

For a long time, and certainly in 1988, a fixture of the conventional wisdom that prevailed held that the transition from authoritarian rule would take place on the left of the political spectrum. The PRI, it was thought, had shifted too far to the right after 1982, and subsequently

* The best justification for a new, unavoidably painful beginning was to unveil the darker sides of the past, and only with a distinct political system could the country take advantage of its long-awaited and much-fought-for democratization.

between 1989 and 1994; its technocratic wing had devoured it and led the country down the road of privatization, trade opening, a free trade agreement with the United States, massive cutbacks in food subsidies, falls in real wages, and an overall predilection for globalization.

All of this, it was argued, was leaving the old left wing of the PRI— the labor and peasant unions, the bureaucracy, the intellectuals, and local leaders—behind and bewildered, in a society where inequality and age-old social resentment were so great that it could only be governed on the left. Moreover, the new urban middle class, especially after the 1982 economic collapse and the ensuing lost decade because of the debt crisis, was too small, too passive, and too upset to act as a counterweight. The future, it seemed, belonged to a two-party system, whereby the technocratic faction of the PRI would either ally itself with the small, provincial, conservative, and Catholic PAN or gradually replace it, and the left wing of the PRI would join forces with the multiple splinter groups on the fringes of the political arena from the old Communist, Trotskyist, Castroist left. The two large fronts would alternate in power, and either the PAN would remain a small party with 15% of the vote at most (about what it obtained in 1988, and in the mid-eighties in local elections), or it would be absorbed by the technocrats.

The 1988 presidential elections appeared to confirm this forecast, as the technocratic elite in the PRI, led by Carlos Salinas de Gortari, "won" the election with 50% of the vote (probably having actually received between 40% and 45%), and the scission on the left of the PRI, led by Cuauhtémoc Cárdenas, officially was assigned 30% (but in all likelihood reached somewhere between 35% and 40%). The PAN remained way behind, at around 15%. These results were magnified in Mexico City, the country's most modern, educated, middle-class region, where the left actually beat the PRI and PAN, two to one.

Although this potential exit from authoritarian rule was not applauded by everyone, it enjoyed the advantage of encouraging two types of continuity. First, it simply formalized the previously existing, so-called pendular system discovered by Mexican and American political scientists since the mid-fifties, according to which even under the PRI boot, Mexico was successively governed by presidents from the PRI right and left wings, insuring balance and mobility. No one was totally left out, and no one enjoyed a lock on power. Secondly, it guaranteed that the center of gravity of the new political system would stay roughly where it had been since the 1920s: the PAN's excessively pro-business, superficially pro-U.S., pro-Church stances would remain on the margins of power, and the fundamental agreement among the basic factions of the old Revolution would now be extended to the two large parties emerging from the democratization, globalization, and modernization paths Mexico was inevitably following.

It was not to be. Indeed, the whole idea was somewhat naive. Yes, Mexico with its social cleavages was theoretically predestined to be governed on the left, but that most likely would occur half a century later, or not at all if the country actually changed. In almost every democratic transition in Latin America or Eastern Europe, the need to reassure conservative elites and cores of power had actually led to exits from authoritarian rule on the right of the spectrum, not on the left. The only notable exception was Nelson Mandela in South Africa, but only because of his immense personal stature, and in fact, the policies he pursued once elected president in 1994 were highly orthodox, conservative ones, particularly in economic and security matters. In Chile, Brazil, Argentina, Spain, Greece, Poland, and El Salvador, the transition took place on the right, logically enough. And so it was in Mexico.

The Mexican left began to collapse as of 1991, at least in comparison to its performance in 1988. Although it united behind the banner of the PRD, and a single leader—Cárdenas—it lost votes in each election, receiving only 17% of the vote in the 1994 presidential sweepstakes, and though it peaked slightly in 1997, in Mexico City and in national legislative races, reaching 25%, it fell back to 17% in 2000.[11] Simultaneously, though, and for all of the reasons many had thought and/or hoped the left would succeed, it did not disappear: it never fell below 17%, and on occasion did better, consolidating its hold on Mexico City, the state of Michoacán (the Cárdenas family fiefdom), and a few other regions of the country.

The surprise, of course, was the PAN. It displaced the left in the 1994 elections, after a virtual, informal alliance with the Salinas administration for six years that allowed it to win several state governorships for the first time in history (Baja California, Guanajuato, Chihuahua). It achieved almost one-third of the national tally after a debate where the PAN presidential candidate performed incomparably better than his rivals. In 1997 the PAN continued to thrive, and in 2000 its candidate, Vicente Fox, finally accomplished what almost every observer had predicted would happen with another choice: it drove the PRI out of the presidency of Mexico. Furthermore, it retained enough of its seats in the 2003 midterm vote to keep governing, and in a squeaker in 2006 won the presidency again, this time with Felipe Calderón.

The moral of the story, and the ensuing complication for Mexico, was that instead of finding itself at the dawn of the twenty-first century with a functioning two-party democracy, or at least with a four-party arrangement endowed with a de facto or de jure runoff system, it confronted the challenge of the most unstable, conflictive, awkward setup: a three-party system where anything goes. Worse still, the specific tripartite formula Mexico gave itself possessed several features that rendered it even more dysfunctional. At any one time after the initial rotation of 2000, each of the three parties could win a national election, be it legislative or presidential. Here is the national pecking order for the five fully democratic elections held in Mexico in recent times: 1997 (midterm legislative): PRI in first place with 38%, PAN in second with 26%, PRD in third with 25%; 2000 (presidential): PAN in first with 43%; PRI in second with 36%; PRD in third with 17%; 2003 (midterm): PRI first with 37%, PAN second with 30%, PRD third with 18%; 2006 (presidential): PAN first with 35.9%; PRD second with 35.3%, PRI third with 22%; finally 2009 (midterm): PRI first with 37%, PAN second with 28%, and PRD third with 12%.[12] In other words, in five votes, over twelve years, the old PRI came in first three times, the PAN twice, and the PRD not even once. But the PRD came in second once, and the PRI came in third once. This is about as fickle, unstable, and unpredictable as it gets, and demonstrates a remarkable degree of so-called voter disloyalty over a very brief period of time. A similar pattern emerges from the gubernatorial elections in Mexico's thirty-two states; in most there are in fact only two competitive parties, but those two vary not only state by state, but in some cases, election by election in the same state.

This arrangement is the worst conceivable one because it almost insures that each party will always have something, and hope reasonably to achieve more. Consequently, parties have no incentive either to compromise or to fight outright with others, preferring instead to build on a vague, nonconfrontational platform that can allow any one of them to remain united, and beat out the other two the next time around. No party has a majority in the overall electorate, and therefore cannot hope to implement its program, whatever it may be. And any significant alliance of two parties against the third (for example, the PRI and the PAN against the PRD) poses the risk of angering significant factions within each of the two allies as well as opening themselves up to charges of cynical opportunism. This enables the isolated party to claim that it alone is principled and to woo disenchanted factions within opposing parties. The situation has remained pretty much unchanged since 1997. The PRD controls the majority of Mexico City, the second most important elective office in the country, with the third-largest budget. The PAN has the presidency, and the PRI enjoys a relative majority in Congress (in 1997, 2003, and 2009), as well as the greatest number of governorships, including those of the two largest states, Mexico and Veracruz.

Why did things turn out this way? For many reasons, of course, but partly because the alternative—i.e., a political party reconfiguration—implied divisions inside each party and a realignment on political and ideological grounds. It meant that the modern, technocratic wing of the PRI would break with the old, nationalist, populist faction; that the reformist, social democratic left would break with the radical, revolutionary left; and that the right-of-center, moderate, modernizing group in the PAN would break with the ultraconservative, ultra-Catholic faction. Each one of these scissions could only come about through ideological, political confrontation, each bloc abandoning its bureaucratic partners and joining forces with its programmatic soulmates.

This simply never happened. After the 1988 break within the PRI led by Cuauhtémoc Cárdenas, there has only been one additional intra-PRI split, involving the teachers' union leader, Elba Esther Gordillo, in 2003. No one significant has abandoned the PAN or the PRD in order to ally itself with a more like-minded group. The reason: any realignment would have entailed, and continues to imply, confrontation with yesterday's allies, followed by convergence with today's newly found friends. But the three-legged stool, as opposed to a four-legged chair or a two-legged individual, is by definition the most unbalanced structure and the easiest one to overturn. It remains untouched since 1988. There is absolutely no reason to believe that this will be altered anytime soon. The inherently unmanageable three-party system, which can only be suppressed and replaced by a two- or four-party structure if a majority-generating, winner-takes-all process is established, will persist, because two-thirds of the votes are required in both houses of Congress to modify the Constitution, and each party always has a blocking third of the seats somewhere, if only in the streets.

As it stands, each one of Mexico's last three presidents has received an electoral mandate successively smaller than his predecessor: Ernesto Zedillo, 49% in 1994, Vicente Fox, 43% in 2000, Felipe Calderón, 35.9% in 2006.[13] The only solution is to force the electorate to decide: to vote in a referendum on critical constitutional matters and in a runoff election between the two leading contenders in the first round. But this clashes with Mexico's aversion to conflict. Why fight with someone if you can get along just fine without bringing disagreements to the fore, and actually imposing definitions through majority rule? While no one disputes the democratic nature of this tacit pact, no one deems it functional or adequate in the face of the country's immense challenges. It is particularly pernicious in terms of managing Mexico's powerful centrifugal forces, which were subdued under a one-party system but now are increasingly destructive, as we shall see in Chapter 9.

They can only be dealt with through a democracy where transparent, open, and explicit confrontation of different regional, ethnic, economic, and political interests simultaneously conciliate Mexican society's yawning gaps *and* allow a majority of its inhabitants to impose democratically reached solutions on recalcitrant minorities. This is not happening, largely because no one wants to bring into the public sphere the obvious, countervailing points of view and interests present throughout the country. The democracy we have neither forces these conflicts nor allows them to be settled peacefully; the consequence is their aggravation.

This, however, is by no means the only practical, democratic consequence of the trait of national character we attempted to describe in the previous chapter. Perhaps the most serious one—the second challenge—involves economic and social policy, or more directly, the absence of competition in Mexican society, and of any self-respecting antitrust regulations or policy. This is where the rubber truly meets the road.

## *Competition and the* Guinness Book of World Records

We have already seen how power has been highly concentrated in Mexico since time immemorial. There is one oil company, one teachers union, one national television network worth mentioning (the others are local, or hobbies for their owners, or destined for intellectuals), one cement company worthy of the name, one electric power generator, one tortilla maker, one bread baker, no independent candidates for elected office, one magnate whose net worth exceeds that of the following ten combined. This has always pretty much been so, at least since the Conquest, which among other matters entailed a complete concentration of land in the hands of the Church and the Crown, and of commerce with one company (the Casa de Contratación), one port (Cadiz-Seville), in one country (Spain). There are myriad explanations for this state of affairs—historical, economic, political—but at least an additional one conducive to its perpetuation today, a cultural factor. And it is perhaps the most malignant consequence of Mexico's conflict aversion: its thorough mistrust and dislike of competition. The economic equivalent of conflict aversion (and of the perpetual Mexican penchant for wishful thinking and the concomitant reluctance to choose between incompatible opposites) is risk aversion. This can be truly lethal for an open market economy, which is what Mexico possesses today. These economies thrive on competition and risk taking, when competition pervades; they founder when monopolies take over and reduce risk taking. This is where Mexico finds itself right now.

Competition inevitably signifies someone's loss and someone's gain, and Mexicans abhor losing. The two can be relative, temporary, or beneficial for the *collective* entity in which the winner and loser compete and the competition takes place. Competing means risk taking, and engaging in confrontation: a loyal, transparent, legal confrontation, or a cutthroat, no-holds-barred, ruthless confrontation, but confrontation nonetheless. Entering into it involves the possibility of defeat, humiliation, and shame, or the destruction of a rival and enemy, who may rise to fight another day. No market economy in the world today enjoys even imperfect competition: monopolies are the name of the game everywhere. But almost all market economies—and union movements, and the media, and political systems—are regulated, in order to avoid the extremes that Standard Oil or AT&T reached in the United States at different moments of the twentieth century. Successful market economies all are at the partial mercy of fanged regulatory agencies—some more fanged than others—which step in when price-fixing, market assignments or cartels, unfair competition, or other forms of monopolistic behavior become too obvious or damaging to society or the economy.

Mexico lacks these institutions (its toothless Federal Competition Commission is not autonomous, and its Justice Department cannot bring antitrust suits). It has done without them partly because, at least until the mid-nineties, Mexico's form of crony capitalism did not need them, and partly because the very notion of the state imposing competition on a society that loathes it remains totally alien to the country, its elites, and public opinion. Nonetheless, an ample and growing consensus has emerged in Mexico and abroad that the main obstacle to the country's future economic growth, and further enlargement of the middle class, lies in this excessive concentration of power. As we have noted, every kind of power is exercised by few: political, economic, financial, media, intellectual, public and private, labor, and so on. More and more experts, from the World Bank and *The Economist* to former Finance Ministry officials and the governor of the Central Bank, from left-wing rabble-rousers to anachronistic conservative free marketers, from novelists like Carlos Fuentes to public intellectuals in the editorial pages of the newspapers, all seem to agree that something has to be done about Mexico's many monopolies. Unfortunately, there is no grassroots movement behind this convergence of elite opinion, and even among those who profess to share these pro-competition views, when push comes to shove, they veer away from specifics, or from taking more public stances.

There are many motivations for this relative indifference, ranging from fear of reprisal to personal ties, but one explanation lies undoubtedly in the aversion to conflict and the reluctance to find oneself exposed someday to competition. It is remarkable to see how an otherwise sophisticated intellectual elite or administrative technocracy, for example, is uncomfortable with anything vaguely resembling meritocracy. With the partial exception of the finance and foreign ministries and the Central Bank, government jobs in Mexico are drastically anti-meritocratic; ours is a large-scale spoils system. And with the exception of the National University's Engineering, Law, and Medical Schools, and the ITAM's (Mexican Autonomous Institute of Technology) Economics Department together with the Monterrey Tech's Engineering Department, there are no Mexican equivalents of the Ivy League, the

U de Chile or the USP (Universidade de São Paulo), Oxbridge or France's *grandes écoles*. This is even more true in publishing, journalism, national institutions, or prizes and medals. Again, the reasons are many, but one stands out: a meritocracy requires competition: some win, others don't; and competition entails strife, which Mexicans continue to detest.

A marvelous illustration of this syndrome lies in the *Guinness Book of World Records,* of all places. As *The New York Times* put it in an article in 2009, "If Guinness World Records ever creates a category for the country most obsessed with being in the *Guinness Book of World Records,* Mexico will surely be in the running."[14] It goes on to list the strange records Mexico has sought to break: largest number of people dancing simultaneously to Michael Jackson's *Thriller*; most mariachi musicians gathered in one place; the longest catwalk and St. Valentine's Day kiss; the largest meatball, cheesecake, and, of course, the biggest taco and tamale. The most recent records were for the world's tallest artificial Christmas tree and ice-skating rink, in late 2009. All of these heroic attempts were carried out, predictably, with full-barreled government support. As Mexican political scientist Carlos Elizondo elaborated, the most surprising thing is why a country that avoids competition at all costs wishes to accumulate Guinness Records: "Why such an obsession with this?" His answer is elegant and enlightening: "For the same reasons we dislike competition. These records are based on noncompetition. The point is simply to make something bigger or with more people. . . . No one else in the world cares. There are no other mayors competing in the world tournament for the tallest Christmas tree, in which we competed and won."[15]

A final harmful consequence of conflict aversion lies in the rules regarding electoral competition. In recent times, that is, in the diaper stage of the country's democratic rule, the reluctance to confront has acquired a particularly destructive, tragicomic set of features, laid down in great detail in the new electoral laws passed in 2007, and which may enjoy a long and happy life.

Mexico has held two basically democratic presidential elections in its history, and two almost democratic ones. Francisco I. Madero's election in 1911 took place in a country just emerging from a thirty-year dictatorship, without any real contenders or electoral laws and customs; and Ernesto Zedillo's victory in 1994 was free but not entirely "fair" (or "equitable," in a direct translation from the Spanish), as Zedillo himself confessed. Vicente Fox's in 2000 was the only truly unblemished one; Felipe Calderón's in 2006 was free and fair, though many considered it tainted. In all three cases, however, the behavior of the Mexican mass media cannot be considered part of a democratic process. They overwhelmingly favored PRI candidate Ernesto Zedillo in 1994 and PRI candidate Francisco Labastida in 2000, and were deeply biased in favor of PRD candidate López Obrador in 2006 until the very end of the campaign, when they switched sides and tilted heavily in favor of Felipe Calderón. The issue was not so much whom they favored, but rather the fact that they clearly backed one candidate against others. All the previous elections were either meaningless (José López Portillo ran unopposed in 1976, and received 96% of the vote) or so profoundly tampered with (1940, 1952, 1988) that they cannot be considered democratic under any definition of the word.

In the two really competitive elections (2000 and 2006), negative campaigning and mud-slinging in the media were commonplace: not more nor less than elsewhere in the democratic world, where either by purchasing media time, or enjoying officially assigned public airtime, or through interviews on TV and radio, the three main candidates gave as good as they got. In 2006, however, one candidate, the PRD contender, Andrés Manuel López Obrador, concluded that he had been unfairly deprived of his victory through various stratagems and subterfuges, but mainly because of unfair negative campaigns waged by his opponents and third parties: the media, the business community, the incumbent president. He dismissed the fact that he had been the media's darling for five of Fox's six years in office, and particularly of Televisa, the television monopoly, and that he brought the private sector's opprobrium upon himself by basically threatening to dispense with it.

In any case, after his defeat, and in an effort to redraft electoral laws acceptable to everyone, the PRI (which fared badly in 2006) and President Calderón (who wanted at all costs to obtain PRI backing for the rest of his agenda), allowed the left to rewrite the rules. And it did so with relish. In the Constitution (Article 6), and in the Electoral Code (Article 233), the losers of the 2006 vote specifically prohibited and criminalized parties and candidates from negative campaigning. The new constitutional language stated: "The expression of ideas shall not be the subject of any judicial or administrative inquiry or prosecution, except in the case of attacks on morality, the rights of third parties, the commission of crimes, or any disturbance of public order."[16]

This was subsequently interpreted in the implementing legislation as banning "expressions which denigrate [national] institutions or political parties themselves, or that incur in calumny of individuals. The General Council of the Federal Electoral Institute has the right to order the immediate suspension of radio or television messages [spots] that are contrary to this rule, as well as banning any other propaganda."[17] Thus Mexico enshrined in the Constitution its penchant for conflict aversion, as if translating traits of national character into law would generate any impact on everyday life, political or otherwise. The only result of this absurd intent was to drive negative campaigning and electoral confrontation out of the areas where it was banned—radio and television—and into those where it was countenanced, if only by omission: mainly, the Internet.

There is a case to be made in mature democracies that have experienced years of negative campaigning and media strife that some type of limitation might be desirable, under determined circumstances, at certain times. There is no conclusive evidence in the literature about whether negative campaigning works or turns people off, whether "staying positive" pays higher electoral dividends than "going negative." We only seem to know that not responding to a negative campaign can be fatal (see John Kerry's Swift Boats in 2004). Except in Mexico, where the reluctance to engage in altercation is such that the best reaction to criticism has been, in several elections including the 2009 legislative vote, to turn the other cheek.

In conclusion, then, Mexico's political, law enforcement, electoral, and antitrust laws, institutions, and practices all serve the country poorly. But instead of originating in the authoritarian system the nation lived with and, as many believed, suffered under for seventy years, and whose disappearance led many to hope that these defects and drawbacks would evaporate with the advent of democratic rule, it turns out they have outlived the ancien régime. The reason is simple. They did not spring from the authoritarian recent past, but from the cultural and historical character traits of the remote past. And once again we confirm what we have suspected: Mexico and the Mexicans made the avoidance of confrontation, contradiction, and strife, on a personal, political, and even international scale, a way of life that permitted, in their time, the survival of a people and the emergence of a nation. Today, this way of life stands in the way of that people and that nation's full entry into modernity.

## CHAPTER 5

# The Power of the Past and the Fear of the Foreign

Few generalizations about Mexicans by nationals or foreigners are as widespread as those underlining the country's obsession with its history and the resulting fear and rejection of "the other." In the following two chapters we will contrast a corresponding trait of character and the material reality it affects and contradicts.

Octavio Paz, in an essay in *The New Yorker* in 1979 examining the differences between Mexico and the United States, emphasized how they were also separated by their different views of the past: Mexico looks back and broods; the United States looks forward and forgets.[1] The notion that the outside world has always been a source of danger and disgrace for Mexicans, that everything coming from abroad threatens the country, is of course hardly irrational. It is well founded in Mexican history. But the country's obsession with the past also springs from how it is read: as a past of oppression and betrayal. Mexico's official history, in almost every reading, is composed of successive episodes of invasion, rape, conquest, treason, and death, all linked somehow to an "other," who is always alien, extraneous, foreign.

We have already stressed how contradictory this notion can be. As the Mexican writer and commentator Luis González de Alba has repeatedly claimed, if today's "us" identifies Mexicans with the conquered Indians of 1519–21, then how come we are all *mestizos*, by definition offspring of Indians *and* Spaniards?[2] How did we manage to descend only from Indians? But behind this oft-denounced paradox, there is both an interesting factual question and an accompanying psychosocial analysis that, while arguably simplistic, does provide some clues to Mexicans' fear of the foreign and their entrapment in the past.

There is a logic to their seeing themselves as more Indian than Spanish, or mono-ethnic *mestizos* rather than products of multiethnic *mestizaje*. In the overwhelming majority of cases during the early years of the Conquest and the colony, *mestizos* were born to Indian mothers and Spanish fathers, hardly ever the other way around. And it is also a fact that the Spanish father was invariably an absent one, to put it mildly. He was literally just passing through, satiating his sexual hunger, and moving on. As Federico San Román has phrased it, embroidering on Santiago Ramírez's thesis, this absence of any father explains both Mexican individualism and conflict aversion. Both were defense mechanisms constructed to guard the abandoned Mexican from a hostile world, where the protective father did not exist.[3] The Spanish procreated with many women without filling the role of fathers or husbands. The first *mestizos* grew up without a father and without an integrated family. The Mexican, then, says San Román, is a chronically unfathered or fatherless being, whose initial bastardy leaves a permanent mark, and who repeats his own history until today. His eyes are always focused on the past, on the same drama, on the same betrayal. That recurrent betrayal, from generation to generation, feeds the historical anger that has much more to do with family disintegration and poverty today than with events of five centuries ago.

## (Re) Writing History

Be this as it may, there is scant room for discussion about the way "Mexican" history began: how and why Cortés conquered the Aztec empire with four hundred men and twelve or thirteen horses. The answer is . . . he didn't. The Aztecs' colonized, oppressed neighbors did, together with a smallpox epidemic that came from Cuba in the summer of 1520, the Aztecs' insistence on taking captives alive for human sacrifice, and their cosmology warning of an imminent debacle.[4] All Cortés accomplished—in one of the most astounding political feats of all time—was to channel widespread discontent, nourished by human sacrifice, cannibalism, blood tributes against the empire, and the world vision of the Aztecs into a funnel of weakness, betrayal, and corruption. But this accurate, close-to-the-ground version of history serves neither as a cornerstone for nation building nor as the raw material of myths and legend.

For that, it had to be the other way around. Thus, our Indian ancestors were defeated by a powerful enemy that took advantage of its technological prowess and the divisions of the "home team" to subdue the country. And so, for the first time, the external "other" wrought its plague and pestilence upon the people of Mexico, not in actual fact, but in the written and oral history of a culture obsessed by history and at the same time familiar with historical underpinnings and how to manipulate them. As Emilio Uranga has put it: "The Mexican always gives the impression of already having lived before, of dragging in the depths of his soul a history and a world that are no longer, but that emotionally, at least, were inerasably engraved in his soul."[5] For him (or her), history is a stone slab borne on the back of a vanquished people.

Mexican elementary school textbooks, even in their current, more modern versions, are inevitably euphemistic about the Conquest. Describing the reasons why the Indians were defeated, they list three. The first "was that the conquered Indians did not feel part of a common political and cultural union. They had different traditions, languages, and customs. There was a long history of wars among them, which had produced hatred and resentment. The Mexicas (or Aztecs) . . . who dominated and exploited the others, were the most abhorred. Many Indian communities saw in the Spanish convenient allies with whom to combat their old enemies. *The conquerors quickly understood this situation and took advantage of the enmities prevailing among the Indian peoples*. In the battles against the Mexicas, the Spanish could count on thousands of Indian allies, bent on liquidating their oppressors. *Little did they know that their fate would be the same as that of the vanquished*." The other two reasons were technology and weapons, as well as a different idea of combat, whereby for the Indian, "nothing brought greater glory than capturing an enemy alive and then sacrificing him [to the gods]."[6] The insinuation in the first reason is glaring: the Spanish tricked the Indians who opposed the Aztecs into combating them, and subsequently annihilated their allies, just as they destroyed the Aztecs!

There is a wonderful tale, recounted by González de Alba, about the first drafting of an official history—and the resulting destruction of the previously accepted version of history—in the territory now known as Mexico. When the Aztecs became independent from Azcapotzalco, roughly a century before the arrival of the Spaniards, their new king, Izcóatl, ordered all the history books (known as *códices*) destroyed and rewritten. The reason: the Aztec people did not receive sufficient adulation or "respect," and as the Matritense Codex stated, "it is not convenient for everybody to know about the paintings [of history]. . . . Those who are subjects will be spoilt and the earth will become crooked, but [the paintings] guard many lies and many in those lies have been seen as gods."[7] Mexico began rearranging history to suit its aims and imagination long before it became . . . Mexico. The contradiction is self-evident. On the one hand, the country insists obsessively on writing and rewriting history, and referring to it; on the other, it "knows" that it can always be redrawn, with the stroke of a pen, in order to achieve certain aims or political purposes. There is nothing as fragile as an official version of history, which can be torn up and redone on a dime, as so many other nations discovered, perhaps none more than the former Soviet Union.

Ever since Izcóatl, then, the country's establishment and its schoolchildren, its elites and its masses, its politicians and mainstream intellectuals have all constructed or learned an "official history," like every other people in the world. That history is somewhat different from others, though, since here the victim is king, defeat is glorified, and foreign influences and agents are decisive and ruthless. Linearity and simplification make the tale palatable and true, as elsewhere. Mexico's "losers," however, generate a gap between fact and reconstruction that is possibly wider than those of other societies. Americans, for example, make up quite a story about the Alamo, a good part of which is false and a small part of which is true. But the defeat, while "heroic" and glorified far beyond what the facts allow, is placed in the context of victory: the success of the Texan Secession a few months later. Mexico places its victories in the context of defeat.

The *story*, as opposed to the *history*, begins with the tragedy of the Conquest, moves on to the devastation of the Black Legend, continues with three miserable centuries of colonization and an ensuing heroic, mass struggle for independence. This was subsequently thwarted by the Americans (1836 and the Texan Secession; 1847 and the U.S. invasion and occupation), the French (through their invasion and occupation in 1862), the Porfiriato, and the selling of Mexico to the United States. It was followed by the Revolution and the angry insurrection against evil "others," all the way to the Zapatista uprising against NAFTA in 1994 and the new national sellout implicit in the free trade agreement. Formulated succinctly, Mexico's official story is one of deflowering from abroad, oppression from within provoked by foreign influence, and an immense fear of the outside "other" definitively corroborated by a "correct" reading of the "real" history. Thus the obsession with history springs from the role assigned to Mexico's martyrdom in that narrative; the best proof of Mexico's status as a "victim country" today is that it has always been one. Likewise, the rejection and terror inspired by the foreign factor today stem from the fixation with past betrayals and defeats. They all go together.*

No wonder then that in 1992, five hundred years after Columbus's arrival in Hispaniola, and in the midst of an ultimately failed educational reform, an enormous brouhaha erupted regarding a *new* version of Mexico's official, free, and obligatory elementary school textbooks. The latter were first conceived and published back in 1959, when the country's last and most successful literacy campaign began. Then president Adolfo López Mateos and his education minister, Jaime Torres Bodet, who had served as UNESCO's second director-general, concluded that the only way to unify educational standards and extend literacy to all was through state-printed, free textbooks in every elementary school discipline, including, of course, history, particularly for fourth, fifth, and sixth graders. Those books were the ones with which Mexico's baby boomers grew up in the sixties and seventies, when population growth surpassed 3.5% a year. They became a symbol of Mexico's social, supposedly egalitarian development, and undoubtedly facilitated the country's initial education drive. They were printed by the millions on state-owned printing presses, and became the constant object of discussions, pressure, and adjustment over the years. The Church sought to limit sex education in the science books, the opposition strove to revise the politically apologetic nature of the civics

---

* Héctor Aguilar Camín and I, in a brief book we published in 2010—*Un futuro para México*—touched upon this fixation, stressing how Mexico has too much past and too little future and must do away with its obsession with history. Héctor Aguilar Camín and Jorge G. Castañeda, *Un futuro para Mexico* (Mexico City: Santillana, 2010).

texts, and even the United States joined the fray by seeking to tone down certain excessively anti-American statements.

But by 1992, on the eve of the NAFTA debate in the United States and an educational overhaul attempted by Salinas de Gortari, the government embarked upon a major reform of the science and history books. It also came in the wake of protests by the former U.S. ambassador, actor John Gavin, about the image of his country and the world in those history texts. The review was outsourced to a group of mainstream historians. But a major protest by the left, the excluded intellectuals, and the teachers union forced Salinas to back down in the end. Only minor modifications were made to the textbooks.

What was so controversial? Mainly the relationship with the United States in the nineteenth and twentieth centuries; the concrete role of a few nineteenth-century heroes; the pros and cons of the Porfiriato; and to a lesser extent, the resistance of the pre-Columbian peoples to the Spanish Conquest. As we have said, every society engages in major debates about children's education and in particular about how history is presented to them; all nations "invent" heroes, who were inevitably more blemished individuals than those described in children's textbooks. Mexico's 1992 debate was no different except that it focused not on whether children should know the "truth," but on defining and interpreting the "truth." In the words of the lead historian in the exercise, Héctor Águilar Camín, the question was whether "someone has considered the profound impact that our tendency to exalt defeats and disdain victories can have on our children's civic culture when they learn the strange things the 'motherland's history' teaches them."[8]

The "strange" things taught to schoolchildren include dating Mexican Independence to 1810, when it actually occurred in 1821; insisting, as the Church now does—it didn't, before—that in 1576 the Virgin of Guadalupe was sighted by Juan Diego, a young peasant who subsequently received proof of her apparition through a stamped image of Our Lady on the shawl in which he was carrying roses; presenting the Revolution of 1910 as an epic for "*Tierra y Libertad*" ("Land and Freedom"), when in fact all the peasants of Morelos wanted was to replace the sitting vice president and retrieve their farm plots from the past.

The historical discussion was directly and deeply rooted in Mexicans' perception of themselves as "losers": victims of the guile of others, humbled, and dignified in defeat but never proud of victory. Mexico is a land, as Octavio Paz puts it, "of superimposed pasts. Mexico City was built on the ruins of Tenochtitlán, the Aztec city that was built in the likeness of Tula, the Toltec city that was built in the likeness of Teoti-huacán. . . . Every Mexican bears within him this continuity, which goes back two thousand years."[9] In a country where everything divides people—geography, ethnicity, religion, and most of all class and money—history is one of the few uniting forces, one of the few areas of consensus. But in order to unite the country, that history must be crafted, and its design cannot be neutral or evenhanded given the inevitable ups and downs, victories and defeats, successes and failures that the "truth" always contains. It is constructed as a tale of insult and injury, of suffering and grief, starting with the fall of Tenochtitlán. Specifically, this tragedy is presented as the bitter fruit of treason (La Malinche, the Tlaxcaltecans) combined with weakness (Moctezuma, the Tarascan kings in Michoacán) and myopic oppression (the Aztecs' brutal, bloody domination of the neighboring peoples).

Worse followed. A fledgling nation stretching from the border with British Oregon to Colombia was rapidly dismembered. It lost its first chunk—roughly 200,000 square miles, the equivalent of Mississippi, Alabama, Georgia, and South Carolina—in 1823 when the Central American nations seceded. During Mexico's first thirty years of inde-pendent life, it had fifty governments, and partly because of that it lost Texas in 1836, and then half of what was left—today's Arizona, California, New Mexico, Utah, Nevada, and parts of Colorado and Wyoming—in 1847. In 1862, Mexico was invaded by the French, and when they were finally expelled five years later, the country, after Be-nito Juárez's interregnum, soon succumbed again to dictatorship, cor-ruption, and humiliation.

But for history to serve as a unifying thread in Mexican nation building, more was required than this dismal narrative of agony, fail-ure, and heroic but futile resistance. Three further ingredients were necessary: the rewriting of history as often and as radically as possible; glorification of the enduring traits of this ongoing tragedy; and con-struction of a wall against the foreign demons who have repeatedly wounded, damaged, and nearly destroyed the country and who pro-vide the leitmotif of its history. This is a clearly defined strain of the national character that permeates every nook and cranny of Mexican life, in every region of its geography, in every heart and mind, and in every law. It ranges from the Aztecs a century before Cortés, to the 1992 children's books debate; from the exaltation of Cuauhtémoc the martyr, to the myriad restrictions on immigrants working and living in Mexico. This strain is the most distinguishing feature of a national culture or character that invariably surprises and confuses the foreign observer. The best proof of this predilection lies in the results of the National Educational Test for middle-school children taken in 2010. Of the three categories—i.e., mathematics, Spanish, which is in fact reading comprehension, and history—53% of the students turned out to be insufficiently educated in mathematics, 40% in Spanish, but only 13% in history; 34% had only an elementary knowledge of mathematics, while 62% did of history, and only 2% performed excellently in mathematics, whereas 6% did so in history, three times more.[10] Thus, in the year 2010, in a country with a GDP per capita of nearly $15,000 (PPP), with one of the world's most open economies, middle-school pupils did three to four times better in history than in mathematics, when if anything it should be the other way around.

Not that this educational obsession with history actually delivers results. Poll after poll demonstrates that despite all the learning by rote and the countless historical holidays the country celebrates (February 5, Constitution Day; March 21, Benito Juárez's birthday; May 1, Labor Day, like everywhere; May 5, the victory over the French at Puebla in 1862; September 16, Independence Day; and November 20, Revolution Day, all in addition to the classic religious holidays), Mexicans in general and schoolchildren in particular scarcely remember their history lessons. While practically every Mexican has heard of Emiliano Zapata or Pancho Villa, only 29% can name the country's first president (Guadalupe Victoria, a singularly insignificant figure); less than half know the year when the struggle for Mexican Independence began (1810); only 11% are familiar with the date of the fall of Tenochtitlán (1521); and just 23% can say when Columbus "discovered" America. The responses are even less accurate for people with only an elementary school education, which is understandable, but they nonetheless underline the futility of the debates over the children's textbooks. A scant 6% of all Mexicans with primary education or less replied correctly to the question of when Mexican Independence was finally achieved (1821). Of the historical holidays mentioned above, none was better known than the most familiar and ahistorical ones in Mexico:

Mother's Day (May 10), Children's Day (April 30), and the Day of the Virgin of Guadalupe (December 12).[11]

## The Ritual Is the Message

But maybe these pollsters, and authors such as myself, have it all wrong. Mexico is eminently a country of rituals; if there is any distinguishing feature of the national character, it is that. Everything is a ritual, a substitute for facing up to awkward realities. There are social-religious rituals: baptism, first communion, *fiestas de quinceaños* or coming out parties, marriage, burial and postmortem mass. There are educational rituals: graduation from elementary school, middle, and high school, not to mention college. There are political and patriotic rituals, beginning with saluting the flag and singing the national anthem every day in hundreds of thousands of schools, and attending ceremonies in honor of the populous pantheon of Mexican patriarchs, organizing parades for each historical date, and celebrating each estate's "day"—Army Day, Navy Day, Teachers' and Construction Workers' Day, Children's and Mother's Day, Architects' and Engineers' Day, Doctors' and Nurses' Day. These are rituals of daily life, involving everything from the perennial *abrazo* or hug to the so-called political *besamanos*, or congratulations offered to someone who has been appointed to high station or has survived in it (akin to the mafiosi kissing their godfather's ring). These never-ending rituals are the social and personal expressions of one of Paz's favorite theses: form over content, or what he later called will for form.

In perhaps his most insightful writings, which mixed aesthetic criticism with soul-searching, Paz repeatedly stressed the Mexican penchant for form: in art, in architecture, in literature, in politics. As he wrote in his introduction to the catalogue for the controversial exposition of Mexican art at the Metropolitan Museum in New York in 1992, titled Thirty Centuries of Splendor, "The theme of this exhibition of Mexican art unfolds before our eyes: the persistence of a single will through an incredible variety of forms, manners, and styles. There is apparently nothing in common shared by the stylized jaguars of the Olmecs, the gilded angels of the seventeenth century, and the richly colored violence of a Tamayo oil—nothing, save the will to survive through and in form."[12]

Paz wrote in a tone and substance devoid of any derogatory or critical connotation. If anything, the poet seemed to think that therein lay the Mexican genius: in bestowing upon the same content—or sensibility—a succession of extraordinary forms, where form itself becomes the purpose, the point, and the passion. As Paz puts it, "Form surrounds and sets bounds to our privacy, limiting its excesses, curbing its explosions, isolating and preserving it. Both our Spanish and Indian heritages have influenced our fondness for ceremony, formulas and order. . . . Perhaps our traditionalism, which is one of the constants of our national character, giving coherence to our people and our history, results from our preferred love for Form. . . . Our devotion to Form, even when empty, can be seen throughout the history of Mexican art from pre-Conquest times to the present."[13]

This proclivity—or emptiness, some would retort—leads directly to the emphasis on ritual. It is the orderly expression of Form. And ritual invades everything, including education. It is quite possible—indeed, highly probable—that the recurrent insistence on names, dates, and heroes in teaching Mexican history to children in a certain way, despite the obvious absence of any quantifiable results, must be found in the ritual itself: the rite is the message. Children do not have drummed into their heads the unending list of episodes of Mexican victimization in order for them to remember them, much less to understand them. The purpose of the exercise is the exercise itself: the teachers' feeling satisfied that they have done their job (whatever the usefulness of the job); the parents, that they have fulfilled their obligation to have their children taught the fundamentals of life (even if they were not learned); the government officials (from the school principal to the minister of education), that they have complied with the law and custom (no matter how silly the law or how fabricated the custom); and the country's political and cultural elites, all gratified by the proven respect for the preordained rite. This process enshrines the Mexican predilection for simulation in a quasi-religious catechism.

These rituals are deeply ingrained in the psyche of the Mexican infant and adolescent, and if they are not assimilated and interiorized on time, they never will be. I did not attend elementary school in Mexico, having lived in New York and Cairo through seventh grade; I then pursued the rest of my education at the French Lycée in Mexico City. So when thirty years later I was appointed foreign minister, a job that despite its political and bureaucratic weakness is steeped in ritual—the foreign minister always sits or stands to the president's immediate left in every official ceremony—I found it difficult to know what to do: when to sing the national anthem, salute the flag, or look circumspect, wistful, or happy, how to greet other ceremony participants—with great enthusiasm, solemn respect, or distant aloofness—or even how to walk a proper distance behind, next to, or in front of the president, depending on the pomp and circumstance of the moment. My utter lack of ingrained familiarity with the rituals experienced in elementary school made me a mediocre standard-bearer for Mexican protocol.* Worse still, I was even less adept at respecting age-old customs of indirect communication, euphemisms, rhetorical flourishes, and elliptical expression. I simply did not respect the rites of power, public discourse, and behavior that Mexican politicians, artists, poets, and dancers all must adhere to. Not only did this get me into a lot of trouble with the public at large, but, more gravely, it also gave grist to my political adversaries, all eagerly seeking to exploit an outsider's apparent weakness. This played to the traditional PRI and Mexican penchant for intolerance toward the "other," especially when that "other" is also an outsider. What I obviously misunderstood was that Form is not a means to an end, an instrument of expression of content, a beautiful (or hateful) recourse for stating something somehow; it is an end in itself, the message itself, the ultimate receptacle whose importance far outweighs what it contains.

This is historical education in Mexico today: a ritual that every child knows by heart, and in the heart; a moment that will be remembered forever, not for the lessons learned or heroes revered, but as a rite of passage. Going to school consists largely in attending the ceremony honoring the flag, the singing of the national anthem, the interminable graduation speeches and diplomas, the ritual of presence. The object of the history that encircles the ritual, its raison d'être, lies in tragedy, in the memories of the vanquished, in their resentment and resignation stemming from constant defeats, always supposedly at the hands of "another," always derived from the subterfuges and deviousness of "forces from abroad," ever ready to take advantage of Mexican hospitality, division or altruism and decency.

---

* My father, who was also foreign minister for three years, also went to school abroad (in the 1920s), also detested diplomatic rituals, and skipped them whenever he could. Nonetheless, he was far better at respecting them than I was when he had no choice.

Once again, the drug issue allows us to clarify the intensity of this vision. Mexico has rightly insisted since time immemorial (actually since the 1960s) that the production in—and transshipment through—its territory of illicit substances is no more responsible for the drug challenge than U.S. consumption. It has always sustained that as long as American demand for drugs remains what it is, Mexican supply will too. It recurrently adds that the United States smacks of hypocrisy when it swears off drugs, since in fact it never does.

Where the question becomes complicated is when anyone replies that, forty years after drugs entered the mainstream of American life, it is evident not only that U.S. demand will not diminish, but also that American society is comfortable with or at least resigned to the status quo. So yes, as the argument goes, the United States is hypocritical and Mexico is sincere, but the U.S. is happy with this situation and Mexico is not. Mexico is idealistically naïve and dignified, the U.S. cynical and deceitful, but Mexico suffers from its disenchantment, and the U.S. regales itself with its scornful indifference. Who is on top, as in the Penélope Cruz film? Again in the official script, Mexico's honesty and nobleness are taken advantage of by the perverse and hypocritical Americans, but Mexicans rarely ask themselves why they are decent and righteous but downtrodden, whereas Americans are mean and lean but get their way. The reason is obvious. Mexico prefers to be right and weak, since it has convinced itself it will always be weak, but at least it will always have the consolation of being right.

## Quantifying Fear and Inviting In the Foreign

As recently as 2004, after the advent of democracy, globalization, NAFTA, and a certain degree of economic prosperity, according to a Centro de Investigación y Docencia Económicas (CIDE) poll, 51% of all Mexicans thought it was bad for ideas and customs of other countries to spread in Mexico; only 27% thought this was a good thing. In 2006 the number dropped to 34% saying it was a bad thing, and rose to 40% saying it was good; by 2008 positive opinions had climbed to 50%, with "only" 33% holding negative feelings.[14] If the question was phrased slightly differently, as in a Pew Global Attitudes Project poll taken in 2009—"our way of life needs to be protected against foreign influence"—four-fifths agreed, and nearly half agreed *completely*. In a

similar vein, in the same year, faced with the question whether globalization was mostly good or mostly bad for Mexico, opinions were
divided equally; when the question was reiterated two years later, this
time defining globalization as greater contact between the Mexican
economy and other economies in the world, a majority was in favor.
Nonetheless, 42% thought that Mexico benefited little or not at all
from foreign investment in general, and they were unswervingly
opposed to it in oil, electric power, and infrastructure. Mexican elites,
however, though polled less scientifically, proved to be highly favorable
on the three counts (oil, electric power, and infrastructure).[15] These
attitudes have undoubtedly helped to protect Mexican culture and
even to enhance its influence abroad, mainly in Central and South
America. But they have proven totally dysfunctional to the country, as
we shall see in the next chapter.

This "fear of the foreign" and mistrust of the outside world does not
mean that Mexico is an inhospitable society. Its hospitality is legendary,
and contributes at least partly to a little-known fact: more nonmilitary
Americans (close to one million) reside in Mexico than in any other
nation in the world.[16] Twenty million U.S. residents visit the country
every year, and there are several hundred million north–south border
crossings, with practically no episodes of violence, aggression, or hostility against any of these visitors.[17] And it *is* true that the foreign factor in
the life of the territory known today as Mexico has always been overwhelming. Thus it is perhaps a symptom of Mexico's dilemma that
despite its repeated attempts to limit foreign influence and intervention, the country has repeatedly experienced it. A nation that prides
itself so much on wanting to be the "owner and author of its own des-
tiny" has, in fact, rarely been so.

Moreover, it has persistently suffered, since birth, from the temptation all Mexican leaders have known—and often succumbed to—of
seeking foreign backing for their domestic endeavors and conflicts. As
the political scientist José Antonio Crespo has documented in a notable
recent book, *Contra la historia oficial*, even Benito Juárez, the hero of
the war against the French, sought U.S. support, first against the conservatives, then against the French, then once more against Emperor
Maximilian after he was abandoned by the French. Juárez signed the
opprobrious McLane-Ocampo Treaty in 1856, which allowed the
United States free passage through the Isthmus of Tehuantepec and

from Sonora to the Gulf of California, as well as the right to intervene in Mexico when "circumstances so warranted," without the consent of its authorities. The treaty was rejected by the U.S. Senate since many members feared it would increase the number of slave states, but Juárez had no qualms about bargaining away swaths of territory and sovereignty in exchange for guns and money.

He did not stop there. During a maritime incident in a Veracruz harbor in 1857, Juárez sought and obtained the armed intervention of two American frigates against the conservative leader Miguel Miramón. Later, he justified his pragmatism in this way: "The success of our sacred cause is assured. The great people of the United States have allied themselves with us. I only regret that the great liberal family has not been able, alone and without foreign backing, to annihilate the reactionary forces."[18] A few years later, with Lincoln in the White House and Maximilian and the French in Mexico City, Juárez's Washington ambassador, Matías Romero, wrote his president that he (Romero) preferred to lose territory to the Americans than to the French, and that the best way of achieving this was "to reach an agreement with the United States whereby we would commit ourselves to cede to them part or all of the territory that Maximilian would cede to the French."[19] An altruistic, proud defense of sovereignty this was not, even if it might have been good politics.

We must now turn, then, to the reasons for this perennially perceived threat rising from the "other," for the sense of danger always generated by the outside world in Mexico. And our point of departure is that the Mexicans' obsessions with their history and with the outside world are inseparable: one is incomprehensible without the other. A clear example is the way Mexico treats foreigners, even those it welcomes, and on occasion worships, but always mistrusts.

### Xenophobic, Me?

Mexico is known today, and profusely thanked, throughout Latin America—and in Spain—for being a nation that welcomed thousands of political refugees from the Spanish Civil War in the late thirties, from the military coups d'état in South America during the mid-1970s, and as recently as the 1980s and 1990s, from Central America's domestic convulsions. Some will temper this admiration with the sobering reminder that economic immigrants from the south are routinely mistreated in Mexico on their way to the United States: extortion, kidnapping, forced prostitution, and human trafficking are the norm.* But by and large the country is fondly remembered in various corners of the world for the warmth of its welcome to foreigners. As we have explained, few people are as hospitable in their homes (*Mi casa es su casa*) and neighborhoods as Mexicans.

What only those who have settled in Mexico realize, though, is how many ramparts, hoops, ditches, hitches, and overall obstacles the nation has erected to keep foreigners from holding certain jobs, acquiring certain rights, and enjoying certain freedoms. All of these impediments are a symptom of the "return of the repressed." Since Mexicans blame foreigners for the nation's setbacks in the past, they are persuaded that they must continue to protect themselves today from them. Article 32 of the 1917 Constitution addresses the matter of restrictions for naturalized Mexicans. It has been amended only twice, in 1932 and 1944, when limitations on naturalized Mexicans serving in the merchant marine and the armed forces were inserted. As an annotated version of Mexico's three Constitutions and hundreds of amendments explains:

> The concern of the 1917 Constitutional Convention for safeguarding national security and sovereignty can be explained by the fact that in the past foreigners located in strategic national security positions betrayed Mexico's interests, threatening national independence. For these reasons, the [Constitutional] Convention sought not only to establish a preference for individuals more intimately connected to the country, but also to forestall foreign intervention in national affairs. Although national identity has consolidated itself over the years, and national institutions have become more robust, the differences spelled out in

---

* The country seems divided about how well or poorly it treats Central and South American migrants entering Mexico illegally on their way to the United States. In a poll taken in October 2009, 45% of those interviewed said Mexico treated undocumented migrants as well as or better than Mexican undocumented migrants are treated in the United States; but 48% thought that Mexico treated them as badly or worse than Mexicans were treated in the United States. "Xenofobia en México," Gabinete de Comunicación Estratégica (GCE), Mexico City, October 9, 2010, p. 7.

Article 32 are still in place and remain valid precisely as permanent catalysts of national identity (whatever this may actually mean).[20]

It is, as we shall see, a disturbing piece of legislation.

The story begins with José María Morelos, one of independent Mexico's two founding fathers, a priest who fought in the region that today carries his name. He picked up the standard of Independence and became its leader when Miguel Hidalgo, the first patriot, was captured and beheaded by the Spanish less than eleven months after initiating the insurrection. Once catapulted into the struggle's leadership, he wrote a major document, almost a Declaration of Independence, titled *The Sentiments of the Nation*. It has become part of Mexican lore as a founding pronouncement, which included a few astonishing proclamations, such as the demand that the only religion permitted in the new, independent state be Catholicism (perhaps understandable for a priest). He also included two clauses, which have remained with Mexico ever since: #9, whereby "Only Americans [meaning Mexicans, in the language of the time] can hold jobs"; and #10, "Foreigners will not be admitted, unless they are skilled artisans capable of teaching and free of all suspicion." So much for the libertarian, open-minded nature of Mexico's Independence heroes. As a contemporary Mexican legal scholar has put it, "the Spanish ceased to be demographic building blocks of the nation, and were transformed into the 'other,' who had to be excluded in order to build an authentic nationality."[21]*

But this was not just Morelos speaking. Until 1994, a president was not only obliged to be Mexican-born, but both his *parents* needed to have been physically brought to life on Mexican territory. Today, according to Articles 32 and 82 of the Constitution and several secondary laws, the following posts are among those reserved for native-born Mexicans (i.e., those born in Mexico, or being the offspring of a Mexican-born parent abroad *and* having requested a Mexican nationality *and* renounced any other nationality): the president, cabinet secretaries, the

---

* Things haven't changed that much. In a poll taken in December 2009, 40% of all Mexicans agreed with the statement that "to be 100% Mexican, one must be Catholic." "Encuesta nacional. Segundo Semestre, 2009," Gabinete de Comunicación Estratégica (GCE), Mexico City, 2009, p. 57.

mayor of Mexico City and every other town, members of the National Chamber of Deputies and Senate as well as of state assemblies, state governors and lieutenant governors, ambassadors and consuls, the CEOs of the social security institutes and the oil and power companies, the rector of the National University and its board of trustees, the rectors of all public universities, the Central Bank governor and its board of directors, the Federal Electoral Institute and its governing council, the Supreme Court, appellate judges, circuit and district judges, and the president of the National and Mexico City Human Rights Commissions. No naturalized Mexican, or one holding double citizenship, can occupy any one of these posts, or countless other minor ones.*

These are not poll numbers or ethereal character traits; they cannot be equated or confused with beliefs or superstitions. These are constitutional provisions in most cases, or tenets of implementing legislation (for example, the Foreign Service Law) in others. They have remained valid and unmovable since 1917, when the current Constitution was ratified, although they were not included in the two previous ones, in 1857 and 1824. Their justification in the Constitutional Convention debates of the time is highly illustrative of the state of mind prevailing then, and now. For example, Francisco Múgica, a delegate to this convention who years later, in 1940, was a whisker away from succeeding Lázaro Cárdenas as president, went further than the letter of the law. He suggested the "need to differentiate among foreigners; some were the 'pernicious ones *par excellence*, like the Spanish and the Americans,' and others belonged to the same linguistic and racial community [of ours], the 'indo-latins.' "[22]

As recently as 2001, when as foreign minister I was able to overhaul the country's Foreign Service Law, the only amendment the Congress rejected was the one allowing naturalized Mexicans to be appointed ambassadors or consuls. Mexico was ready for democracy, an open economy, respect for human rights, legal abortion, and same-sex marriage in its capital, but not for full rights for its citizens by choice. The same opinion prevails with regard to less distinguished but much more high-profile positions. In a poll taken in 2009 on whether naturalized Mexicans should be allowed to play on the country's national team in

---

* The same poll also showed that 69% percent of all Mexicans thought that in order to be 100% Mexican, it was necessary to "have been born in Mexico." Encuesta Nacional. Segundo Semestre, 2009, Gabinete de Comunicación Estratégica (GCE), Mexico City, 2009, p. 53.

the World Cup soccer finals, 61% said no, because, as 78% believed, they had acquired Mexican citizenship only out of athletic convenience; 70% believed that they "do not really feel Mexican."[23] Another poll found that 81% thought naturalized Mexicans should not be allowed to become members of Congress, and 73% believed that they should be banned from occupying public university presidencies. Most ominously, between 66% and 76% of Mexicans expressed their opposition to foreigners of whatever nationality coming to work in their country—a far more xenophobic stance than in the United States.[24] And their reason was peculiarly Mexican: out of fear, from weakness, as this quote from a Constitutional Convention delegate in 1917 illustrates:

> We are a weak grouping . . . which is why the foreigner will always be stronger in Mexico than anywhere else, and also why the naturalization of foreigners in Mexico is a legal procedure, but not a real concept. It is not a positive fact; the foreigner comes to Mexico and is naturalized but does not become assimilated to the Mexican people. It is enough just to speak to any foreigner, even those who have spent some years in Mexico, or to see his demeanor, his ways, his aspect, to see that he does not mix in with the general mass of Mexicans; his biological type and his natural physiological qualities are closer to those of his previous motherland, whereas those of the Mexican ethnic type are not present. No matter how much he says he loves Mexico . . . it is not true, he loves his business, not the country. Now that the Revolution has triumphed, we know that they have all been against the Revolution.[25]

These were the words of Congressman Paulino Machorro Narváez. Better still: as Congressman Epigmenio Martínez put it, "Practice has shown that those with foreign blood always care for their blood, never for that of others."[26] Not surprisingly, Mexico's sporadic attempts to invite immigrants or settlers have been singularly unsuccessful. Ironically, even the leftist or anarco-revolutionary factions in Mexico, like the Flores Magón brothers just before the Revolution, included in their program the prohibition of hiring Chinese workers, who had already come to Mexico to work on the railroads.[27]

With the exception of the presidential restriction, these tenets are inconceivable in countries of immigrants, like the United States and

Canada, or Argentina, Uruguay, Brazil, and Chile. The problem is that Mexico is not a nation of immigrants, and has never been one. The refugees who came from Spain numbered barely 25,000; those who fled Pinochet in Chile after the 1973 coup that ousted Socialist president Salvador Allende did not total more than five thousand; the entire Jewish population in Mexico, mostly second-generation Mexican-born, barely reaches fifty thousand. If provisions such as these existed in the United States, for example, Henry Kissinger and Madeleine Albright would not have been secretaries of state, Arnold Schwarzenegger would not have been governor of California, and none of the Cuban-American members of Congress, mayors, or ambassadors would ever have served their adopted country. More pertinent to Mexicans, however, is the fact that millions of naturalized Americans of Mexican origin—including those made eligible for U.S. citizenship after the 1986 immigration amnesty, as well as those to come in the next legalization—would also be banned from countless jobs in American government and society.

These are not the only rights reserved for native-born Mexicans. For nearly two centuries now, resident or naturalized foreigners in Mexico have been excluded from a number of occupations and everyday rights. These range from serving in the armed forces to owning property and realizing investments in various areas of the economy. The most peculiar—and futile—restriction is the ban on foreign titles to beachfront property. From the 1917 Constitution onward, Article 27 stipulates that foreigners cannot own land along the country's three borders, or on its beaches. The rationale for this prohibition lies in the incessant claims presented by American citizens, and taken up by Washington, against the Mexican government during the nineteenth century and through the 1940s, regarding properties that were either in the hinterland, or along the poorly defined border, or straddling it. Understandably enough, this eventually provoked a reaction from Mexico.

For those in the hinterland, it established the so-called Calvo Clause in Article 27 of the Constitution, whereby any investor or property holder in the country, simply by owning anything, ipso facto renounced his or her rights to seek protection from a foreign government. Subsequently, the implementing legislation for border and shore areas was altered first in 1937, then again in the early seventies, soon after adoption of the law creating the *maquiladora,* or in-bond assembly plant, industry on the U.S.-Mexican border. By definition, the factories were located as close to the border as possible, in order to hasten the arrival of inputs and the reshipment of finished products.

Beaches were placed off-limits as an extension of the historical precedent. By the end of World War II, though, Americans began hoping to acquire property in one of the world's more beautiful sea-and-desert areas, the renowned region of Baja California, generally referred to as "Baja." Across the border from San Diego, one hundred miles south of Los Angeles, the Pacific side of the 1,500-mile peninsula became immensely attractive to surfers and snowbirds; soon the Sea of Cortés, also known as the Gulf of California, would be rightly baptized as the "world's aquarium" by Jacques Cousteau. Thousands of Americans and Canadians sought to build and own beach houses around La Paz, and mainly in San José del Cabo and Cabo San Lucas, at the tip of the peninsula. The problem lay in the land title: the Mexican Constitution banned them from holding property. That said, everyone in Mexico, starting with the peninsular authorities and including the Tourism Ministry (or its equivalent) in Mexico City, strongly encouraged foreign investment. The solution was marvelously Mexican: individual fifty-year, renewable trust funds for forbidden zones, or *fideicomisos en zona prohibida,* were set up to purchase beachfronts, and prospective U.S. homeowners became the majority holders of the shares in the trust funds. The system has functioned since the 1940s, with only one minor snag. American banks have rejected mortgage applications backed by trust fund deeds, and so the actual number of investors has remained far lower than it would have been otherwise. But Mexico has refused to even consider modifying Article 27, so, on the one hand, the restriction remains in place. On the other hand, it is waived or circumvented through legal subterfuge. And on the third hand, this tool has limited the beneficial impact of the entire exercise for employment and national development.

A similar simulation has occurred, perhaps inevitably, with the restrictions placed on naturalized Mexicans from high office. The most powerful and influential public official in Mexico's recent history, other than its successive presidents, has arguably been José Córdoba, Carlos Salinas de Gortari's chief of staff, advisor, and erstwhile friend. Between 1988 and early 1994, Córdoba wielded immense power, which he applied with intelligence and hard work. He could not be appointed to the cabinet since he was a French-born and -raised naturalized Mexican, so Salinas simply made him de facto prime minister and his formal title was Chief of the Office of the Presidency), a job not contemplated by the restrictions, since it didn't exist. Once again, a way was found around the absurd limitations, but this did not lead to their suppression, just to their being systematically respected only in the breach.

There is another bizarre constitutional provision, Article 33, which has been both the butt of jokes by and a source of fear for foreigners ever since it was drafted. It states, in a nutshell, that foreigners must refrain from any type of political participation in Mexico, and can be deported, without hearing or appeal, if they violate the statute.* Those from abroad, mainly Latin Americans, often refer to it mockingly as the "*masiosare*" article, in reference to a memorable verse of the Mexican national anthem, which begins, in reference to the motherland: "*Mas si osare un extraño enemigo profanar con su planta tu suelo . . .*" or "Now, if a foreign enemy were to dare to profane your soil with his foot . . ." They sarcastically refer to Mexicans in general, as some Mexicans do to themselves in the context of political discussions, as *masiosares*: extreme and eccentric but also hypocritical nationalists, who wave flags and denounce foreigners, but emigrate or go shopping to the United States at the first opportunity.

## Mexico's Zip Code

This leads us directly to the central question of Mexico's relations with the "rest of the world," which, almost always, means the United States (Spain is only occasionally the object of scorn or resentment). It is an ambivalent, love-hate, confused, and confusing relationship, which is just as mysterious and on occasion as incomprehensible to Mexicans as it is to foreign observers. It can be exemplified by a couple of soccer stories that suggest the depth of Mexican atavisms and contradictions in regard to the real "other."

* Although this article is not new, it touches a chord in Mexico. According to a poll carried out in October 2009 on xenophobia in Mexico, 66% of all Mexicans believed that foreigners who live in Mexico have no right to criticize the situation of the country. "Xenofobia en México," Gabinete de Comunicación Estratégica (GCE), Mexico City, October 9, 2010, p. 8.

In February of 2004, Mexico and the United States were competing for the North American slot at the Athens Olympic Games soccer finals. This is not as big a deal as the World Cup competition, but nonetheless prestigious. The last game was scheduled for Guadalajara, located in the central-western region of the country. Some American team members had made a few disparaging remarks about their rivals, and one had reportedly urinated on the stadium lawn just before the game began—not exactly the type of behavior that would ingratiate them with the home team public. In any case, as the duel heated up, some fans began to hurl all sorts of projectiles at the Americans, and a small but significant minority of the Jalisco Stadium's fifty thousand fans started chanting, toward the end of the game as the Americans were about to go down to defeat: "Osama, Osama, Osama," in obvious reference to 9/11.

Similar episodes occurred five years later in Mexico City, when the two teams squared off, this time for the 2010 World Cup finals, with the fans from the 100,000-strong Aztec Stadium booing the U.S. national anthem and tossing garbage and liquids at the American squad. That evening, like a few weeks before in a previous game, hooligans celebrating Mexico's victory had attacked American-looking bystanders, who were actually Dutch, at the Independence Monument in downtown Mexico City. They attempted to force their way into the Maria Isabel Sheraton Hotel, where the foreigners had barricaded themselves for protection. Not dissimilar episodes of anti-American sentiment, fervor, and resentment had surfaced in the U.S. home games, which took place in Houston and East Rutherford, New Jersey, and which were hardly home games. The immense majority of the spectators were Mexican. Of course, it is also true that violence, passion, and outbursts of nationalistic excess or xenophobia disrupt soccer games all over the world (some readers may remember a France–Algeria match played in Paris some years ago, where thousands of Algerian fans booed the playing of the "Marseillaise"). And on occasion, the passion becomes political, with racist or fanatical overtones. But hailing Osama bin Laden before a U.S. soccer team barely three years after 9/11 perhaps went beyond the pale.

What made the Guadalajara incidents in particular more revealing and contradictory than other, equally reprehensible, outbursts were the peculiarities of Jalisco state and its capital. Jalisco has been, since the late nineteenth century, one of the four largest migration-sending states in Mexico. Along with Michoacán, Guanajuato, and Zacatecas, it had traditionally accounted for more than 70% of all emigrants leaving for the United States, and still today is the leading outmigration state in absolute terms. Not only do hundreds of thousands of its sons and daughters work and live in the United States; through their remittances, they support many other hundreds of thousands who stay home. In addition, Jalisco, its capital, and the surrounding towns on Lake Chapala, like Ajijíc and Chulavista, include some of the oldest U.S. retiree colonies in Mexico, dating back to the fifties and sixties. Everyone gets along splendidly, and clashes or arguments are virtually unknown.

More importantly, Jalisco is home to Puerto Vallarta, the sea resort originally made famous by Elizabeth Taylor and Richard Burton in the 1960s, when they were shooting John Huston's *Night of the Iguana* and he was snatching her away from Eddie Fisher. Today, it is Mexico's third-largest tourist spot, after Cancún and the Mayan Riviera. Ninety percent of its vacationers are American—no longer the Hollywood jet set of yesteryear, but a much more Joe Six-Pack, time-sharing, supermarket-shopping crowd that nonetheless provides jobs to thousands of *jaliscienses*. So the fans at the stadium were endangering not one but three golden-egg-laying geese: migrants and remittances, U.S. full-time residents, and tourists. Worst of all, they *knew* all of this. There are few inhabitants in the state that do not have family north of the border, or who do not work, one way or another, in the tourism or hospitality business. So why in the world would they place these benefits at risk, even partially and temporarily? Perhaps it is not all that surprising, given the education Mexican children receive regarding American evil and trickery, along with the PRI-driven encouragement of anti-American prejudice and even rage, always in search of a foreign scapegoat to distract the populace from its own shortcomings. But it still requires explanation.

### Ducks and Ambivalence

It begins with one of Mexico's most notable character traits, that of admiring Americans and at the same time enjoying insulting them, deceiving them, and taking advantage of them. The joke is as old as both countries' common history, but still worth repeating; I first heard it twenty years ago as told to me by Guillermo Sheridan. Two duck hunters, one on each side of the river that serves as part of the border, suddenly detect the same prey and shoot at it simultaneously; down comes the duck in the middle of the dried-up shallow stream. The American grabs it by the tail, the Mexican by the neck, and both begin to fight over who shot the duck and should keep it. Finally the Mexican, in a notable display of maturity, suggests that instead of fighting, they settle the matter peacefully, through a contest. They will each lay their shotguns down and kick each other as strongly as possible, wherever it hurts most (not hard to guess), and whoever does not cry out gets the duck. The Mexican requests only that given his size and history of malnutrition, and so on and so forth, he go first. The American accedes, confident that his strength and Wheaties upbringing cannot fail him. The Mexican sprints and kicks the American in the groin, the U.S. hunter doubles over and almost faints, but remains silent, and is about to return the favor, when the Mexican smiles and says: "Hey, dumb *gringo*, keep the duck."

Polls and surveys, focus groups, case studies, local research, and just about every type of probe have been carried out in Mexico to ascertain the nature of our citizens' attitudes toward the United States. None of these efforts can be considered to be truly and definitively accurate; the responses not only vary in regard to the questions but also to the moment when they were asked, the region in which the study was drawn up, the age group involved, or the sequence of questions and premises involved. We would not even contemplate attempting to resolve these enigmas here; but we do believe that some polls, particularly when they have become historical surveys and show consistency, as well as some studies and data that demonstrate patterns of behavior or belief, can be relevant and indicative of where things stand.

The first irrefutable point is that Mexicans mistrust the United States. According to one series of polls carried out by the same experts between 2004 and 2008, 43% of the population harbored this sentiment the first year of the surveys; in 2006 the number grew to 53%, and in 2008 (before Obama's election), it had reached 61%. Mexicans also conserve a certain dismissive attitude toward Americans, summed up in Spanish by the complex word *desprecio*, that can only be poorly translated as "looking down upon." In the above-mentioned surveys, 32% of those interviewed expressed *"desprecio,"* 34% admiration, and 38%

resentment toward the United States. These numbers vary somewhat by region (the north is in general more positive toward the U.S., the south less), by age (the younger more positive, the elderly less), and by political inclination (left-of-center PRD sympathizers more negative, PAN and PRI adherents more positive). And maybe in the most revealing conclusion, 46% of all Mexicans consider their country's proximity to the United States as more of a problem than an advantage, while 45% think the opposite; this last belief has been growing since 2004.[28]

Conversely, and just as significantly, Mexicans systematically rate the United States as one of the three or four countries they have the most favorable opinion of. The U.S. ranked in the number one slot in 2004, number two in 2006, just behind Canada, and seventh in 2008, before Obama's election. After his victory in 2009, Mexicans held the most favorable opinion of the United States among twenty-four countries surveyed by the Pew Global Attitudes Project, with the exception of six, and by tiny margins: Kenya, for obvious reasons, Nigeria, South Korea, India, France, and Israel.* Similarly, although support for the following proposition has dropped over the past few years, even in 2008, as the Bush administration came to an end and American prestige was at its lowest point in years all over the world, stunningly and schizophrenically 45% of all Mexicans supported the idea of their nation forming a single country with the United States, if this entailed a higher standard of living, with 51% against. In 2006, the equivalent figures had been 54% in favor, 44% against; in 2004 the numbers were similar to 2008.[29] The realism of this proposition is irrelevant; what counts is that so many Mexicans support it.

This inclination dovetails with the statistic that is time and again quoted in the U.S. press and in the American immigration debate: that between one-third and two-fifths of Mexico's people would immigrate to the United States if given the opportunity. The variations in the propensity to depart depend largely on Mexican perceptions of the state of the U.S. economy, and of how quickly they can find a job, given the

---

* Because of the Arizona immigration law approved in June of 2010, this perception changed dramatically, but probably only for a while. In the 2010 Pew Survey, the favorable opinion of the United States held by Mexicans fell from 69% in 2009, after Obama's election, to 56%, after Arizona. Just before passage of SB1070, 62% of Mexicans continued to have a favorable opinion of the United States. Pew Research, "Obama More Popular Abroad Than at Home, Global Image of U.S. Continues to Benefit," Washington, D.C., 2010.

reports they receive by phone almost every day from friends and family north of the border. The percentage has rarely topped 40% and so far, at least, has never dipped below 30%; the legality of the procedure makes a difference to less than a third of those wishing to migrate.

This is perhaps the crux of the matter. A very considerable number of Mexicans express their disposition to leave their country. This does not imply that they actually will depart, or even that they really want to, but rather that they are disposed to do so. It does, however, purvey a sense of their state of mind and pragmatism in regard to the United States, as well as the upside of the negative feelings already described. The breakdown in the statistics is almost as interesting, though equally ambiguous in regard to authentic intentions. The south of the country—much poorer than the rest—is the least desirous to depart; the center—the traditional sending region—the most inclined in this direction. A logical, but tragic, figure reveals that eighteen- to twenty-nine-year-olds are the most willing to emigrate: fully 51% of this cohort confessed its "intention" (with the caveats mentioned before) to expatriate itself, when the national average in this particular poll was 40%. Finally, and perhaps counterintuitively, Mexicans with a high school or college education were found to possess a greater penchant to go abroad; those with no education showed the lowest (only 19%, half the national average) proclivity to try their luck in *El Norte*.[30]

Obviously these data contrast with Mexicans' self-defined identity as much more Latin American than North American, as well as with their more intense desire to be part of Latin America than of North America. Belying this sentiment is the undeniable fact that Mexico is more North American than ever. In 2008, roughly 11% of all native-born Mexicans resided—legally or otherwise—in the United States: the highest share in history. Many of them currently possess both nationalities (around 3 million).[31] A great deal more will do so with the passage of time, especially if the 6 or 7 million illegal Mexicans currently in the United States are amnestied sometime soon.*

---

* Here, as elsewhere, we use the terms "illegal," "undocumented," and "unauthorized" as interchangeable synonyms. This is not to say we dismiss the political connotations—in both Mexico and the United States—of each word. The advocates of immigration reform, amnesty, and a migrant workers' program in both nations avoid the term "illegal" and use the other two; the opponents of reform emphasize the illegal nature of immigration without proper papers. The two sides have a point; we simply alternate the use of all three for stylistic reasons, acknowledging the debate but not engaging in it here.

But most importantly, this confirms the oft-cited ambivalence of Mexicans toward their neighbor to the north. That ambivalence, already evident in the laws, customs, and poll numbers outlined above, can also be illustrated by the following opinions. On the one hand, a majority of Mexicans favor foreign investment in their country, knowing full well that this means essentially U.S. investment. While the majority felt in 2004 that Mexico obtained some benefits from foreign investment in general, in that year, and even more so in 2008, 70% thought that foreign investment should continue to be banned in oil exploration, production, and distribution (meaning basically gas stations), and 60% felt roughly the same way (a bit less drastically) about electric power generation, telecommunications, and the media.[32] Three-quarters of the country's inhabitants believed in 2004 that Mexico obtained large or some benefits from foreign investment; the numbers have varied over the years somewhat, but not significantly. In other words, Mexicans want foreign investment, but not where foreign investment wants to go: an understandable stance, but not a terribly realistic one, and evidently one that evades adopting a binary—yes or no—position on a critical matter for the country in the years to come. This is a symptom of what lies behind the beach issue—the rejection of the Principle of the Excluded Middle described in Chapter 3—except that given the sums involved—drilling one well, successful or not, in the deep waters of the Gulf of Mexico can cost up to $200 million— the petroleum equivalent of the legal subterfuges for oceanfront property are unlikely to persuade the oil majors, or even service providers like Halliburton or Schlumberger.

A similar reluctance to stand up and choose or be chosen—in violation of the same Aristotelian law—appears in Mexico's geopolitical location. To the question "Should Mexico seek greater economic integration with Latin America, North America, or be a bridge between the two?," 32% chose the first option, 18% the second one, and 41% the third one; among the so-called elites or leaders who were also queried, the equivalent numbers were 62% for the bridge, 24% for North America, and 11% for Latin America.[33] Again, the best of both worlds— being a so-called Bridge of the Americas, like the one that straddles the Panama Canal—is deemed preferable to a clear definition. And again, it constitutes an act of sheer wishful thinking, since the rest of Latin America clearly perceives Mexico as no longer a full-fledged member of the region, because of pre-NAFTA economic integration, NAFTA itself, immigration to the United States, and other factors. Likewise, the U.S. begrudges Mexico its lack of solidarity and support in difficult junctures, with conduct unbecoming that of an ally, partner, and neighbor, at least according to the American definition of these notions, which does tend to equate an ally with a subordinate. In addition, neither of the two parties—Latin America and the United States—views Mexico as a bridge between them, because neither needs one; this is not unlike the U.K.'s occasional and futile claim and hope to be a bridge across the Atlantic between Europe and Washington. In both cases all parties have sufficiently direct communications and bonds so as to forsake any third-party assistance in this regard. If anything, the only way Mexico could become more useful to Latin America would be if it got closer to the United States and was able somehow to share its hypothetical "special relationship" with Washington.

Mexicans prefer to avoid choice and pursue all good things simultaneously, whether it be to remain a country of traditions as well as family values *and* enter modernity; to belong to Latin America *and* have a closer relationship with the United States; to enjoy the benefits of an open market economy but *also* the cultural and political icons of sovereignty and *dirigisme*; to have elections with contending candidates *and* have everyone agree on everything; to live under the rule of law *and* insure that traditional usages, as well as a certain sense of individual justice, endure. In their contradictory way, Mexicans want to engage in the delights of belonging to the rest of the world, *and* to keep the rest of the world out of Mexico; they want to conserve their individualism, their distaste for altercation, the walls around their homes and gardens, *and* become a middle-class, open, hospitable society.

In a survey carried out by GAUSSC, a Mexican polling firm, in 2009 that included a chapter on so-called Mexican idiosyncrasies, a Mexican pollster addressed six polar or binary, substantive questions to 2,500 Mexicans over the age of eighteen, offering them the possibility of choosing one of the two terms involved, or to abstain from choosing either. The dichotomies were: Should children be taught Mexican history and the story of Mexican heroes, or should they be taught English and to use computers? (the second choice came out on top). Should Mexico become more like the United States, in order to create a greater number of jobs, even if this means losing traditions, or should it conserve its traditions, even if this means creating fewer jobs? (the two came out equal). Is it more important for Mexico to maintain its sovereignty, even if the well-being of its population does not improve, or should it seek to improve the well-being of the population, even if this were to make the country less sovereign? (the second option won hands down). Should Mexico have good relations with Cuba and Venezuela, even if this angers the U.S., or have good relations with the U.S., even if this angers Cuba and Venezuela? (the second option beat the first one, two and half to one). Should the border between the two countries be open to migrants, trade, and tourism, or should it be closed so that drugs, arms, and drug money not cross? (option A won). And finally, are foreign companies in Mexico committed to the country because they create jobs, or are they not committed because they do not create jobs? (option A came out on top).[34] Mexicans responded to the simplistic, dichotomic questions, phrased somewhat artificially but deliberately as mutually exclusive, with rather modern, open-minded attitudes.

But the most interesting result of the study was that on average, approximately a third of the total declined to take sides, considering themselves neutral. While it could be argued that this was because they didn't know what to answer, or considered the questions excessively Manichaean, it can also be interpreted as part of the great reluctance to choose, even when the choice is hypothetical and almost imposed upon the sample. Most of those interviewed would probably hope to achieve both aims, even if they knew they could not.

There is a magical, almost mystical note to Mexico's wishful thinking.* It surfaces among the nation's most cynical politicians, its most ruthless businessmen, its most sophisticated and cosmopolitan writers.

---

* Back to soccer: In the 2010 South Africa World Cup a phone poll (middle class and upward) showed that 40% of Mexicans thought their team would make it to the quarter finals, which had not occurred since 1986, when the tournament was held in Mexico and there were only twenty-four teams in the competition (in 2010 they were thirty-two). And 24% thought Mexico would do even better than that, reaching the semifinals or the final, while 11% believed Mexico would be world champion. In other words, 64% of all Mexicans with phones in their homes thought, or hoped—that is the issue—that Mexico would do significantly better than it ever had done before. There was no solid reason to sustain this faith, and obviously it was not confirmed. Mexico fared exactly the way it did in every World Cup competition since the 1930s, neither better nor worse. But two-thirds of middle-class Mexicans, for some strange reason, thought that playing on the other side of the world would make a difference. It did not. "Confían en el Tri," *Reforma* (Mexico City), June 10, 2010.

It is ever present, and never confessed to; it is ubiquitous and recurrent, without ever being truly acknowledged. It has a link to cultural roots: time heals all, and since it does, the passage of time itself will make all things possible. The archetypical Mexican song refrain of *"Con el tiempo y un ganchito, ha de resecarse el mar"* ("With time and a little hook the sea will dry up") sums it up well. Those goals or objects of desire, unreachable today, will be attained tomorrow, even absent any other factor. Why? Because, in fact, mutually incompatible aims are always within reach potentially; only time is necessary to make them happen. Time being the cheapest commodity around, anything can be accomplished just by waiting. How this jibes with one of the most open economies and societies in the world is another matter, which we will now attempt to discover.

## CHAPTER 6

# At Last: An Open Society, an Open Economy, an Open Mind?

When those of us who grew up in Mexico during the 1960s were able to travel abroad—a tiny minority of the population—one of the main events of the year was the holiday visit to San Antonio, or El Paso, or Houston, or San Diego. For Houston and San Antonio, and sometimes El Paso, the voyage was by car; otherwise by plane, though this was not quite as productive. Productive? Yes, since at least one of the main purposes of the journey was to purchase *fayuca*: contraband electronics, food, clothes, gadgets of all sorts, unavailable in Mexico and quite accessible, price-wise, in the United States. Instead of the obsolete TV sets manufactured in our country, we could buy Sony Trinitrons; instead of rancid peanut butter, we could obtain Skippy; instead of highly flammable Terlenka windbreakers, we could don Members Only jackets.

The only problem was how to get them into Mexico without paying duties (they were onerous), or excessive bribes (moderate ones were okay). The car or station wagon would be filled to the brim, with maybe a small television on top of everything, highly, even ostentatiously, visible. When we stopped at the secondary customs inspection, some twenty miles into Mexico, the on-duty official would make believe he was searching for drugs, guns, money, or high-value contraband, and all of a sudden, lo and behold, he would discover the small TV. With deep regret and shame, he would convey to us his irreversible decision to confiscate it, together with a stern warning to refrain from introducing forbidden goods into the country, since they took jobs away from Mexicans, and besides, "*Lo hecho en México está bien hecho*" (loosely translated: Mexican stuff should be good enough for you). And we would be on our way, with our *fayuca*, or American stuff, nicely stashed away under blankets, children, coats, and suitcases.

The difficulties of sealing a border with the United States were present not only at the physical frontier. Stories about the Mexico City airport flourished, each one more imaginative than the other. I remember when cameras were installed above the customs inspection stations; the officials simply glued cardboard blinders on the lens. When the first red-green light system was inaugurated, customs inspectors manipulated the frequency so that red would almost always flash, allowing them to demand their "*mordida*," to "bite" travelers for their bribe, more often.

Given all of these ploys and the infinite corruption of the Customs Agency, in the mid-seventies President Luis Echeverría found an ingenious way, or so he thought, to kill two birds (cousins of the duck we met in the previous chapter) with one stone. He needed to employ the Chilean refugees whom Mexico had generously welcomed after the Pinochet coup in 1973, and he had to find and appoint honest customs officials at the Mexico City airport. So he named the Chileans, who actually *were* honest and efficient. Unfortunately for them, and for Mexico, they were also totally unfamiliar with local customs and celebrities. One day they found nothing better to do than to inspect the dozens of Louis Vuitton suitcases brought back from Paris by an aging but proud Mexican actress; not only did she not give up the ship (actually, the contraband), but she raised such a nationalist ruckus that the following day Echeverría was forced to fire the Chileans. So much for that idea.

Fifteen years later, in the midst of one more of our recurrent and disastrous economic crises, affecting the balance of trade and the exchange and interest rates, and driving prices to the sky, a new generation of officials abandoned the fight against *fayuca*. In 1987, deciding that discretion was the better part of valor, in one fell swoop they removed tariffs and quantitative restrictions on most Mexican imports from the rest of the world. By then, entire neighborhoods of Mexico City (mainly Tepito, but also street-vending malls like Coapa, Peritianguis, and others) had become entrepôts of contraband from abroad, on occasion even offering guarantees on illegally imported refrigerators. They had fitting rooms for expensive dresses, warranties on electronics, and on-demand capability for goods not in store: just like the Mall of America. Contraband did not completely disappear, since the Mexican sales or value-added tax was still higher than in the U.S., but the incentive to bring in goods illegally diminished drastically. The drive to the American border towns of McAllen or Harlingen was no longer worth it.

## Trading with the Enemy

This was the beginning of Mexico's trade liberalization, which climaxed with NAFTA and was enshrined in the agreement with the United States and Canada. By 2008, practically everything could be imported into the country from its North American partners duty-free, including used cars, corn, beans, powdered milk, and fructose syrup, the last restricted products on the waiting list since 1994. Mexico had become one of the most commercially open economies in the world, where imports plus exports over GDP reached 55%, twice the U.S. number, more than Japan, and a level similar to various Western European nations like Spain, the U.K., France, and Italy, though slightly less than Germany.[1]* This represented a major shift for Mexico, which traditionally, like most Latin American economies, based its growth on the domestic market; foreign trade, even after the country again became a major oil exporter in the late seventies, never amounted to more that 20% of GDP.[2]† Perhaps until then the character traits described in the previous chapter were functional to building an unfinished nation, an industrial economy, a national market, a defensive posture against a hostile and distant outside world. No more, not with the numbers summarized below.

Today, while NAFTA has been much less of a resounding success than most of its advocates hoped and advertised back in 1993, a major-

---

* Exports reached 28% in 2009, and imports 29% in 2009. Exports plus imports were 57%: World Bank, "Exports of goods and services (% of GDP)" and "Imports of goods and services (% of GDP)" (Washington, D.C., 2010).

† Exports were 8% in 1970, and imports 10% in 1970. Exports plus imports are 18%.

ity of Mexicans are nonetheless attached to it and would not wish to see it repealed. When it was rammed through Mexican society and a rubber-stamp Congress in 1993 by Carlos Salinas de Gortari, his colleague, friend, and counselor, Spanish prime minister Felipe González, was convinced that had it been submitted to a democratic debate and a referendum, it would have lost.(Or so he confided to me years later.) More importantly, Ulises Beltrán, Salinas's pollster at the time, reached the same conclusion, not dissimilar to what has occurred in several European countries along the path to the European Union.[3] But today no one seems to want to revoke NAFTA; the proof lies in the fact that the left-of-center PRD opposition, which has had a strong voice in Congress since 1994, has never tabled a resolution to abrogate it, even though the treaty clearly stipulates that this can be accomplished with six months' notice. The Mexican middle classes would not be happy campers if that were to occur.

As might be expected, the opening to foreign trade did not really mean "foreign." As always, for independent Mexico, the "world" has meant the United States. Ever since 1895, the U.S. has been Mexico's most important trading partner, concentrating around 70% of all imports and exports in the 1890s, 100% during World Wars I and II, and anywhere between 65% and 70% in the 1970s–80s, and 80.6% of its exports today, though recently a somewhat smaller share of its imports, due to a brief spurt in purchases from China. The next largest partner, China, represents a paltry 7.5% of Mexico's foreign commercial transactions; the entire European Union accounts for 8%, and the largest Latin American share, corresponding to Brazil, barely 1.3%.[4]* The absolute totals for non-U.S. trading partners are not negligible, reaching several billion dollars in some cases, but the relative totals are largely irrelevant. So opening up to "the rest of the world" was another Mexican euphemism; it meant opening up to the neighbor to the north. Nobody thought it through in detail, but the result is that today Mexicans mistrust and are highly ambivalent about the inhabitants of a country with which their wide-open economy does virtually all of its trade; more significantly, that trade today constitutes more than half of all its economic activity. Something has to give, or the mistrust and

---

* Mexico's foreign trade with Brazil represents 1.28% of its total sales abroad. Subsecretaría de Comercio Exterior, *Exportaciones e importaciones totales de México*, Secretaría de Economía, 2010.

trade will eventually neutralize each other and paralyze Mexico. This is partly what has happened since 2000, when the initial NAFTA élan began to run out of steam.

There are many reasons why NAFTA started faltering so soon after its conception, but a few stand out. These were, chiefly, the restrictions on investment in energy, tourism, retirees' hospitality, infrastructure, and cultural industries that sprang directly from the already described passions. That said, despite decades of efforts, now formalized in free trade agreements with the European Union and Japan, among others, Mexico has proved unable to diversify its foreign trade. There is absolutely no reason to believe that policy will ever trump geography on this score. Mexican businessmen, let alone the executives and strategists for multinational firms established in the country, are accustomed to exporting next door, and have no desire whatsoever to venture far away when they can enjoy the luxury of selling to the world's largest market, just across the fence or the river.

The "truly existing" Mexico, not the one most of us have in our heads, will always have only one noteworthy trading partner, and it will always have to combat—or accommodate—the protectionist temptations of that partner. We believe Mexico should draw the logical conclusion from this fact, and peel away the atavisms, curtailments, laws, regulations, prejudices, and legitimate grievances that are seared on occasion into its very soul. But it is quite understandable that other voices may hold a contrary opinion, and that, thanks to modern technology, globalization, a deliberate policy, and a national, consensual effort, they might hope to truly diversify the country's trade patterns, aligning them with the salient traits of Mexico's national character. In our view, this effort would prove fruitless, and furthermore the new Mexican middle classes would not likely countenance its consequences if it did succeed: higher prices and fewer foreign goods. But what makes no sense at all is the idle insistence on maintaining two diametrically opposed postures: on the one hand mistrusting, "dissing," or containing the United States, and on the other, possessing one of the world's most open economies and one of the world's largest concentrations of trade with one partner.

This ambivalent attitude appears particularly incomprehensible given that its results are so far quite mediocre, despite Mexicans' reluctance to admit this. Since Mexico's unilateral trade opening in 1987, or since NAFTA came into law in 1994, its economic growth has averaged less than 3%. Even if we start in 1996, after the 1995 debacle, the average remains approximately the same.[5] It's not exactly evidence that the current course is working. This is especially relevant if, as expected, Mexico continues to lose part of its manufacturing export base to China, and finds itself forced to move up the value-added chain into services, or higher tech sales abroad. This process began as early as 2000, and it will in all likelihood further concentrate the country's business with the north, while at the same time making the existing restrictions more damaging to trade and investment, though perhaps not to national pride. It will become particularly valid in one area where Mexico has a huge comparative advantage over practically every nation in the world. And that is tourism: close to 90% of all visitors to Mexico travel from the United States.[6]

## *Spring Breakers and Retired Baby Boomers*

Once again, the numbers do not pan out for the country. Although it is an unquestioned player in the international tourist arena, ranking tenth in the world, it could perform far more competitively. Even if we include one-night stays just across the border, its 20 million tourists compare poorly with those visiting Spain (57 million) or Italy (40 million).[7]* Further, a more realistic number for Mexico's tourists might be 13 million, which corresponds to those who spend at least one night in the interior, not just on the border. Regrettably, Mexico is not taking advantage of some of the special attractions it has to offer, above all, to American visitors, be they spring breakers, honeymooners, or tree huggers. Nothing is more important to the country, and this was acknowledged as long ago as the Alliance for Progress. Tourism constitutes its number one industry in terms of employment, with nearly 2.5 million direct and indirect jobs; its number-three single generator of hard currency; and it represents the only economic activity that is at least partially spread out through various parts of the nation.[8]

---

* Mexico: 21.5 million international tourist arrivals in 2009; Spain: 52.2 million international tourist arrivals in 2009; France: 74.2 million international tourist arrivals in 2009; Italy: 43.2 million international tourist arrivals in 2009.

Mexico should be welcoming far more tourists to many more destinations, spending more money each day per person. We have to move
people away from the traditional beach resorts—Cancún, Mayan Riviera, Puerto Vallarta, Los Cabos, Mazatlán—to "new sites"—Puerto
Peñasco, Careyes, Costa Maya, Huatulco—and to old, deserted ones—
Acapulco, Ixtapa-Zihuatanejo—and mostly to other attractive spots.
Mexico's tourist attractions are almost infinite: archaeological ruins,
colonial cities, major modern, urban centers, old *hacienda* luxury
hotels, spectacular canyons and jungles. But all of these need infrastructure—airports, hospitals, highways, and, more than ever, security—in order to attract investment in hotels, restaurants, restoration,
and advertising. The country is far from matching its potential to
become a major world-class tourist destination; it should be receiving
well over 50 million travelers every year.

This is the case as far as traditional tourism is concerned. In practice, at least in the short term, we are moving in the opposite direction.
Visits declined by 6% in 2009 over the previous year. The reasons were
no secret (H1N1, the war on drugs, insecurity, the worldwide recession), but even in the absence of these problems, our market share is
not growing.[9] When Cuba comes on line as a major destination for
Americans, we will face even stiffer competition. So in addition to
doing the "easy" things necessary to entice more guests in a traditional
manner to traditional resorts, we must branch out in two directions
that only the Caribbean countries can also partly attempt, although
most lack the educational, infrastructure, living standards, and even
security (which, despite our problems, we have, or had). Those directions are snowbirds and retirees, two groups that on occasion overlap
but that can be addressed as distinct markets.

For all sorts of motives—flexible work schedules, more discretionary income for certain population groups, work-at-home through
the Internet and broadband—upper-middle-income Americans will be
able to spend longer periods away from home, albeit not necessarily on
vacation. What they are looking for are convenience, cost, and security.
These translate into good transportation and communications, entertainment attractions, health services, and hospitality facilities. Long-
term visitors will also want their dollar to go significantly further than
at home, so they improve the quality of their lives—and escape the cold
or the heat—by spending three to six months of the year away. And,

just as importantly, they will expect security for both their property and themselves.

Mexico is the one country that satisfies the first condition—proximity—and the only one that can fulfill most of the others. The Dominican Republic, Jamaica, and Cuba, for instance, lack the touristic and national wherewithal to deliver these services and guarantees. They are close to certain areas of the United States—Florida, the East Coast—but very far from others: the West Coast, the Midwest, Texas. Conversely, some regions of Mexico are near to just about any part of the United States. And the country could become a haven for prosperous, though not necessarily wealthy, American midcareer professionals whose children are in college or a bit younger, who want to spend a few months of the year elsewhere, in an environment where they can work, live differently and better, with everything they are accustomed to back home. No other country can truly compete with Mexico for this market.

Mexico is similarly well placed in the contest for baby boom retirees, although here we are in uncharted territory: no country really competes with Florida and the Southwest yet. And indeed, probably only Mexico can. Large numbers of Americans born during the postwar demographic bubble (between 1945 and 1950) are retiring as they reach sixty-five, a new batch of senior citizens. They are quite unlike their parents; they grew up in the sixties, and are reaching retirement age in far better health than others before them. They are far more worldly and open-minded, with more resources available for their retirement; and many have expressed a wish to discover alternatives to Florida, Arizona, or Nevada as their place of late-life residence.

First, it will be necessary to reform the Constitution so foreigners can directly and transparently own beach property, obtain a mortgage if they want one, put their home in their sons' or daughters' names, insure that when they pass away their assets will belong to their estate, as they have stipulated, and not as some government bureaucrat or congressman may determine. Short of this, Mexico will simply not seduce the baby boomers, despite all its attractions. Second, this means top-flight, insurance-covered, next-door health care (at least at a primary level), where the common, but not life-threatening, illnesses that this stage of life inevitably entails can be treated easily, quickly, and competently. This is a health-conscious generation. It requires international airports no more than one hour away, with multiple flights to the main U.S. hubs, and no difficulties in entering or leaving that could delay a medical transfer. There are already flights stateside from twenty Mexican cities, but they correspond chiefly to migration patterns, not to tourism or retiree flows. The current number of flights for those flows is by no means sufficient.

Third, this means offering baby boomers the amenities of life typical of their station in life: golf, peace and quiet, movie theaters and DVD rentals, cable TV and concerts or shows, good restaurants and pleasant hotels for their friends, traditional Mexican service and hospitality, Walk–Don't Walk signs to cross the street, stores where they can purchase Mexican goods that will make their stay different, together with the American ones that will make them feel at home. Eliminating price gouging and shakedowns is not a realistic goal, but it is possible to limit these abuses and discourage the national pastime of rooking Americans.

Lastly, and perhaps most decisively, this means bestowing upon these residents a legal and financial situation that is secure, simple, and expeditious: residence or immigration papers, receiving their Social Security check and being able to exchange it for pesos at the going rate without being taken to the cleaners. It involves knowing that their insurance covers treatment in Mexico—a big if, and one that we have been attempting to negotiate, so far unsuccessfully, with major U.S. companies and Medicare since I was in the Foreign Ministry in 2001. It also requires a fair tax status for this potentially invaluable and immense tourism market. It can be done, but only in Mexico, only with Americans (and to a far smaller extent with Canadians), and only if Mexico wishes to suppress, or at least control, the demons of its character from the past.

A better illustration of tourism's paradoxes lies in the internal debate that took place within government circles of both countries between 2002 and 2005 regarding the issue of "pre-clearance." This somewhat technical mechanism consists simply in having U.S. Customs and Immigration agents—today called Customs and Border Protection—clear American and non-American travelers to the United States at the point of origin abroad. Countries that have already established this system are Canada, Ireland, and the Bahamas. On taking a plane in Montreal or Dublin, for example, visitors bound for the United States pass through customs and immigration at the local airport, and do not pass again when they land in New York or Chicago; their arrival is classified as a domestic flight. The advantage for the point-of-departure country is that it can receive and dispatch flights destined for the United States to and from noninternational U.S. airports, since Customs and Immigration have already been cleared. This increases tourism, since it allows direct charter flights from airports in the U.S. that otherwise would have to apply for costly federal government permits to process foreign passengers.

In the case of Mexico, the Fox administration sought in 2002 to negotiate a pre-clearance agreement with the U.S., initially in Cancún. It was thought that this would encourage travelers from cities with only domestic airport facilities, such as Memphis, Nashville, several in Alabama, the Carolinas, and perhaps as far as St. Louis, Kansas City, Oklahoma City, and sites in northern Texas. But just as important, it was also believed that given the immense panic, or outright security hysteria, unleashed by 9/11, it would be wise for Mexico to slip in under the American security perimeter or bubble, and indeed extend it to North America as a whole before Washington began slapping restrictions on travel from other countries to the U.S.—which it did a few years later—that would inevitably hurt Mexico more than just about anybody else. As it happens, such restrictions were imposed anyway.

From the start, things didn't quite work out. Having American Customs and Immigration agents screening Mexicans (since they could not inspect only Americans) on Mexican soil was anathema to the interior and justice ministries, as well as to numerous intellectuals and politicians. Explanations—for example that there was no substantive difference between refusing Mexicans permission to board in Cancún, or to order them home from Miami—were to no avail. There were already dozens of DEA and FBI agents in Mexico; Canada was perfectly satisfied with the procedure; it would protect Mexico from a future U.S. backlash and bring more tourism now, create jobs now, improve living standards now. But the very notion of American agents denying Mexicans anything in Mexico proved intolerable.

A couple of years later, the idea was revived under a new tourism minister, who approached it more assiduously than his predecessor. Progress was made, even on the prickly issue of whether U.S. officials could bear arms in Mexico, a matter that had always been a subject of arduous negotiations with DEA agents. But the talks eventually collapsed, for two reasons: the cost of pre-clearance, which by 2005 the Bush administration was unwilling to pay, and the risk for members of the several shifts of Customs and Border Protection employees who would have to live in Cancún. That resort was already a dangerous city infested with drug traffickers and gangsters, although it would get much worse as of 2007. The owner of the Cancún airport, Fernando Chico Pardo, financed several trips by U.S. officials to visit housing and schools for agents who might eventually be posted there, all in vain. When the deal had been possible, Mexican nationalism held it up; when that nationalism waned, Washington was no longer interested.

### Immigration and Investment

Immigration is of course the area that overshadows all of Mexico's relationship with the United States. Many years ago we signed a temporary worker agreement with Canada that provides visas today for slightly more than fifteen thousand Mexicans per year. In contrast, the number of those who legally or illegally seek jobs in the United States every year oscillates between 250,000 in a trough to perhaps 450,000 in a peak year. Thus, for all practical purposes, Mexico, which is a significant sending country by world standards, "sends" everybody who leaves to the United States. Virtually 100% of the between $20 billion and $25 billion in remittances shipped home every year originates in the U.S. This represents approximately 2% of GDP, three times what it was in 1985, the first year the Central Bank attempted an estimate.[10] Part of the increase stems from the fact that current flows are much better tabulated than before. All of this has been going on, of course, for more than a century: there is nothing new under the sun.

Mexicans have of course always possessed an ambivalent attitude toward immigration to the north, but the reality is devoid of ambiguity. Approximately two in every five Mexicans have family in the United States; 30% or 40% of all Mexicans say that they would leave if they could; and Mexico has today, at the nadir of its outbound migration evolution, one of the highest shares in the world of native-born population residing abroad.[11] The total has reached more or less 11%, that is, several times what it was in the sixties and seventies, less than El

Salvador (16.4%) or Ecuador (15%), but more than Guatemala (9%), Algeria (2%), Turkey (6%), Morocco (8.6%), or Egypt (3%).[12] The main difference lies, however, in the concentration of residents abroad: Ecuador has some people in Spain and elsewhere in Europe in addition to the United States, Egypt in several areas of the Persian Gulf, the Philippines in many countries. Mexico has virtually all its migrant eggs in one big American basket.

Since there is no likelihood that Mexicans will start immigrating to other destinations, or that they will stop emigrating anytime soon, it appears almost certain that at least for another couple of decades a significant share of the country's population will reside in the United States. If they are legalized, these Mexicans will once again come and go incessantly, as their countrymen and women with legal status do now, and as even those without papers did continuously until the mid-nineties, when migration circularity was interrupted. Their impact on Mexican society will expand, bringing new ideas, skills, habits, and attitudes to the poorer neighborhoods of the large cities they left, and to the villages where many of them were born and raised. Insularity, fear of the foreign, and reverence for a supposedly common past are simply not compatible with the extraordinary churning of people that circular and legal immigration entails. The two forces clash constantly, and will do so increasingly in the near future: Mexicans who live, work, marry, and age in the United States cannot, with fewer and fewer exceptions, hold the same views about the country they have tacitly adopted, as those foisted upon their compatriots who stayed home. If the United States is the source of all of Mexico's ills, why in the world would anyone want to go there? It's not just an example of the old maxim, "If you can't beat them . . . join them." Millions of Mexicans do join them, and indeed tens of millions of them are modifying their attitudes toward the U.S., even though the official, conventional, and archetypical perspective remains fixed in the popular imagination, both at home and abroad.

Moreover, if there ever is an immigration deal between Mexico City and Washington that includes amnesty and a migrant worker program, it will inevitably also require Mexico to curtail further illegal emigration. This would add another ingredient of incompatibility with the specter of the perils of the past and with self-identification as victims of the outside world. Does the country want legalization of its undocumented expatriates and a legal path of entry for future flows, or does it wish to maintain the pretense that it holds no responsibility for dissuading or deterring illegal departures (despite standing Mexican law)?

For its part, foreign investment, like foreign residence, works at cross purposes with Mexico's attitudes, laws, and current set of incentives. Back in the seventies, when the economic model of import-substitution industrialization ran out of steam, foreign direct investment from abroad represented 0.87% of GDP—a tiny figure, less than half of the equivalent for Canada but four times below the corresponding figure for the United States, and similar to Spain's at the end of the Franco, statist, corporatist, protectionist era.[13] And it accounted for at most one twenty-fifth of total yearly investment in Mexico, foreign or national, public or private. In other words, the country was clearly reluctant then, as now, to open up to foreign investment, banning it from many sectors, such as oil, electric power, the media, and mining. But at the same time, Mexico did not really seem to require resources from abroad, insofar as it was annually saving and investing a hefty sum of its GDP—more than a quarter—with the foreign component playing a minor role.

When the domestic savings rate dipped, and inflows from abroad became indispensable during the mid- and late seventies, Mexico needed to find a way of sustaining previous growth rates. Like just about every nation in the so-called Third World, it therefore sought external credit, of which there was plenty, thanks to billions of petrodollars available around the globe after the quadrupling of oil prices in 1973. It was only a decade later, when, crushed by the debt crisis and reduced to virtually no economic growth at all, that Mexico found itself obliged to court foreign investment and adjust its laws accordingly, and join the General Agreement on Tariffs and Trade (GATT) in 1985. NAFTA, although technically a trade agreement, was in fact intended much more as a guarantee of continuity and orthodoxy in macroeconomic policy for foreign investors who liked what they saw in Mexico—investment from abroad had begun to climb—but were still unwilling to take the plunge.

The Salinas de Gortari government eliminated various restrictions on inflows from abroad, such as the 51% Mexican ownership rule for many companies with foreign affiliations. It allowed foreign ownership of mines and secondary petrochemical plants, and implemented changes in intellectual property regulation. And after NAFTA became law in 1994, a noticeable initial increase in foreign investment *did* occur, from below $12 billion per year on average during the previous five years, to more than $15 billion on average between 1996 and 2000, reaching almost 3.5% of GDP yearly.[14] But there was softness in these figures. Part of the rise stemmed from one-time-only or nonrecurrent purchases of Mexican state- or privately owned firms (steel, banks, insurance, telecommunications, airlines); and much of the truly new investment continued to spring from Fortune 500 companies present in Mexico for decades. The thousands of small and medium-size enterprises from the United States, Europe, and Japan that Mexico expected and needed did not come about, in view of the lingering legal and bureaucratic obstacles.

By 2005, foreign investment share of GDP was back down to 2.5%, and in 2008, admittedly a bad year, it dropped further, to 1.8%.[15] More worryingly, for the first time since 1960, in the third quarter of 2009, foreign direct investment turned negative: firms were disinvesting more than they invested, at least during those months. Today Mexico is capturing a shrinking slice of the world's investment pie, whereas countries like Brazil, whose economy is roughly 17% larger than Mexico's (depending on the year, the respective exchange rates, and the price of certain commodities), are receiving twice as many dollars, euros, and yen from abroad. Mexico invests a greater share of its product (20.4%) than Brazil (16.5%), but foreign investment represents a far larger share of Brazilian overall investment (19.6%) than in Mexico (8.7%), despite Brazil's being as nationalistic and inward-looking a country as Mexico.[16]

### *Growth, Gaullism, and* Gringos

Mexico's real challenge is to grow. In order to achieve this, it needs far more domestic and foreign investment, public and private. Oil in the deep waters of the Gulf of Mexico, at more than seven thousand feet below the surface of the sea, can only be found and extracted through massive outlays by huge companies, whether oil giants or service providers, in association with Pemex. Millions of new jobs can only be created by thousands of new midsize firms investing for the first time in

Mexico for the domestic market and for reexport to the U.S. Mexican infrastructure—ports, airports, highways, power grids, and so on— and education can only be ramped up to world standards with financing, both public and private, from abroad, meaning largely the United States and, to a lesser extent, Canada.

None of this can happen today, given the obstacles posed by the country's laws and attitudes. And they are many: the absence of competition, the monopolistic practices of business, the regulatory agencies' lack of teeth, the overall crony nature of Mexican capitalism, and the overt protection enjoyed by, among others, the media, oil, and electric power. All this insures that only the brave or reckless will dare to venture into Mexico if they lack the tools—the size, the right connections, and experience—to overcome these obstacles on their own. No one claims that the drawbacks to foreign investment often denounced in Mexico are unreal or insignificant. This "foreign" investment is generally financed with local resources, rarely benefiting the balance of payments; the technology it introduces tends to be both antiquated and expensive; it caters more often to headquarters' needs and sensibilities than to those of the local economy; it is rarely in for the long haul. But all of these deficiencies cannot alter the fact that Mexico today will find it extremely difficult to grow if it does not attract two or three times the amount of investment from abroad that it is receiving today, specifically from firms with no previous presence in Mexico, and in higher value-added sectors than before. If one accepts that the traits of the national character outlined in the previous chapter are real, they do not permit this, even if a government were to prove bold enough to change laws and customs in order to proceed in this direction.

Although the analogy might seem strange, what Mexico needs is a Charles de Gaulle, a leader capable of adapting the country's psychology to its reality. This recourse to a foreign parallel is less abrupt than it may seem at first. Only a transcendent historical figure like de Gaulle in France could bring this about in Mexico, and there is no leader of equivalent stature on the horizon. De Gaulle persuaded the French to bury their resentments and grievances against Germany precisely because of the role he played combating the Nazi occupation of France in World War II: he was practically the founding father of modern France thanks to that role. Between 1958, when the Treaty of Rome established the Common Market and de Gaulle returned to power, and

1963, when he and Germany's chancellor Konrad Adenauer signed the Elysée Treaty, which put a new Franco-German alliance at the heart of the construction of Europe, de Gaulle transformed French attitudes toward their previously despised and feared neighbor. The general understood, knowing his people like no one else, that a pro-German policy was indispensable for France, but that it would never fly if French hearts and minds were not won over. So he included massive schoolchildren exchanges in the Elysée Treaty, as well as other similar provisions, and an unspoken but vigorous admonition to his compatriots: no more calling the Germans "*sales boches*" ("dirty krauts"), even in their absence. He grasped that it was impossible to leave behind three wars (1870, 1914–18, 1939–45) and millions of French dead if the people of France did not set aside their anti-German resentments in all walks of life.

There are few expressions more common in Mexican everyday conversation than "*pinches gringos.*" The qualifier can be loosely translated as "lousy," "fucking," or "asshole" Americans; the noun "*gringo*" has roots as mysterious as the treasure of Moctezuma. The etymology of the word, which is also used in a more generic fashion elsewhere in Latin America, varies from country to country, and the list of its roots is never exhaustive. In Chile, where it refers to practically any foreigner, it is said to stem from the use of any incomprehensible language often referred to generically as Greek, which in Spanish is *griego*, which can rapidly become *gringo*. Another anecdote states that when British and American engineers built Chilean railroads, and established the traditional semaphore, stop-and-go system, they would always shout "red-stop," "green-go" (thus *gringo*), to the Chilean railroad workers. In Uruguay, where the term designates people of English origin, some suspect that it springs from the expression "*drink and go*" always used by Brits in Montevideo downing a quick beer or tot of rum; in nearby Argentina, the term referred to Italian immigrants, basically because they did not speak Spanish, *gringo* being a generic term for anyone who didn't know the local tongue.[17]

Finally, and most importantly, in Mexico two historical origins are offered, both obviously unproven. The first comes from the use of colors to differentiate between various American battalions that in 1847 invaded and captured the capital. Several were green (their designation, not their uniforms), and their marching orders were voiced out constantly and stridently: "Go, green, go." The other root lies in the song "Green Grow the Lilacs," originally an Irish melody that was chanted recurrently by American troops in Mexico. Its first verse is "Green grow the bushes," which was rapidly translated intro "*gringo*" by Mexicans who heard the American invaders belting it out in battle or on the march. Some Mexican scholars have insisted on the non-Mexican etymology of the expression, even dating it back to *Don Quixote*, where in Cervantes's second chapter he refers to a shepherd in love, and says that he could not understand a word, because everything he heard was in "*griego o gerigonça*," that is, incomprehensible. Again, *griego* or *gerigonça* can easily become *gringo*, meaning someone who cannot be understood in the language he speaks.[18]

Today, the term is clearly pejorative, although on occasion it can be admiring, as when followed by an exclamation mark. But it is more generally muttered behind Americans' backs, and encapsulates perfectly all of the paradoxes and mazes of the Mexican perception of the United States and its inhabitants. Mexico needs something like a de Gaulle to convince itself that it can no longer utter these words, because the only way it will ever stop thinking about them is by no longer pronouncing them. An interesting precedent—as well as an appropriate response to those in Mexico who object to American references to Mexicans as "spics," "greasers," "wetbacks," or "beaners"—lies in the American predilection for political correctness, and what it has wrought in the U.S., despite its heavy-handedness and occasional obnoxiousness. Derogatory expressions in reference to Mexicans, Mexican-Americans, Latinos, and so forth are just not acceptable anymore, and are gradually disappearing from public *and* private discourse, perhaps less rapidly than would be desirable, but consistently. We are a long way from there in Mexico. As we are also far from banishing the other despicable expression of "*pinche indio*." Mexicans from all walks of life, including the members of the indigenous communities themselves, resort to this derogatory expression or term incessantly, using it to designate and offend someone they consider to be uncouth, poorly groomed, lacking in social graces, and, in general, poor. Political correctness of this sort has not yet made it to Mexico in this case either.

Getting to where we should arrive means, among other things, of course, carrying out a profound revision of elementary school history and civics, or social studies, textbooks, not only regarding Mexico's complicated issues with the United States during the nineteenth and twentieth centuries, but also about the state of the world today. Where does Mexico belong? How can it separate its current worldview from its obsession with history? Can it find and consolidate a location in the world compatible with its needs and the desires of its people? Should it set aside history in order to do so? Short of clear answers to these questions, and the changes their answers impose, most of the ambitious and necessary reforms spelled out by numerous Mexican intellectuals, businessmen, and a sprinkling of politicians about the country's ties with the United States will remain in limbo. Before describing some of these possible reforms, and providing a few insights into what Mexican society really wants in life, the story of 9/11 in Mexico can serve as a somber illustration of the emotional, intellectual, and political challenges the country confronts.

That day's tragic events in New York and Washington took place in a peculiar context of U.S.-Mexican ties. President Vicente Fox had just returned from a highly successful visit to the U.S. capital, where he had been hosted by George W. Bush at the first state dinner of his term, applauded by a joint session of Congress and by a second meeting of legislative leaders, feted by the U.S. press on its front pages. Fox was further informed by Bush, Secretary of State Colin Powell, and National Security Advisor Condoleezza Rice that, despite the known reluctance of Congress, the administration would attempt to deliver on its promise of some sort of immigration deal by the end of 2001. The specifics were not entirely clear, but private conversations by senior officials in both governments suggested that a compromise could include a legalization process for Mexicans in the United States without papers, as well as a temporary worker program for new migrants at a level well above the existing legal flow, though below the total illegal sum. Bush had made his first trip abroad as president to Fox's home in Guanajuato back in February of that year. Overall, despite the intense dislike that both countries' punditocracy felt for the two "cowboys," public and published opinion in the two nations coincided in detecting a new era in relations and a new place for Mexico under the American sun. It lasted five days.

When news of the Twin Towers disaster hit Mexico, there were three types of reactions. The official one, logically enough, was headed by Fox, who called Bush that day and extended his sympathy and sup-

port. The second one, of Mexican society at large, was of strong solidarity with the United States, together with a wisp of foreboding that
Washington would retaliate against somebody, and this would not benefit Mexico, or anybody, for that matter. The third was more complicated. This response was generally muted and indirect, or, some might
say, hypocritical, though a few demonstrators voiced it explicitly in
their banners and chants. It consisted of a gamut of sentiments ranging
from glee to smug condescension. The United States got what it
deserved; after all, hadn't it bombed Hiroshima, Nagasaki, Vietnam?
And it translated into a none too subtle, though elliptical, warning to
the Fox government: don't even think of unconditionally endorsing
any reprisal that Bush might order.

The ambivalence spilled over into policy and politics on two scores.
First, there was a deep division within Fox's cabinet as to whether he
should promptly travel to Washington and New York to personally
extend his condolences to Bush, New York mayor Rudy Giuliani, and
the American people, as Tony Blair, Jacques Chirac, and countless others did during the first days after the attacks. Alternatively, since he had
just been in the U.S. capital, perhaps he should wait a couple of weeks,
until the American team was under less pressure and tension. The interior minister, Fox's closest aide and his purported heir-to-be (in fact, he
lost out to Felipe Calderón in 2005 in the race to become the PAN candidate in 2006), as well as his chief of staff, were opposed to excessive
gestures of sympathy and support. They thought that a dignified, sober
approach was more fitting, especially since they were negotiating
important domestic issues with the left-wing PRD and the old, nationalistic PRI. Further, since they had been led to believe that Bush would
soon invade Afghanistan (he did, on October 13), they considered that
Mexico should offer only lukewarm backing to that venture. On the
other side, I as foreign minister and a few other presidential aides
believed that Fox should travel to the United States as soon as possible.
On September 12, I said: "This was not a time to nickel-and-dime our
support for the American people and their government."

The discussion was complicated by a singular feature of Mexican
politics at the time. Until 2008, whenever the president left the country
he was required to seek authorization from Congress. So if Fox had
wished to travel immediately to Washington, he needed first to find a
window with the Bush administration, then to resolve the divisions

within his inner circles, all the time facing the risk that Congress might veto his trip. It took me until October 4 to get Fox to Washington and New York; he went on the Larry King show before that and stated unambiguously that Mexico stood side by side with the United States at that moment of trial.

The Mexican position nonetheless continued to appear unsatisfactory to the chattering classes on both sides of the border. One segment of the commentocracy and political elite decided that the government had been excessively accommodating, forthcoming, and ebullient with Bush, especially since Fox's visit was followed just ten days later by the invasion of Afghanistan. But another part concluded that Mexico had snubbed the United States, since Fox's delay in traveling to Washington implied a reluctance to display our solidarity in public. The so-called Mexico experts in the U.S. reached the same conclusion, without offering any evidence that anyone in the Bush administration shared their point of view. Several years later, I asked Colin Powell whether there were any grounds for thinking that Mexico had been slow and tepid in its support; nothing of the sort, he replied. In the end, the Mexican government, myself included, ended up pleasing no one: on the one hand being seen as too friendly with the U.S., and on the other as not friendly enough.

The true issue, however, was identified by Jeffrey Davidow, then the United States ambassador in Mexico, a career bureaucrat from the State Department with an enormous load of chips on his shoulder, but an acute observer of Mexican mores, if not of local politics. He understood that the problem was not the Mexican government's reaction to 9/11. It was Mexican society's response. This did not reflect the closer bilateral ties generated by NAFTA, or the impact of Fox's visit to Washington, or the fact that dozens of Mexicans, or perhaps many more, according to a comment Mayor Giuliani made to me on October 4, when we visited Ground Zero with him, died in the World Trade Center disaster. Quite simply, there was no outpouring of broad Mexican sympathy, support, and solidarity for the tragedy befallen its neighbor. *Fox's* supposedly slow response would be forgotten; Mexican *society's* coolness would not.

What this shows is that, in the absence of a fundamental shift in attitudes, such as those carried out by de Gaulle in France, the social and economic transformations Mexico requires are implausible. As long as Mexicans remain persuaded that their oil is better left under the ocean floor than exploited in association with foreign petroleum companies, the laws will not change; and if they do, the legal, political, and even violent challenges to any relevant constitutional amendment will sabotage their intent. As long as Mexicans continue to consider that their beaches enclose a strategic national interest, and cannot be sold to foreigners (meaning Americans), the country will persist in being a second-rank, though first-rate, resort spot, depriving its citizens of the millions of additional jobs the industry can provide.

## What About Obama?

Similarly, Mexico will again miss the boat if it does not recognize the extraordinary opportunity represented by the Obama administration, led by a president who perhaps for the first time in recent history is capable of grasping and following a visionary agenda (more so than Bill Clinton) with his neighbor. Certainly the time has come for both countries to start detailing—or at least imagining—how their relations can be transformed: a North American Economic Union, or Common Market, with full mobility of capital, labor, goods, and services; with infrastructure and social cohesion funds along European, Marshall Plan, and Iraq lines, and a common antitrust approach; a unified security commitment, against both organized crime and potential terrorist threats; a single currency and permanent supranational institutions, at first devoted strictly to trade issues, but later to broader economic and social matters, including labor rights, the environment, and human rights in the broadest definition of the term; and finally, far away in the future, a venture into certain political areas and the crucial realm of the rule of law. At first sight, this may seem like an overambitious agenda, one that could take decades or longer to implement, although it is certainly being increasingly contemplated.* It may also seem far removed from the current mood of American and Mexican public opinion. But it is the one path that promises rewards for both countries.

* See, for example, the work of the North American Forum, chaired by George Shultz, Pedro Aspe, and Peter Lougheed; COMEXI and Pacific Council on International Policy, "Managing the United States–Mexico Border: Cooperative Solutions to Common Challenges"; and Robert Pastor's new book, *The North American Idea.*

Most thoughtful Mexicans agree with many of these proposals, but believe, not unjustifiably, that the United States, particularly the conservative heartland, would never go along with them. That may be true today, but the situation is not static. Americans have a record of modifying their stances when persuasive arguments are presented to them, are openly debated, and when they are given the option to choose. They decided to support the United Nations (after rejecting the League of Nations a quarter century earlier); they always backed the Marshall Plan, granted under far different circumstances, but that cost, in today's dollars, far more than any ambitious development agenda for Mexico ever would; and they decided to support NAFTA, largely because it didn't really matter to them. Paradoxically, Americans have also subscribed to the idea, for different reasons and with a different strategy under Bush and Obama, of an exorbitantly expensive process of nation building in Iraq and Afghanistan, arguably two countries where their interests pale compared with Mexico.

If Mexico were to submit such a vision during the Obama era, at first it would almost certainly be laughed out of court. On second thought, however, Obama and the sophisticated people working with him might grasp that nothing is more in the United States' interest than a modern, prosperous, democratic, and equitable Mexico. And they might then conclude that endorsement of this or a similar agenda offered the best and fastest—and perhaps the only—way to achieve this goal. One additional advantage, while not of the same importance, might be Washington's role in the new world order. The United States needs additions to its roster of friends, allies, and credentials in the post–Cold War international arena; solid relations with a stronger Mexico would improve America's standing in the world.

Washington lacks reliable, constant, durable ties with midsize, mid-development, mid-influential countries, such as emerging economies comparable in political weight with, say, Canada, Italy, or Australia. Mexico can be one of these allies, if its neighbor seizes the chance the moment offers; not many others fit that description. The U.S. could use a positive story to tell the world about its contribution to a lasting and substantial rise in the living standards of what are still referred to as developing countries. For Washington, Mexico could become the North American equivalent of the Northern European nations' success in lifting Ireland, Spain, and Portugal by their bootstraps in the 1970s,

1980s, and 1990s. For this to happen, the United States has to change, but so must Mexico. And for us, once again, the main obstacle is the Mexican national character. Perhaps a change in Mexican attitudes toward the United States is not impossible, and part of the heavy lifting in this realm has begun. Interestingly, according to one poll, Mexicans today, despite their misgivings, when offered the choice of European-style integration with North America or with Latin America, opted for North America by a narrow majority.[19]

The tale is often told of how when Spain's Socialists came to power in 1982, barely seven years after Franco's death, they asked themselves what country they would like theirs to resemble. The response was France and Germany. In their view, Spain's problem was Spain: they did not want to see Spain remain the Spain of the past, and to avoid that, they saw Spain's solution to be Europe. Inspired by this episode, the Mexico City magazine *Nexos* asked Mexicans, in late 2009, in the course of an incipient national conversation about Mexico's future, what country they would like theirs to be like. The results were remarkable.

When the question was asked without offering examples to choose from, the answers were: the United States, 31%; China, 6%; Canada, 5%; Brazil, 5%, Spain, 4%; and none of the above, 34%. The proportion of those picking the U.S. ranked above the national average among men as a whole, among thirty- to forty-nine-year-olds, rural dwellers, the inhabitants of the north of the country, and PRI sympathizers. When offered five specific choices—the United States, China, Brazil, Spain, and Cuba—the answers were even more startling: the United States, 34%; China, 9%; Brazil, 7%; Spain, 6%; and Cuba, 2%; none of the above, 29%. The breakdown by groups was similar to the open query, but with nuances. The preference for the U.S. was higher than the overall average among thirty- to forty-nine-year-olds and among higher-income Mexicans, and it reached a remarkable 50% in the central states of the country, probably because this region has always experienced the highest outmigration.[20]

The poll was somewhat skewed by the peak of Obamania in Mexico and the world, as well as by the severity of the 2008–09 economic crisis for Mexico, where the economy contracted more, 6.5%, than in any other major country. Economic considerations were dominant in people's thinking, and the main justification for choosing the U.S. was its economic strength. Another poll, taken at the same time and again asking for a country that could serve as a role model for Mexico, produced similar results: the U.S. with 37%, Canada with 8%, then Japan, France, Germany, and Spain, each with 3%. When the question was phrased more indirectly, but perhaps more revealingly—"If you had to entrust your children's future to someone who lives abroad, where would you want that person to live?"—the answers were the U.S., 38%; Canada, 14%; then Spain, Germany, Japan, and France, each between 7% and 5%.[21]

## Ready for Change?

Despite the distortions introduced by their timing, the outcome of these surveys was totally unexpected by most analysts, and showed what other statistics, as well as several historians, had already surmised. Mexico's business, political, intellectual, and even religious elites were the last barricade, the only surviving depository of the trait of national character described in the previous chapter: the obsession with the past and the dread of the external. Mexicans on Main Street, it seemed, were finally leaving this baggage behind, even if their leaders of all stripes and in all walks of society were not.

In the meantime, the lingering impact of those traits paralyzes Mexico in an area of political endeavor that is of less relevance than others we have reviewed, but that nonetheless increasingly affects the daily lives of its citizens. Foreign policy, and Mexico's role in the international arena, is dramatically constrained by the straitjacket of the past and the foreign. This has led a country of 112 million inhabitants, with the world's twelfth-largest economy, and a unique geographical location, often to vanish from the world stage or, when it seeks a more active role, to face major domestic opposition or rejection.

Whether at the United Nations, in Central America, on climate change, or regarding the defense and promotion of human rights and democracy, let alone in dealing with the United States, Mexico is forced to oscillate between rhetorical attachment to abstract principles—nonintervention, self-determination, absolute sovereignty of states—enshrined in its Constitution, and a realpolitik diplomacy that confuses or irritates a good part of its elites. But the reality is that those abstract principles, which (like most other countries from Latin America, Africa, and Asia) Mexico could apply only sporadically and when its national interests were *not* at stake, are less and less relevant to a modern, middle-class, democratic, and market-based society. On the other hand, Mexican society, or at least its leaders, is rubbed the wrong way by a foreign policy that separates Mexico from the rest of Latin America—where its heart lies but its interests do not—and from what used to be called the Third World. It is rapidly rendered inoperable in part.

When Mexico adopts positions at the United Nations or at the Organization of American States that correspond both to its objective importance and to its ever-tightening links with the United States, the left, the intelligentsia, part of the PRI, and even the Church and the business community complain. The position of the Church and the business elite is perhaps oddest. They do not lament Mexico's convergence with Washington, or its upholding human rights in Cuba or Venezuela, or its alignment with the G-8 on climate change because they reject these positions per se. Rather, they feel these positions do not merit a fight with the left, its newspapers and pundits, its foreign allies and domestic sympathizers. They see them as ultimately minor matters. Conversely, when Mexico does side with Hugo Chávez, the Castro brothers, Iran, or Nicaragua, they view the costs of doing so as minimal and the benefits as considerable. Since frequently—though not always—Washington cuts Mexico some slack on these questions, the conclusion becomes self-evident: Mexico is better served by pursuing a traditional, "nonaligned," moderately anti-American course, without resorting to U.S. bashing but nonetheless befriending regimes that do. This tactic translates rapidly into a default solution. It is the option any Mexican president or foreign minister chooses, unless for reasons of conviction, vision, or contrariness, he or she decides otherwise. It is what has been labeled the PRI "chip" present in every Mexican official's mind.* The problem, of course, is that this default stance is misunderstood by most of Mexican society. Instead of recognizing it as a second or third best option, Mexicans believe that this approach

---

* Mexican officials, whatever party they belong to, have what many called a "PRI chip" in their mind. They react and respond to stimuli of all sorts in the same way, which is the way the PRI ran the country for the past eighty years. The reason is simple: the PRI simply reflected the basic traits of the Mexican psyche, not the other way around.

corresponds to the country's international interests, to its history and tradition, and to its very soul.

Consequently, the government's views are often misunderstood by its foreign partners, and by Washington in particular. They react with incredulity, dismay, or cynical resignation to what they perceive as Mexico's persistent hypocrisy. In their view, Mexico continues to espouse causes, allies, and so-called principles that it knows full well it has outgrown yet cannot convince itself to abandon because of seemingly petty domestic considerations. Mexico's international posture tends then to be dismissed by many as unreliable, inconsistent, and contradictory—or simply introverted and irrelevant—especially on issues that are not of great import to Mexico, although they may be to others.

In the next installment of this soap opera, Mexico discovers that it actually possesses an agenda with the U.S. or Canada or the European Union, and seeks the comprehension and sympathy of their respective governments in order to move that agenda forward: immigration, drugs, pandemics, and tourism, among others. Sometimes its requests are well received, despite its ambivalent behavior on other items; but on occasion, Washington or London or Tokyo responds with a "Where were you when I needed you" smirk, or, more justifiably, with a "We have domestic political considerations to attend to also, by the way." Likewise, if for another motive, Mexico is forced to side with Washington or the richer countries on a bilateral or multilateral issue of import to them, even though it may seem inconsequential, Mexican society ends up more confounded than ever. It feels that national sovereignty has been sold out for no good reason.

Any Mexican government's options are limited by the national character traits we have described, either as they are lived by society at large, or as they are expressed by vocal and powerful elites. It often cannot establish international commitments or be taken at its word, since, as Leonard Cohen's song goes, everybody knows that it will be abandoned either by its people or by its neighbor. At the same time, Mexico cannot utilize its strongest card in its dealings with Latin America or other regions, i.e., its "special relation" with that neighbor, because society won't allow it. The final outcome is an obstinate tendency for Mexico to punch way below its weight in the international arena, to find its foreign policy reduced to the bare essentials of its links with

Washington, and to constantly discover that even this relationship is
often poisoned by American mistrust or neglect, all too frequently provoked by Mexican hypocrisy. It is a vicious cycle.

The only solution would be for a government to brave the fires of
national character, not only for two or three years, as was the case with
Fox between 2000 and 2003, but persistently, until a series of policies
are locked in by international covenants or other instruments. In the
end, the outcry would almost certainly be far less strident than antici-
pated, and in so doing, Mexico would be carving out a role for itself in
the world far more consonant with its economic, political, and social
realities than the one long imposed by its history and phantoms. But it
would take a courageous chief executive to follow this path, sown with
all sorts of tricks, traps, treason, and traditions. Since the line between
courage and foolhardiness is a fine one, there is little hope that this trait
of the national attitude will be soon abandoned. But it will be difficult,
if not impossible, for Mexico to thrive if somehow it does not find a
way to break out of this impasse.

## CHAPTER 7

# Illusory Laws, Lawless Cynicism

Perhaps the most frequent attributes attached to Mexican life and society are corruption and lawlessness. As Jorge Portilla emphasized, "The first in a list of typical and daily facts [that make up our national character] is the *mordida* [the bite or bribe], which carries all of the guilt of our national disgraces."[1] We shall discuss in the next chapter how relevant and dysfunctional these perceptions and features are to current affairs in Mexico, but here our purpose is to describe and explain Mexicans' attitudes toward corruption and the law. This is perhaps the most delicate task we have set ourselves, since the stereotypes in these domains are more entrenched than elsewhere, and also tend to be more often extrapolated than others. For the purpose of clarity, we have deliberately dissociated violence, crime, and delinquency from corruption and weakness of the rule of law, mainly because, as we showed earlier on, Mexico is not today an especially violent country, nor has it been in the past, and crime presently is neither more widespread nor more serious than in other Latin Americans societies, nor worse today than before.

Conversely, corruption, the sporadic and isolated nature of the rule of law, and impunity do go together, like most evil things. As in Graham Greene's *The Lawless Roads* and *Another Mexico*, lawlessness breeds corruption; corruption perverts the legal and justice system, which inspires virtually no confidence among society's members. Hence it encourages them to break the law or in any case to have scant respect for it, since they can get away with practically everything. The issue is not so much whether Mexico is corrupt or not (there is not much argument about that); it is also not whether it is more or less corrupt than other Latin American nations (slightly less, according to surveys) or whether there is dreadfully little respect for the law in Mexico (an undisputable assertion) or if disdain for the law is greater elsewhere in the region (Mexico stands around the median). The fundamental question is if the origins of this disregard for legality and the concomitant proliferation of venality lie in traits of the national character that permit, and indeed promote, them, or whether they are more linked to a political system that, fortunately, is passing from the scene.

The first indication suggests that the political system is not necessarily to blame, despite what many scholars, pundits, public intellectuals, and pro-democracy activists, including myself, had long believed. It now seems that the corrupt and lawless political system of the seventy-year PRI ancien régime was much more a consequence than a cause, much more an effect than a driver. The PRI was a mirror of Mexican society and its members, not a molder or a creator. Mexico began becoming less corrupt, and somewhat more respectful of the rule of law, before that system faded away, and it has remained intolerably corrupt and lawless more than a decade after the beginning of its extinction through rotation in power. At the same time, however, the age-old arguments, whereby we are all irremediably and congenitally corrupt because of the Spanish, Catholic, *mestizo*, "patrimonialist" heritage are even more false and unacceptable, so a student of the country is left somewhat mystified. These ills are secular and cultural, but not ontological or resistant to change. It is in the general vicinity of history, attitudes, and structures that we are most likely to find explanations, if not the definitive answer, or remedy.

### The Colonial and Nineteenth-Century Heritage

The original sin and first seed of corruption emerged almost certainly with the Spanish *conquistadores*, viceroys, and *encomenderos*, who brought with them the classic expression from the homeland: "*Se obedece pero no se cumple*," or "*Obedézcase pero no se cumpla*" ("We obey but we do not comply," or "Obey the law but do not comply with it"). In the strictest sense, the expression sprang from the Castillian custom (though some scholars also extend it to the Kingdom of Navarre) whereby the law was obeyed but its application could be suspended until its ultimate execution was submitted for final consideration to the king, who was humbly beseeched by an offended party or community to amend the law and take into account their best interest.[2] Some legal scholars have argued that this medieval custom represents an early version of the Mexican figure of *amparo*, not dissimilar though not identical to writs of habeas corpus. They sustain that it was never meant to be an instrument for subverting the law, but simply a mechanism that allowed distance and time to be taken into account. How could the king rapidly determine if an edict or ruling in Mexico City was fair or not, when it took months to come and go to the old country? And in any case, the original version of the proclamation was not open-ended: if the king decided that the law was just, it had to be applied; strictly speaking, this was the equivalent of a temporary injunction, not a permanent override.

Whatever the reason, the tradition was quickly transformed into a form of protection for the colonies from disinformation or ignorance in Spain. It became a peculiar manifestation of home rule, or local autonomy, where everyone made of necessity a virtue. The Crown had no choice but to acquiesce to local needs, and the colonial administrators did not and could not violate the formal principle of monarchical authority. The roots of this ruse may have consisted in the complicated legal structure of New Spain. The Crown owned everything and only "entrusted" Indian villages (that is the meaning of the term *encomienda*), i.e., their evangelization, their well-being, souls, land, and power, to a *conquistador*, who in exchange received the levies normally paid by the Indians to the Crown in the New World. But in fact the Crown held very little sway over the *conquistadores*.

They in turn needed the acquiescence of the king of Spain, and soon of Emperor Charles V, to establish their rule and legitimacy over other local powers, indigenous and extraneous—the conquered and the Church—but they felt able to act in situ pretty much as they liked. There was a tax to pay, there were monopoly trade restrictions and laws regarding protection of the indigenous populations, but the Crown had no way of enforcing them, other than through the same *conquistadores* or their descendants. An appropriate compromise was reached. The subjects in the New World accepted the nominal authority of the Crown in Madrid and of its representative, the viceroy of New Spain;

they paid most of their taxes, respected most of the trade impositions, and, up to a point, defended their own interests by not entirely destroying the indigenous population. But they ran things on their own locally, paying only lip service to the monarchy's edicts and regulations. This was the beginning of the separation between law and fact, between a de jure world and a de facto one, between the outward, rhetorical, and even reverential respect for the law in the abstract, and the emergence of a path in everyday life totally decoupled from that law.

This simulated adherence to the rule of law planted the seed of what Octavio Paz and others have called the "patrimonialist" nature of colonial governance, and which lingers on today. The poet uses a marvelous example from the regency of Marianne of Austria in the seventeenth century to make his point. Her prime minister, Fernando Valenzuela, facing a dire financial situation for the monarchy, decided to consult with the court theologians whether it was licit to auction off high offices, in particular the viceroyalties of Aragón, New Spain, Nueva Granada or Upper Peru, and Naples. The theologians found nothing in the laws of God or man that prohibited this sale. As Paz says, "The corruption of the Mexican public administration is basically only another manifestation of the persistence of the ways of thinking and feeling exemplified by the dictate of the Spanish theologians."[3] In his view, patrimonialism represents the intrusion of private life into the public sphere. Under a patrimonial regime, the borders between the public and private spheres, between the family and the state, are vague and fluctuating; more specifically, "If everyone is the king of his house, the kingdom is like a house and the nation is like a family. If the state is the king's patrimony, how can it not also be the patrimony of his relations, friends, servants and favorites?"[4] Centuries later, this would translate into what Claudio Lomnitz would call a national ideology: "The formal adoption of a State ideology . . . had as its reward the personal benefits that state institutions bestowed upon their members. Personal benefit and national interest coincided within state culture, in the same way that state ideology coincided with institutional state practice."[5]

The viceroy of New Spain knew he possessed great leeway in dealing with his subjects, both by mistreating them more than the Crown formally acknowledged or tolerated, but also by handing out favors, perks, riches, and privileges freely, according to his own interests and preferences. He "owned" the colonial state, to the extent there was one—and by the late sixteenth century at least the trappings of one had emerged; and thanks to his largesse, he was able to dole out as parts of his "property" slices of the very state itself. To illustrate briefly how this feature of colonial governance has endured, a poll taken in 2003 inquired whether people thought a public official should be able to enrich himself in office as long as he "delivered the goods": 48% said yes.[6] Public office became the premier instrument of social mobility, since land, trade, and the labor force belonged to the Church or the Crown, or to a small elite enjoying their continued favor. Enterprising *criollo* or Spanish young men became corrupt bureaucrats for the same reasons that led Jews in late medieval Europe to become moneylenders, then bankers. This was the only lucrative activity open to them.

The second great link in the historical chain of corruption and disregard for the law was forged with Independence. Almost all of the republics in today's Latin America and the Caribbean were born between 1808 (Haiti) and 1825 (Colombia). They adopted liberal constitutions modeled on a combination of the U.S. founding document, the French Declaration of Human Rights, and the philosophy of the eighteenth-century Enlightenment. These constitutions enshrined separation of powers, federalism, respect for human rights, and elections, albeit with restricted suffrage and sovereignty residing in the popular will: nothing was omitted. The problem resided in the totally artificial, or fictitious, and often cartoonlike nature of the documents' relevance or applicability to the social, economic, and political context they were destined for. As Samuel Ramos put it, highlighting the absurdity of it all, and quoting a colleague of his, "the first text of the United States Constitution known in Mexico was a bad translation imported by a dentist."[7] Or, as a major political and intellectual figure of the post-Independence years, Fray Servando Teresa de Mier, remarked about the vigorous and unreal debate raging in Mexico in the 1830s between federalists and centralists, "I would cut my own neck if any one of the participants knew what kind of a species a federal republic was." While the disconnect between the written text of the law and the historical reality it addressed was typical of all of Latin America, with the possible exception of Brazil, which conserved its monarchy or empire until late in the century, it was perhaps more acute in Mexico (and perhaps Peru) than elsewhere. The country, as we observed earlier, had a constitutional representative democracy on paper, and fifty governments during its first quarter century of independent life. No wonder the paper didn't matter.

So from the start, Mexican society was imbued with the quite logical notion that the law was meaningless, and that this was a forgivable sin. Everyone of consequence understood that there were no elections, no separation of powers, no federal republic, no economic freedoms, no civil liberties; everyone also accepted that this did not represent a major dilemma. The problem was that almost no one recognized that by maintaining the colonial era's tradition of ignoring the law, Mexico was perpetuating a birth defect that would plague it for nearly two centuries. The gravity lay in the flagrance and stridency of the gap between constitutions that came and went (two in the nineteenth century, another in the twentieth, with, as we saw, 489 amendments in less than a hundred years of existence), and the workings of everyday life and the ongoing activities of civil society. Under these circumstances, it was almost impossible to instill in the population any attachment to the law, to the incipient and practically useless justice system, or to contracts, honesty, and transparency in government or society. Documents, laws, and words themselves acquired a remarkably contradictory nature. On the one hand, society attached a reverential, almost magical virtue to them: a signature on a document (as in the popular expression "*papelito habla,*" or "paper talks") or a public commitment in a speech was considered tantamount to reality. On the other, everyone well knew that political jargon and legalistic gobbledygook were meaningless.

The corollary, as during the colony, was corruption. Since nothing could be achieved by applying the law, everything had to be accomplished by purchasing privilege or selling off segments of power. Different factions fighting for power would place hunks of sovereignty on the auction block in exchange for diplomatic recognition, credit, and arms from abroad; the Church defended itself from reforms that threatened its wealth and authority by hiring conservative allies who in turn enticed foreign princes to rule Mexico; liberals sought American support, time after time, in exchange for one perk or another. And among individuals, matters of business, labor, markets, and justice were resolved by bribes, payoffs, kickbacks, scams, and deals.

It took more than half a century for a modicum of order to be established. Only after Juárez defeated the French, Maximilian, and the conservatives, "restored the republic," and then died peacefully in his sleep five years later, was it possible for the Porfirian age of stability and order to commence in 1876. It lasted for more than thirty years and brought huge economic progress and social change to the country, albeit neither new respect for the law, nor limitations of any sort on the venality of public life. Díaz himself, and some of his closest aides—Justo Sierra, the education minister; José Yves Limantour and Matías Romero, the financial architects of prosperity; and perhaps a few others—were known for their personal honesty, as Juárez had been, but the rest succumbed to either Juárez's or Díaz's famous and oft-repeated aphorisms. Juárez: "*Para los amigos, justicia y gracia; para los enemigos, la ley*" ("For friends, justice and grace; for enemies, the law"); and Díaz, referring to journalists and critics: "*Ese gallo quiere maíz*" ("Those chickens want their cornfeed").*

## The Revolution and the Law

In one of the most illuminating examples of Mexican acceptance of corruption, a stew of similar "*boutades*" sprang up over the years. These folkloric expressions surfaced during the Revolution and in its aftermath. Álvaro Obregón, the real victor of the 1910–17 epic, who became president in 1920 and was reelected in 1928, only to be assassinated before taking office, coined the timeless refrain "I have never met a general who could resist a fifty-thousand-peso cannonball." And in fact, from the 1930s and until 2003 at least, Mexican military attachés posted at some two dozen embassies abroad received their salaries in dollars; their monthly tax-exempt wage totaled $22,000, plus whatever spare change they could pick up from sending home all sorts of goodies through the diplomatic pouch.

Corruption most flourished during the period of consolidation of the PRI regime, that is, after 1940, once the basic trappings of the political system created by Presidents Plutarco Elías Calles (1924–28, and de facto, 1928–34) and Lázaro Cárdenas (1934–40) were installed, and especially after the end of World War II. And, with it, Mexicans

---

* The written accent in proper Spanish falls on the i, but the saying is still pronounced with the phonetic accent falling on the *a*.

invented immensely imaginative one-liners to characterize it, starting with the one we quoted at the very outset of this work: "*El que no transa, no avanza*" ("Whoever doesn't trick or cheat, gets nowhere"). A couple had to do with honesty in public office: "*No roba, pero se le pega el dinero*" ("He doesn't steal, but money sticks to him"); "*Fulano de tal es honesto, pero honesto, honesto, honesto, ¿quién sabe?*" ("So-and-so is honest; but honest, honest, honest, who knows?"). A classic one has generally been attributed to one of Mexico's wealthiest and most powerful politician-businessmen ever, Carlos Hank González: "*Político pobre, pobre político*" ("A politician in poverty is a poor politician"). And about how the newly inaugurated spoils system actually functioned: "*No les pido que me den, sólo que me pongan donde hay*" ("I am not asking for money, just to be appointed where I can get some"); "*Vivir fuera del presupuesto es vivir en el error*" ("To live outside the federal budget is to live in error"); and "*Amistad que no se refleja en la nómina no es amistad*" ("A friendship that is not reflected in the payroll is no friendship at all"). Finally, on corrupting others: "*Con dinero baila el perro, si está amaestrado*" ("Properly paid and trained, a dog will dance"). And most triumphantly: "*¡La Revolución hizo justicia!*" ("The Revolution finally meted out justice!").

The opposition or dissenters were not exempt: "*No les cambies las ideas, cámbiales los ingresos*" ("Don't bother to change their ideas, just change their income"). Even the press, infinitely corrupt until the late seventies (and in many cases, still today), came up with its own self-deprecating and sarcastic catchphrase, exalting the bribes, or *chayote*, it received systematically to report favorably on business, government, labor unions, and celebrities: "*Sin chayo, no me hallo*" ("Without my bribe, I am lost"). Once again it was Cantinflas who best illustrated Mexico's unwavering cynicism with regard to corruption and disrespect for the law. But innumerable Mexican comedians, working at the equivalent of improvs, known as *carpas*, also made hay in the 1940s and 1950s over the immense wealth accumulated by officials of the time, particularly under the Miguel Alemán administration (1946–52), including, according to just about everybody, the president himself. Roger Bartra places the comedian at the center of the discussion: "Cantinflas's message is transparent: poverty is a permanent state of stupid primitivism that must be vindicated hilariously. . . . Thus there is a perfect correspondence between the corruption of the people and that of the government: this people (Cantinflas) has the government it deserves, or conversely, this corrupt and authoritarian government has the people best suited for it, the one that Cantinflas-like nationalism provides as a subject of domination."[8]

The jokes and cynicism all conveyed the same meaning. Mexicans accepted corruption as a way of life—it was seen as "the 'oil' that makes the wheels of the bureaucratic machine turn and the 'glue' that seals political alliances" (as Alan Riding quoted an anonymous source in 1985). They resigned themselves to lawlessness, especially when it became explicitly political, through the repression of government opponents that began in earnest and became systematic in the late 1940s. That was when the Communist Party was banned as the Cold War got under way, and the main independent labor confederations were domesticated and transformed into sweetheart unions. No one respected the law, and no one could manage without corruption; since a justification had to exist for this state of affairs, two rationales began to emerge. First, laws that were deemed unjust did not have to be abided by; second, the only way to get around an unfair justice system was through corruption, either as a victim or as a perpetrator.

## A Special Species of Laws

The link between corruption and the absence of the rule of law, as well as Mexicans' attitudes toward both, grew tighter with time. Since the applicability of many laws was utterly unimaginable, the country approved law after law that was never meant to be applied, following the age-old ritual of simulation. This was particularly flagrant in regard to international treaties or conventions, for which implementing legislation was never drafted or passed, but also for some curious constitutional and electoral provisions. What all of this wrought was a new incentive to break the law. Often there was literally no alternative, since it was almost impossible to respect the law. This led to what Mexican essayist Jaime Sánchez Susarrey labeled, in a marvelous analogy with Latin American literature, "Mexico's magical legalism."[9]

On the foreign front, human rights conventions, labor rights clauses, and environmental regulations in treaties were all signed and ratified (though ratification was occasionally postponed) but were sel-

dom translated into domestic legislation that would make them binding and relevant; for example, in the late nineties, Mexico accepted the
binding nature of the Inter-American Human Rights Court but as late
as 2010 refused to actually modify its laws when the Court called them
violative of international human rights law. Not many ordinary Mexicans followed these convoluted processes closely, as might be expected
anywhere, but this gap between foreign commitments and internal
enforcement cast a shadow on the nation's international image. It led to
charges of hypocrisy and bad faith, implying that the word of a Mexican official meant nothing since he or she never acted upon it. And it
"infected" a broad cross section of Mexico's political and intellectual
elites with the same disease: you can subscribe to all the international
conventions you want, and pass all the domestic legislation you wish.
None of this really matters, and the proof is that not even foreign obligations carry any weight.

The Constitution was not only endlessly amended; its original programmatic or aspirational nature was reinforced as the years went by.
When foreign observers wondered why the 1917 foundational document was so long-winded and multifaceted, Mexican jurists and sincere constitutional scholars, as well as apologists of the PRI regime that
emanated from that text twelve years after its signing, all offered the
same response. The Constitution was much more a list of hopes, aims,
and desirable aspirations than a normative document. Perhaps because
it grew straight out of seven years of revolutionary strife, and two years
of interminable debates, it could not have been otherwise.

It included normative articles, such as Article 27, which stipulated
national sovereignty over natural resources and community land
tenure; or programmatic ones like Article 3, which laid out an entire
educational program; or a combination of both such as Article 123,
which attempted to place labor–management relations into a more
socially responsible and acceptable framework. But as the letter and
spirit of the text became further removed from Mexicans' daily lives,
this initial, noble virtue was distorted and transformed into a debilitat-
ing vice. Every time a social grievance emerged and could not be truly
addressed (almost always), a constitutional amendment was drawn up,
establishing a right to redress. Squatters without homes protested and
received . . . a constitutional amendment guaranteeing them a right to
housing, but no homes. The unemployed protested, demanding work

and received . . . a constitutional amendment guaranteeing them a right to work, but no jobs. The ill and those poorly attended at the national health service facilities protested, demanding better and quicker treatment and received . . . a constitutional amendment guaranteeing them the right to better health, but no doctors, clinics, or medicine. The parents of the poorly educated protested, demanding better preschool education, and received . . . a constitutional amendment guaranteeing every toddler two years of pre-K–12 schooling, but no funding. And so on.

By definition, none of these rights could ever be claimed, and the respective secondary legislation was never even crafted, much less approved. But the dissident and the disgruntled, those authentic Mexican believers in the magic power of the written word, felt that their concerns had been at least partly addressed. They backed off, halfway satisfied that they had obtained half a loaf, and went home to fight another day. The Constitution turned into a Christmas tree, lit up with unachievable goals, unexercisable rights, and unfunded entitlements. It became an additional factor in perpetuating the centuries-old dismissal of the law. The law was a wish or an objective, not a norm that everyone was obliged to comply with, in sharp contrast with the legal and constitutional tradition north of the border, where mostly aspirational law is an oxymoron, and norms are respected because they exist, not because they are fair.

In addition to treaties and the Constitution as examples of the country's illusory legality, in multiple domains of political, economic, and social endeavor, Mexico enacted plain-vanilla laws that quite simply could not be obeyed. The silliest example was the gender quota for congressional election lists, established in 2003. That year, as a result of a long struggle by women in Mexico to gradually conquer equality in the country that made machismo famous, a gender clause was inserted into the federal electoral code. Quotas or affirmative action were deemed to be the only lever with which to impose some degree of equality where abysmal differences prevailed. Given that the number of women elected to Congress had stagnated at a negligible level, outgoing legislators decided that Mexico's peculiar electoral system required a healthy dose of gender parity. Of the first five slots in each party's list for the five national electoral districts, two had to be women: either the first and third, or the second and fourth.[10] The logic was that since only the first five candidates in each list were assured victory, parity had to be established in that small, privileged universe. Previously, although 30% of the total slots in each regional district were reserved for women, political parties generally assigned women to the slots lower down, knowing they would not be elected. So now women would be elected come hell or high water, in all parties' caucuses, whether they liked it or not.

This made sense, except that it neglected Mexicans' infinite wiles for getting around rules and regulations they dislike, or which they consider excessive or impossible to abide by. Women were duly registered on the rolls as provided for by the law; parity was fully respected; they were successfully elected, as were their nominal deputies or substitutes in case of death, illness, a better job, or resignation. As soon as they were sworn in, after the 2006 elections and mainly after the 2009 midterm vote, nine congresswomen elected through this provision promptly resigned, and were immediately replaced by their "deputies," who not only just happened to be men, but in several cases, the titular legislator's husband, boyfriend, father, or brother. The ensuing scandal forced the temporary beneficiaries of gender equality to postpone their resignation for a few months, but just before Christmas in 2009, they were able more or less to surreptitiously surrender their seats to their male comrades without anyone noticing. So much for affirmative action, Mexican style.

### Just Laws or Laws Period?

Understandably, this bundle of historical, constitutional, international, electoral, and subconscious or deliberate aberrations has left Mexicans with a dismal view of the law and its transcendence. This alone would explain and even justify the opinions most Mexicans hold on whether laws should be obeyed or not, or under what conditions they should be respected. But there is an additional ingredient in this explosive mix, which must be considered before moving on to the polls, the laws, and the views Mexicans have of them. It has to do with the confusion long felt by many Mexicans about the difference between law and justice, particularly since "justice" almost always has a silent—or strident— qualifier: *social* justice. Laws are seen either as distant, unfair, and benefiting only the rich and powerful, or as instruments of social policy:

agrarian reform, labor rights, sovereignty over natural resources, combating poverty, guaranteeing health and education, and so on. In a poll taken in 2005, three-quarters of all Mexicans stated that, in "general terms, in Mexico laws are not *'justas'* " (which can be translated as "fair" or "just"). Seventy-one percent believed that the law in Mexico does not apply equally to everybody.[11] They are not viewed as designed to allow an economy to work, to deliver equal treatment and due process to all, to insure that institutions—from markets to elections, and including contracts, property rights, and protection from arbitrary authorities—function properly. They are perceived by many Mexicans as utensils with which to guarantee certain outcomes, not as ends in themselves.

Thus the lodestone of the law is not its *compliance*, regardless of its *justice*; instead, the *justice* of the law determines its contingent *compliance*. Unjust laws are not to be respected, and until they can be changed, there is no civic obligation to obey them. Add to this the Spanish cum Mexican legalistic tradition that gave birth to the term *leguleyo*. It describes a person and a comportment obsessed with legalisms devoid of any substance or context, and which leads every self-respecting Mexican to have strong opinions about such and such a law, or such and such a verdict, sentence, or ruling by any given court, on any given day. The upshot is predictable: I will not abide by this law, because I consider it to be unjust; I will not accept this court finding, because I consider it to be incorrect; I will not comply with this ruling, because I consider it to be illegal. The result is chaos. Perhaps the best recent example of how everyone is entitled to his own opinion of the law, including judges whose rulings are viewed as little more than opinions, lies in the admittedly weird conclusion the federal magistrates of Mexico's Federal Electoral Tribunal reached regarding the 2006 presidential election.

As we have already narrated, that election was a matter of acute controversy in Mexico. The result was very tight (Calderón defeated left-of-center rival Andrés Manuel López Obrador by less than half a percentage point) and the campaign process, as well as election day proceedings and tabulation, were considered fraudulent by the losers' supporters (35% of the voters), and initially by a few more Mexicans.[12] In addition to specific charges of ballot box tampering, the opposition felt that the incumbent president, Vicente Fox, and the business community had violated electoral legislation. They had taken sides and, especially in the case of Fox, campaigned actively for Calderón. The business community had underwritten negative radio and TV spots against López Obrador, associating him with Venezuela's Hugo Chávez, and labeling him a "danger for Mexico." These acts, as such, purportedly broke the law.

In Mexico's perplexing electoral system, the tally and results are decided and announced by the Federal Electoral Institute, which also organizes and supervises the vote. However, conflicts and challenges are resolved by a special Federal Electoral Tribunal, separate from both the Electoral Institute and the Supreme Court, whose rulings cannot be appealed, and whose magistrates are elected by a two-thirds majority of Congress. The legislation and constitutional amendments that gave birth to this odd arrangement date back to 1996, and were approved by unanimity, even by the left-of-center PRD. The magistrates were also ratified unanimously, mostly in 1996, and later, as either they retired or, in one case, passed away. In other words, the legal setup and the actors themselves were all approved by the "victims" of the presumed electoral fraud of 2006. And while this did not mean that no fraud took place, its supposed "victims" had their day in court and access to due process, under a law that they had drafted and before magistrates they had voted in.

The Federal Electoral Tribunal rejected the PRD and López Obrador's charges of egregious tampering, turned down his demand that there be a recount (which Calderón refused, perhaps, in hindsight, mistakenly), and ruled that Fox's and the business community's interference in the electoral process was not conclusive or a game changer. In a nutshell, the court resolved that Calderón won the election fair and square, that Fox meddled but didn't break the law, and that the left's claims were invalid.* The most damning, and simultaneously contradictory, or even bizarre, line of the equation, however, emerged in the court's opinion, a worthy example and marvelous specimen of Mexican legal doublespeak, whose confusion can be best preserved in as literal a translation as possible: "President Fox's statements became a risk for the validity of the election which we are hereby judging, which, if their possible influence had not been weakened by diverse concurring acts and circumstances that we have also analyzed, could have rep-

---

* It is true that Calderón's refusal to recount votes threw a veil over the results, and that Fox was less than diplomatic about the legality of his acts.

resented a major element that could have been considered determinant in the final result, if they had been accompanied by other irregularities of importance that had been substantiated."[13]

What the court attempted to convey in this incredibly byzantine language was that Fox's acts could have jeopardized the fairness of the elections, if they had made a difference, but since there was no evidence that they did, and there were no other detectable vices in the process, they were insufficient to nullify the vote. With an alarming degree of cowardice or compromise—or both—the magistrates ruled that the elections were legal, and that although Fox didn't behave very nicely, he didn't break the law. Even by Florida 2000 standards, this was not a model of clarity, courage, or conviction. But the law was the law, and only the courts "speak" the law.

The PRD challenged this ruling in the streets, and lost. It couldn't appeal the verdict, since it had ratified the legislation denying the right to appeal, and it didn't even attempt to take it to the Inter-American Human Rights Commission or Inter-American Human Rights Court, since it would have been laughed out of both, given that domestic legislation approved by the PRD had been applied. But it did contest the verdict in the tribunal of public opinion, where a surprising number of commentators, including some legal scholars, suggested that the electoral court finding was illegal, or unfair, or ignorant of the law. López Obrador himself declared, "To hell with our institutions," and began his campaign for the 2012 elections in 2006, refusing to recognize Calderón as the elected president, and repeating incessantly that the judgment was against the law. How anyone, pundit, constitutionalist, or aspiring president, can declare an unappealable ruling illegal, when that same person, or his or her party, or his or her allies, voted for the legislation and the judges in question, is a symptom of Mexico's approach to the law. The law becomes a matter of opinion, and one opinion is as legitimate and authoritative as any other; if the law does not suit me, it is a bad law, and I don't accept it.

## Teach Your Children

Before examining what the Mexican man in the street thinks about the law, it's worth delving into what a select and crucial sector believes, since its influence on society is immense: elementary and middle school teachers. A survey was carried out in 2002 by the Este País Foundation and magazine, and it provided a trove of data on what the people who educate our children think about life in general, and about the law in particular. The first terrifying result involves values and their respective hierarchy. Having a choice of six options—honesty, respect for others, respect for the truth, tolerance for the ideas of others, solidarity, and respect for the law—respect for the law came in dead last, and in a spontaneous question, it didn't even figure. When asked what the consequences of this attitude might be, more than a third responded that middle school graduates were likely to evade norms, rules, or the law. But it gets worse.

Only 41% of Mexico's more than 1.2 million unionized public school teachers thought that the population should always obey the law; eight out of every ten were convinced, perhaps understandably, they would not be treated fairly by the justice system if they were accused of a crime they did not commit, given the system's venality. And almost half of the nation's schoolteachers would, in case they were *justifiably* stopped by a traffic cop, try to "dissuade" the policeman from giving them a ticket. The political corollary of these views, which we have already encountered, is that among teachers even more than in the case of Mexicans from all walks of life, half disapprove of the use of public force to preserve law and order, even when crimes such as forcibly occupying public buildings, holding officials hostage, or blocking highways are committed while pressing social or economic demands.[14] The teachers' union is not a model of competence or honesty, but neither is it a hotbed of radicalism. Indeed, Latin America's largest union was a mainstay of the previously existing PRI corporatist system, and a bastion of support for the new PAN-led democratic regime that was inaugurated in 2000. It is led by one of Mexico's most remarkable, controversial, and feared women political leaders, Elba Esther Gordillo, generally referred to as La Maestra (The Teacher).

She came up through the ranks of the union in the 1970s and 1980s, becoming the closest aide and mistress of the ancestral leader, Carlos Jonguitud, whom she subsequently helped defenestrate in 1989. Then president Salinas de Gortari, who wanted to carry out a cosmetic cleanup of the major public sector trade unions, supported her actively in this effort. She has ruled the organization with an iron fist ever since, in the noble tradition of other Mexican (and American, and French, and Italian, and Spanish) labor leaders such as Fidel Velázquez, for example, who dominated the entire labor movement from the late thirties until his death in 1999. Gordillo was a stalwart PRI member and figurehead, who ran and won an internal election for secretary-general of the party in 2002, and was elected congresswoman or senator on various occasions. In 2003, however, when as leader of the PRI caucus in the lower house of Congress she allied herself with PAN president Vicente Fox, and supported his attempt at major tax reform, she was expelled from the caucus and the party for the equivalent of treason.

Elba, as her friends call her, proceeded to form her own political party, composed essentially of the teachers union, which obtained almost 4% of the vote in the 2006 election, and was instrumental in Felipe Calderón's photo-finish triumph. She was rewarded with appointments of her son-in-law as deputy minister of education (for primary and middle schools), and of other aides to head the Social Security Institute for public employees, the National Lottery, and a few other minor posts. After Cuauhtémoc Cárdenas in 1987, she has led the only significant schism from the PRI, with generally modernizing, democratically inclined ideas on the political front, but with a narrow, often counterproductive educational agenda, and with a reputation for corruption and excess that follows her everywhere. In most polls, she figures as the most unpopular of the country's political leaders.

Elba Esther Gordillo is exceptionally seductive as a politician, and exceptionally loyal as a personal friend, though not always as a political one. She represents the epitome of the weakness and potential resilience of Mexican political creativity, thanks both to her horrendous reputation for corruption and her singularly modernizing and democratic views. She embodies all of the traits of the Mexican character we have discussed, and all of the realities of Mexican society we have described. According to published reports, every month, the Finance Ministry withholds 1.2 million teachers' union dues before transferring their wages to state governments who actually pay the teachers; those monies are deposited directly into the union leadership's accounts, accountable only to the National Executive Committee, which is in turn accountable only to Gordillo. According to some calculations—the government refuses to publish the exact figures—this represents approximately $10 million per month, or a bit more than $100 million per year. This is her kitty. Other published reports explain how Gordillo obtained a great margin of discretion to manage the union's quotas, and how she dispenses it with exquisite magnanimity and cold calculation.[15] And it is widely believed by public opinion that she dips into it for her own expenses, which are not trifling: several houses and penthouses in Mexico City and its surroundings, a reportedly luxurious home in San Diego, handbags women on Park Avenue would die for, and one, two, or three private jets (owned or leased by the union), depending on her needs at any one time.

She is unjustly held responsible by most Mexicans for the pathetic state of the country's education—this was the case before she took over the leadership, and no minister of education since 1989 has seriously attempted to subdue her—but at the same time remains the only fulcrum on which an educational Archimedes could conceivably lean on to transform that frighteningly mediocre education. She can charm the pants or the skirt off any interlocutor she encounters, and infinitely exasperates her closest friends through her informality, her chaotic work style, and her incredible lack of punctuality. By the end of a day, she has accumulated tardiness of well over a couple of hours, which even by Mexican standards is pushing it. She can be soft and caring with her grandchildren and "her teachers," ferociously arrogant with subordinates, and ruthless with adversaries.

Gordillo finds herself in the twilight of her power and relevance, and will probably be remembered far more for her vices and the damage she wrought than for the pluralism and modernity she brought to the union, or for sporadically but undeniably striving to further indispensable political and economic reforms in the country. If subservience to monopolies has to be banished to the historical dustbin in order for the country to progress, the teachers union and Gordillo should probably lead the way, followed by many others, be they union leaders, tycoons, or bureaucrats. But no one can countenance the incredible disrespect for the law that the nation's teachers profess without concluding that the same disregard in society as a whole is somehow their responsibility, and their own neglect for the law is somehow *her* responsibility. She has run the union for two decades now, and its drawbacks and guilt are hers too.

## Why Should I Respect the Law?

If this attitude is unmistakable among teachers, it is just as evident among Mexicans at large, although it is often contradictory. Mexicans generally believe (5 on a scale of 1 to 10) that the government doesn't respect the law, that "people" don't respect the law (5.6 on the same scale), but that they themselves, that is those polled, do (7.2 on the scale). So who are the Mexicans that don't respect the law? The others, obviously; not me! But on the question of respect for the law, the most damning and revealing numbers emerge in a series of polls carried out by the Ministry of the Interior between 2001 and 2008. In the first year, to the question "Do you think *el pueblo* [the people] should obey laws even if they are *injustas* [unfair or unjust]?," 71% said no; to the query "Can the people disobey the law if it is *injusta*?," an astounding 58% said yes. In subsequent polls (2003, 2005, and 2008), the answers to analogous queries were similar. In late 2009 to the question "If a law affects you or seems unjust to you, what do you do?," 77% said: "I will obey it even though I don't like it," but 18% said "I will not obey it and will not follow it." This is a direct reflection of the trait we detected among teachers, and which was quantified as far back as 1993 among Mexicans in general, regarding the priority they attach to the rule of law: "Mexicans would prefer to live with a minimum of laws, believing they are a necessary evil."[16]

This view of the world and of law and justice is inextricably linked to corruption. Mexicans are obviously not congenitally corrupt, nor are they "culturally corrupt," victims of a national character that will accompany them until their deaths as individuals and as a society. Rather, if the law doesn't work and is meant to be neglected, the only solution for infinite challenges in everyday life, work, business, education, academia, family structures, and government is corruption. Corruption doesn't breed disrespect for the law. It is the low hierarchy of the law, the dysfunctional nature of the system, and the emphasis on the need for laws to be "fair" in order to be respected that breeds corruption. The two aspects become mutually reinforcing, however: corruption undermines an already defective justice system, and generates greater skepticism about the law, which becomes even more despised as it is increasingly considered corrupt.

This has led Mexico to be perceived as the epitome of Latin American corruption—which is saying a lot—not only by others, but by Mexicans themselves. In a series of polls taken in 2006–08 across the hemisphere, Mexico appears as the second most corrupt country in the Americas, after Haiti, and just ahead of Bolivia, in terms of so-called victimization, that is, people who offered a bribe, or were forced to pay a bribe at least once during the last year (the percentage was 37%; the least corrupt country was Chile, with 9%). Mexico's rank improved slightly in 2008, becoming "only" the third most corrupt society in terms of victimization, with 30%, compared to Uruguay, the lowest, with 9%. Even Brazil placed better, with only 11.5% of its people having been victims of corruption. A Pew Global Attitudes Project poll carried out in 2009 in Mexico provided a similar result. To the question "How often have you had to do a favor, make a gift, or offer a bribe to a government official in order to obtain services or a document that the government is supposed to provide?" the answer ranged from 38% in 2002, to 31% in early 2007, to 34% in spring 2009.[17]

As far as the view of graft among public officials is concerned (a far more subjective notion), Mexico fares somewhat better, placing halfway between the worst (Jamaica, Argentina, Guatemala) and the "best," Canada, the United States, Uruguay, and Chile. According to the experts responsible for the poll, the inconsistency between the percentages of victimization and perception of corruption in the case of Mexico may be due to the fact "that everyday, petty corruption in Mexico is greater than systemic corruption," although scandals in the media about corruption (often false but always strident) make this statement dubious; another explanation may lie in the different amounts of money involved. Neither victimization nor perception of corruption, however, has dropped significantly since the advent of representative democracy in Mexico, as many people expected. Corruption was part and parcel of the PRI system of old, but it was Mexican before it was priísta, and its origins lay in the ancestral contempt for the law.

This assessment becomes even more robust when we break down the numbers by population groups, and no longer just analyze them in the aggregate. According to the multiple regression exercises carried out by the pollsters and statisticians, women have a lesser propensity than men to engage in bribery, younger people are more susceptible to be victims of corruption ("shakedowns" if one prefers), and most surprisingly, the higher the educational level of the cohort under study, the more probable that they will fall prey to, or engage actively in, corrupt acts. Out of every ten Mexicans who confess to having been victims of corruption, four have obtained a higher education (college and high school) degree, and three have completed middle school.[18] The reason

for this paradox seems apparent, yet counterintuitive: the more education, the greater the disposable income available for bribes and graft.
Similarly, higher education groups are more likely to be singled out as
targets of corruption by the authorities; and since we saw that there is
nothing in Mexican education that dissuades people from engaging in
these practices, they do.

## Corruption Forever?

Most Mexicans seem persuaded that the age-old corruption in their
midst will never come to an end, although simultaneously they believe
that other countries are, in the final analysis, just as corrupt. There is a
deep ambivalence in our attitude toward corruption, in that everyone
engages in it one way or another; everyone knows that given the disregard for the law, there is often no choice but to engage in it; everyone
knows that it is a regressive tax, since only those who have money can
*billetear* (pay off or bribe) others, whereas those who lack money, by
definition, cannot resort to such subterfuges to attain their objectives,
and therefore are less likely to achieve them. Most everyone also knows
that what the specialists refer to as systemic corruption has diminished
in Mexico over the last fifteen years, not only thanks to a series of legal
and administrative restrictions, but due to the nature of democratic
governance. It is much harder to rip off the state with a powerful,
opposition-run Congress, a free press, and international treaties and
contracts constraining domestic leeway, even if high-level officials were
equally wont to engage in illicit activities. If in addition, for genera-
tional, social, and economic reasons, they are less disposed to do so
overall, big-time graft will inevitably decline. It has. The fortunes accumulated in the forties, fifties, sixties, and even the seventies by cabinet
secretaries, presidential staff members, governors, and heads of state-
run enterprises are now almost impossible to assemble on that scale,
although every now and then cases occur. There is a link between more
democratic governance and less corruption, though not an automatic,
immediate, and sufficient one. It is much more complicated to steal,
and even more difficult to avoid detection.

The downside consists in the persistent and thriving varieties of corruption, now much more visible and resented than before. More visible

because of sunshine: Congress, the press, the opposition, and foreign observers can see what was heretofore invisible; more resented, because an open, democratic, middle-class society is more easily scandalized or outraged than a traditional, closed one that frequently resigned itself to its fate. Daily-life corruption—the traffic cop on the corner, the bureaucrat at the motor vehicle division, the health inspector at the restaurant, the *ejido* commissioner in the village, the building permit office at city hall, the teachers union promotion officer, the municipal policeman supervising street peddling—is not much different from the sixties. Yes, young people are worried about getting caught DUI at night in Mexico City, because there are far more stringent regulations and checkpoints every weekend; but when I was a teenager, we were quite terrified of driving a motor scooter, or later a car, without a license.

Likewise, one will not necessarily meet many more people today than half a century ago who refuse to "find another solution," to "fix things," to *arreglarse* (settle manners differently). They existed then and now, but up to a point they are either heroes or fanatics, outliers not only because everyone else engages in everyday, petty corruption, but because the system is based upon it. There is a huge cost to being honest in Mexico at the street level, in daily life. The attitude most Mexicans adopt lies in going with the flow, whether this means, for the opulent, remodeling a home without a permit, purchasing pirated movies at the corner market, having luggage brought in by bodyguards at the airport, or obtaining related loans at a bank they own shares of (witness the bank collapse scandal of 1995), or, for the poor, paying off a school official to ensure their son or daughter passes their exam, or a union official for a permanent job, or the municipal authorities to sell goods on the street. Everyone would prefer it to be otherwise, since the cost this entails for the country is obvious and immense, but no one can afford to be the first to break definitively with the pattern. Hence, the perpetuation of these mechanisms since time immemorial.

To all of this we must add an additional factor, which is not new, but that is now more ostensible than before: the corruption wrought by organized crime, and Mexico's approach toward this type of perversion of the public trust. Drug cartels, kidnapping gangs, and organized holdup and car theft groups have belonged to the landscape for decades, and it is uncertain whether they are more powerful, ruthless, and violent than in years gone by. For its own political reasons, the Calderón government portrayed them, and the state of affairs, during his term as part of a general breakdown of law and order, but neither the country's citizens nor its history corroborates this perspective.

During the 2006 presidential campaign, none of the candidates made crime busting a central or even secondary feature of their platforms and barnstorming; similarly, the public and the media ignored them. There was a perception of increased insecurity in Mexico during the second half of 2006, as the outgoing administration loosened its grip on the country, but the data for all of those years—from the mid-1990s to 2006—tend to show that homicides, kidnappings, holdups, and petty crime were all on a downward slope. The cruelty of some gangland murders was gruesome and shocking—beheadings, torture—but the spectacular aspects of this violence belied the numbers involved. What had become increasingly true, since the later years of the previous decade, was that Mexicans were learning a great deal more about the potency and reach of the major drug cartels in their country, thanks to the media and the political system. Their reaction to these phenomena was also becoming more vocal, though not substantively different. The traditional approach of looking the other way, however, had ceased to be that easy, or indeed possible at all, and this placed Mexican society in quite a pickle.

Most polls show that the country's inhabitants support what the government calls its war on drugs, but doubt it can be won. Mexicans prefer combating the cartels, but do not wish to pay too high a cost for doing so; a majority approve of the use of the military in the war on drugs, but not in their backyard, and voice concerns about human rights violations. Society deplores insecurity and petty crime, but does not necessarily blame organized crime for these ills. And most Mexicans are understanding, if not sympathetic, to the plight of their compatriots in the police, the military, and low-level government offices when they are offered the choice of *plata o plomo* (money or death).

If all of this sounds highly contradictory, it is. Ultimately, Mexicans continue to believe, with some truth, that their country and government are carrying the United States' water. Mexicans see no good reason why they should not allow drugs to flow north, thus evading the price of a war that Americans do not wish to wage on their own soil, particularly in the case of cocaine, which Mexico does not produce.

At the same time there is a widespread feeling that the drug business has for decades infiltrated all levels of public administration, as well as the political and now electoral arena. The nation's citizens fear and repudiate this state of affairs, but are nonetheless resigned to it, since "all politicians are always corrupt" and drugs are just another manifestation of this ancient drama. They suspect that the "real" drug kingpins remain free and protected, and will continue to do so, as the impunity that reigns supreme in the rest of the judicial system applies equally to them. Corruption, the absence of the rule of law, and impunity stemming from the drug trade are not seen as something different from the same vices in other domains. If anything, Mexicans suppose that the abstract ills came first, and their specific manifestations—drugs, crime, the corruption of the PRI, the incompetence of the PAN—arrived later. They may nostalgically and inaccurately regret the PRI past, thinking that during its regime these ills were under control, and that, in exchange for corruption, they received bountiful benefits: subsidies, public works, jobs, and a certain sense of security. They long for that era, having nonetheless fought for its conclusion and embraced the delights of democratic disorder. On drugs as on so many other issues, Mexicans want to smoke their joint and have it too.

The drug plague affects Mexico in many ways, but perhaps one is the most worrisome and poisonous. It has widened the traditional and abysmal gap between the law and reality. Simulation has been a mainstay of the Mexican way of life for centuries, and the status of organized crime today is nothing more than the freshest expression of this age-old sin. Making believe that drug consumption in the U.S. is illegal (when in fact it is increasingly tolerated), that trafficking in Mexico is strictly illegal (when it has been occurring for decades), that illegal arms smuggling from the U.S. is new (when it dates back to the middle of the nineteenth century), and that it is not in Mexico's interests to receive between $9 and $39 billion for its drug exports every year (making this probably our first source of hard currency, above oil, tourism, or remittances) are all examples of a profound hypocrisy that broadens the chasm between the law and reality. The United States bans illegal immigration, prostitution, drug consumption, and gunrunning, and still suffers from these ills, but Americans do not have to construct a functioning legal system today. They have one already. We don't, and we must build ourselves one, but an excess of simulation renders this task more laborious, or frankly impossible.

Which leads to our next point: Mexico's traditional views of the law and corruption will no longer do today and, in fact, constitute an insurmountable obstacle to the country's progress. As we shall now attempt to show, acquiescence to corruption, impunity, disrespect for the law, simulation, and drafting laws that can never be abided are tantamount to perpetuating the absence of the rule of law. Mexico has no way out of its drug wars or tax take travails, of its low investment rates and informal economy, unless it changes its attitudes toward the law. This is not occurring.

CHAPTER 8

# The Law of the Land, or the
# Land of the Law?

Mexico's lawlessness, corruption, and impunity are not a product of spontaneous combustion. Nor were they always totally dysfunctional to the country's way of life and progress. The origins of these flaws are known, and their dire consequences were touched upon in the previous chapter. What we must concentrate on now are the specifics of those consequences, and how the attitude responsible for the lawlessness, corruption, and impunity must now change. Short of this attitudinal transformation, all of Mexico's judicial, governmental, and economic reforms will continue to fall short of expectations, and the country will have no choice but to muddle through, something at which it has become quite an expert since 1982.

There are various effects wrought by venality, impunity, and disrespect for the law that have left a devastating trail through Mexican society. The national character traits behind these flaws directly contradict any solution to the following four of the country's chief challenges.

The first involves what has unfortunately become Mexico's trademark over the past few years, and that has stigmatized the country abroad and bloodied it domestically: organized crime, narcotics trafficking, and the failed war on drugs unleashed in 2006. Mexico was not an especially violent country before 2006, and indeed, homicides, kidnappings, holdups, and petty crime in general had been diminishing over the previous fifteen years. But the overall equation has changed, and for one reason or another, the absence of the rule of law in this regard has become a crucial problem for the nation.

The second challenge is Mexico's informal economy—a decimating plague. According to some estimates, more than half of the country's economic activity takes place underground: it is off the books, illegal, on occasion prosperous, and always chaotic. Its ramifications range from the classic street peddler to the meager property tax take; its magnitude dwarfs any other aspect of national illegality, and undermines the credibility of any combat on other fronts.

The third challenge stemming from the dismissal of the law and the acceptance of corruption can be found in the vicious cycle that takes us back to the very beginning of these pages. Mexican society is highly individualistic, because civil society is so weak. Civil society, in turn, is as disorganized and impotent as it is partly because citizens have never felt that they can influence events of any sort: at large, or in their neighborhood, their children's schools, or their local clinic. In other words, they are citizens in name only. And this reluctance to assume political or social responsibility springs from the corruption, lawlessness, and impunity that have bred such a degree of cynicism in society. Mexican civil society will never organize itself until the country's attitude toward the law changes.

Finally, and from a different perspective, modifying the nation's perceptions of the law, and creating a lasting, broad-based respect for it, could be one of the unifying features of the future landscape. Today, Mexico has splendidly reemerged as a radically diverse place. It traditionally was so, even before the Conquest, then assumed the mantle of uniformity for most of the twentieth century, and is now a mosaic where each part enriches the others and the whole. The single most important factor of unity from the middle of the last century—the sense of a shared, common history—is now either fading, or has become counterproductive. What can take its place, knowing that the substitute must be less artificial and more constructive than before? The rule of law, perhaps.

## Drug Wars

The best way to begin is with a quick description of Mexico's greatest self-inflicted dilemma in recent years: its bloody, strident, and unwinnable war of choice on drugs. Some facts are in order. Mexico is a producer of poppy and hence heroin, of marijuana and methamphet-

amines; cocaine is foreign, since for climatic and topographical reasons
coca leaf does not grow there. Mexico's role in the cocaine trade has
been, since the mid-eighties, that of a conduit for shipments from
Colombia, Peru, and Bolivia, where all of the world's powder is produced, to the United States. Mexico remains a tiny consumer of drugs
in comparison to wealthier countries, or to the rest of Latin America.
There is some dispute about whether consumption has increased or
remained stable over the past fifteen years, but no one questions its
scant absolute dimensions. The National Addiction Surveys showed
that between 2002 and 2008 the number of drug addicts in Mexico
rose from 307,000 to 465,000—a 50% increase in six years, but barely
the equivalent of 25,000 additional addicts each year, in a nation of 112
million. The percentage of the population considered addicted is
0.4%; in the U.S. it is above 3%.[1] There are many other statistics we
have quoted elsewhere in this regard, but a more credible source might
be Mexico's former commissioner to the United Nations Office on
Drugs and Crime mission in Vienna:

> Mexico entered the consumer market late, and thus its accumu-
> lated incidence of drug consumption is minor. In this late arrival
> cocaine abuse stands out, although it is still considerably lower
> than in the United States. . . . Drug consumption shows a trend
> toward growth. The consumption of any drug (once in a life-
> time) rose from 4.1% in 2002 to 5.2% in 2008; the largest growth
> was for cocaine, which grew from 1.2% to 2.4%. We found
> no increase in hallucinogens or inhalants, and a small jump
> in methamphetamines (from 0.1% in 2002 to 0.5% in 2008).
> For every drug user in 1988, there were two in 2008, marijuana
> being the drug of choice, with 1.6 users in 2008 for every user in
> 1988.[2]

In other words, for the drug of choice, there was a growth rate of
less than 2% per year between 1988 and 2008; given a yearly population
increase of about 1.5% during that period, the rise is practically negligible. The same is true for incidence of drug use (at least once in a lifetime) and prevalence (once in the last year): Mexico's numbers are far
below those of the United States, and of countries like El Salvador,
Argentina, and Chile. As the Mexican middle class expands, these per-

centages will grow, though they will still not justify a major campaign against abuse. The oft-repeated notion that once the Colombian cartels began to operate through Mexico, and started paying their local colleagues in kind, leaping rapidly to a national consumer boom, is simply not borne out by the government's numbers, or by the United Nations' statistics, or by the market. The price differential between unloading a kilo of cocaine in Mexico and doing so on the street in New York remains overwhelming. The ratio is more than eight to one.

For all practical purposes, drugs produced in—or shipped through—Mexico all proceed to the United States. That's the market, not the Mexican *jeunesse dorée*, or the poorer kids in the large city slums, or even the police and soldiers who have smoked marijuana at least since the Revolution of 1910. One of the hit songs of that time was "*La cucaracha*," an old Spanish tune, to which new lyrics were added in view of the circumstances, and which many Americans might recognize. It referred directly to Victoriano Huerta, the hard-drinking, pot-smoking military dictator who assassinated Madero in 1913, and was himself overthrown in 1915: "*La cucaracha, la cucaracha, ya no quiere caminar, porque no tiene, porque no tiene, mariguana que fumar*" ("The cockroach [Huerta] doesn't want to walk anymore, because he has no more marijuana to smoke").

From Huerta to contemporary teenagers, all of the above-mentioned segments of society, as everywhere, do abuse illicit substances. But their market is irrelevant compared to the hundred million Americans who confess to smoking a joint (inhaled or not) at least once in their life, or to the 10 million hard-drug addicts in the U.S., or to the 30 million U.S. citizens who acknowledge having taken a puff during the previous month.

Violence and corruption are generally and accurately associated with the drug trade. Yet there are violent countries where the trade is still minor (principally Central America, parts of Brazil, and Paraguay, just to mention Latin America), and there are nations where drugs do not in themselves entail violence: poppy and heroin in Afghanistan, coca leaf in Bolivia, hashish in Morocco, marijuana in Mendocino County, California, where probably half of the grass consumed in the U.S. is now cultivated.

American demand for drugs, and the role of the United States as a purveyor of weapons and precursor chemicals, are important factors in

Mexico's travails, but they are neither new, nor likely to change. The United States, unlike what the Calderón administration (and to some extent Hillary Clinton) claimed, has in fact admitted for many years that its demand for drugs is partly responsible for the supply originating in Latin America. Witness a brief series of statements made by American presidents over the past forty years. Richard Nixon in 1971: "We must now candidly recognize that the deliberate procedures embodied in present efforts to control drug abuse are not sufficient." Gerald Ford, in 1976: "Drug abuse is one of the most serious and tragic problems in this country. . . . The cost of drug abuse to this nation is staggering." Jimmy Carter, in 1978: "This administration recognizes that drug problems cannot be solved unilaterally but require concerted action by the world community. Drug abuse is exacting an ever greater toll on the citizens of developed and developing countries." Ronald Reagan, in 1983: "Drug abuse in the United States continues to be a major threat to the future of our nation." And in response to a question in 1988: "Q. President [Miguel] de la Madrid [of Mexico] says that demand is the big problem with this drug thing. Reagan: Always has been." And perhaps most eloquently, again in 1988: "The casual [U.S.] user cannot morally escape responsibility for the action of drug traffickers and dealings. I'm saying that if you are a casual drug user you are an accomplice to murder. . . . Thanks to the efforts of Nancy [Reagan's] Just Say No campaign, Americans are understanding that the permanent way to end the drug menace is to deny the drug pusher his market—to stop demand." And Reagan's successor, George H. W. Bush, in 1989: "Americans cannot blame the Andean nations for our voracious appetite for drugs. Ultimately the solution to the United States drug problem lies within our borders . . . stepped-up enforcement, but education and treatment as well. But you and I agree with the courageous Virgilio Barco [then president of Colombia], who said that if Americans use cocaine, then Americans are paying for murder. . . . As long as there are Americans willing to buy drugs, there will be people willing to sell drugs, and people willing to kill as a cost of doing business. There's a connection between the suppliers and . . . weekend users that can never be forgotten." His son George W. Bush in Mérida, in 2007: "I made it very clear to the president [Calderón] that I recognize the United States has a responsibility in the fight against drugs. And one major responsibility is to encourage people to use less drugs." So Hillary Clinton was not making a dramatic new admission when she declared in Guatemala in 2010 that "the United States under the Obama administration recognizes and accepts its share of responsibility for the problems posed by drug trafficking in this region. . . . The demand in the large market in the United States drives the drug trade. We know that we are part of the problem," or when she categorized U.S. demand for drugs as "insatiable."[3]

Yet despite minor ups and downs, American consumption has remained more or less constant over forty years. This was the case despite Carter's attempt to liberalize incarceration criteria and Obama's "nonapplication" of federal anti-marijuana laws in states that legalize it, medically or otherwise, or Nancy Reagan's "Just Say No" campaign and George W. Bush's born-again moralism. The type of drug varies— marijuana in the sixties, the seventies, and the first decade of this century, crack and cocaine in the eighties and nineties, crystal meth and other designer drugs after 2000—but overall demand remains essentially stable. American society, under conservative Republican presidents or moderate and liberal Democrats, simply does not feel that a major effort on this score is necessary or desirable. The crusade is not attractive from a budgetary or a civil liberties perspective; if anything, since 2000 the trend seems to be the opposite. While the pros and cons of demand and harm reduction, of hyper-penalization and decriminalization of drugs in Mexico and the United States, began to be discussed earlier this century, a major campaign to reduce consumption in the United States is still pending. And will remain so. Mexico's traditional lament that it's the Americans' fault is partly true, but vain.

This is no less true with arms trafficking. Even if the United States were to repeal the Second Amendment (the right to bear arms) and/or reinstate the Assault Weapons Ban that expired in 2004, it remains unclear that this would eliminate the supply of arms to Mexico's organized crime groups. It might make procuring weapons more difficult and expensive, but it is hard to believe that the huge number of rogue gunrunners and arms manufacturers in the world would not fill the void. Since no legislative initiative is on this score expected from the United States anyway, it is a moot question.

With this background in mind, it is evident that Mexican attitudes toward impunity and the rule of law stand in the way of the policy changes needed to remedy this state of affairs. The first turns on the extent of the state's control of the country. Traditionally, the Mexican state has ceded small or broad swaths of its territory to local *caciques*, student groups, squatters, and self-designated guerrillas. With time, patience, and sporadic bursts of repression, the state would eventually reclaim those forsaken spaces, although others would soon emerge. The most recent and newsworthy example was the Chiapas uprising in 1994–95. The Salinas and Zedillo administrations, through negotiations and a massive army presence, forced the Zapatistas to retrench to their jungle bastions, but then left them alone. Subcomandante Marcos's minions charged fees and tolls to enter their "liberated" zones, checking and shaking down every visitor, delivering credentials to some and denying them to others, and held sway over this part of the territory. The Mexican military could have reconquered it overnight, but Salinas, Zedillo, and, later, Fox, and indeed even Calderón, chose not to do so. They preferred to cohabit with the indigenous peoples' putative army indefinitely.

The same is true of other cities, villages, and regions in the rest of Mexico, but unlike in Chiapas, the "occupiers" have been either local political bosses who made themselves useful to the state or federal authorities or, more recently, slum or drug lords, not guerrilla heartthrobs. This has been a fact of life for decades in Guerrero (where some may recall how in the sixties and seventies Acapulco Gold was cultivated almost freely), Sinaloa, Durango, and Chihuahua. There were immense landholdings or communities where the local and state police would not venture, and where the army only penetrated in the context of a highly publicized, one-time-only operation. These arrangements worked well for years, then became unsustainable in a democracy, and led Felipe Calderón to unleash a lengthy and unwinnable war on drugs, through which he sought to restore the rule of law and recover the chunks of national territory supposedly taken over by the cartels.

In a sense, Calderón tried, possibly in good faith, to accomplish what the political parties did with gender equality: impose by force the application of laws that could not be fulfilled, insinuating nonetheless that a deal could be struck once the balance of power between the state and the cartels had attained a new equilibrium. Instead of changing the laws and adapting them to reality, the Mexican president, like all his predecessors, sought to alter reality and adapt it to the law, knowing full well that this was impossible and counterproductive. It would add only one more feather to the cap of simulation and disrespect for the law. As late as mid-2010, there were more areas of the country exempt from central state control than when the war began in late 2006, more cities where the drug lords acted in the light of day, more highways and neighborhoods where the police refused to enter or transit, and where the army could only appear briefly and superficially. Mexico has proved unable to recuperate the command and control of previously lost zones, despite more than 34,000 deaths between 2007 and 2010, a terribly tarnished image abroad, and a burgeoning number of human rights violations by the police and the military, all of which have aggravated the cynicism of society. The only imaginable, long-term solution to this challenge, with all its complexities and relativities, implies a radical transformation of Mexico's relation to the law.*

## Violence, Mérida, and a National Police

Another challenge is violence itself. Mexico does suffer, and has for decades, from drug-originated, indiscriminate violence, the absence of law and order, and the extreme venality of local police and authorities. This has been true traditionally in border states such as Tamaulipas, Chihuahua, and Baja California, as well as in off-border, drug-producing states like Sinaloa, Durango, Michoacán, and Guerrero. The same calamities affect localities that have become crossroads or clearinghouses for the drug business, without sharing a border with the

---

* There is at least theoretically an alternative: a Mexican equivalent of Plan Colombia, that is, a massive injection of U.S. money, advisors, instructors, hardware, and software over a sustained period of time. At least through 2010, this seemed inconceivable on both sides of the border, but Mexican attitudes were changing. In a poll carried out by GAUSSC in late 2009, given the option of choosing between the two following statements: (A) "To fight drug traffickers more effectively, the army *does* need the help of the United States military"; and (B) "To fight drug traffickers more effectively the army *does not* need the help of the United States military," 47% chose A and 36% chose B. In another poll taken in March 2009, to the question "Would you agree to the United States' sending troops to fight drug traffickers," an astonishing 40% said yes; in 2007, 22% had said yes to the same question, posed by the same pollster. "National Survey," GAUSSC, Mexico City, December 2009. "50% 'Mi opinión sobre la Sra. Clinton mejoró con su visita a México.' 57% 'Sobre el narcotráfico dijo lo mismo que dijeron otros gobiernos,'" Demotecnia, Mexico City, March 2009.

United States or being significant producers. They all experience violent death, homicide, and kidnapping statistics comparable to countries such as Colombia, El Salvador, Brazil, Venezuela, and Guatemala,
the most violent societies in Latin America. But these realities must be
placed in context, in order to understand the real magnitude of Mexico's challenge in its war on drugs.

The national average of crime and violence reached an all-time low
in 2007, at 9.7 yearly, willful homicides per 100,000 inhabitants, and
climbed up to 14.7 in 2009, as a result of President Calderón's war. This
is still much lower than in the above-mentioned countries (El Salvador
has 49, Venezuela 48, Guatemala 43, Brazil 39, Colombia 36), although
of course, as already stated, higher than the United States and Europe.[4]
The average masks big gaps, however, between states and regions.
Sinaloa and Chihuahua have the highest indices, with 43 and 42 homicides per 100,000 inhabitants; Guerrero, Durango, and Baja California
range from 27 to 30.[5] These numbers, as well as the newspaper head-
lines and local nightly news on television, make Prohibition-era
Chicago look like an affluent suburb of Zurich or Geneva. But there
are large areas of the country where crime and insecurity are almost
unheard of. Mérida, Yucatán, is one of those cities, with fewer than 2
willful homicides a year per 100,000 inhabitants, that is, nearly one-
sixth the national average, and twenty times less than Sinaloa.

The capital of Yucatán is an elegant, melting-pot city of approximately 700,000 inhabitants, although the metropolitan area amounts
to almost a million, making it the country's twelfth largest.[6] The nearby
extraordinary archaeological ruins of Chichén Itzá and Uxmal bear
witness to the sophistication and wealth of the long-lost, enigmatic
Mayan civilization of more than one thousand years ago that its inhabitants descend from. Mérida was founded in 1542, just twenty years
after the fall of Tenochtitlán, and later came to be known as "la Ciudad
Blanca"—the White City—nominally because of the whitewashed
French, fin de siècle mansions of Paseo de Montejo, named after its first
Spanish ruler, Francisco de Montejo y León. But it also carried the title
because it was, and partly remains, a somewhat racist community, in a
somewhat racist country.

During the prosperous years of the *henequén* or hemp boom at the
turn of the twentieth century, the aristocratic landowners who built
those mansions, importing stained glass windows and wooden stair-

cases from Paris, treated their Mayan laborers pretty much the same way plantation owners treated their slaves before the Civil War: like slaves.* The Mayans revolted several times, as early as the middle of the nineteenth century, in the infamous Caste War of 1847–53, and again at the end of the nineteenth century, under the banner of indigenous rights and the *cruz parlante* or Talking Cross. The struggles always involved preserving their syncretic religion, their dignity and pride, their language and their customs. Each insurrection was dealt with brutally by central Mexico, which was unwilling and uninterested in constructing any kind of link between the rest of the nation and the Yucatán Peninsula. Until 1898, just to visit the capital of the country, one had to travel by ferry from the Gulf port of Progreso to New Orleans or Havana, and then back to Veracruz and by train to Mexico City. The rail link to Campeche at the end of the nineteenth century stayed cut off from Coatzacoalcos in Veracruz and the rest of the country until the 1950s.[7]

Mérida is to a considerable extent Yucatán. Fifty percent of the state's inhabitants live in the larger conurbation, which today includes a thriving city devoted to tourism, *maquiladoras,* the state bureaucracy, and universities, as well as trade with the United States from Progreso.[8] But it is a town where, in addition to the intrinsic beauty of its architecture, layout, and vegetation, one can actually enjoy these marvelous attractions, stroll the streets as late as one likes (generally a good idea, given the midday heat) without the slightest fear of being held up or harassed, let alone murdered, raped, or beheaded, as occurs all too often in certain other Mexican communities. Mérida is also, together with Oaxaca, the seat of Mexico's finest cuisine.

It will one day turn into a major retirement area for graying American baby boomers, if Roberto Hernández is to be believed. He is one of Mexico's wealthiest businessmen, who sold the country's largest bank to Citigroup in 2001 for $12 billion, and became a great benefactor of the region. But this will happen only if Mérida remains safe and

---

* As in the comments of U.S. consul G. B. McGoogan in *Progreso,* writing on March 19, 1911: "The peons on the large haciendas are really chattels of the owner. Many peons are born, live and die on the same plantation. . . . The peons are paid very little, and some are treated very badly and whipped and punished in various ways. They become like enraged animals subdued by their keeper." SD 812.00/1084, U.S. Department of State, Washington, D.C.

friendly, as well as far removed from the rest of the country's drug wars. It is so for now. Two of the last three U.S. presidents have visited there (and Barack Obama will also, one day) precisely because the security arrangements are easier.

Yet its fortune does not lie in an honest, well-trained, well-equipped municipal or state police force. All of Yucatán employs only 4,626 state policemen and -women; Mérida has a bare-bones 380 town cops, since nothing but the downtown area is under municipal police jurisdiction. The city police were deemed so corrupt that until 2003 law enforcement was in state hands.[9] These state forces are as crooked, ill-prepared, and useless as the rest of the country's; the community is prosperous, but not rich; the social and economic indicators are certainly not Mexico's highest, by any means. Mayans are known as a gentle, courteous, and nonviolent people, but they have had, throughout their history, bouts of conflict, revolt, and repression. Furthermore, the city's geographic location is attractive to the drug cartels shipping their wares from Colombia. It is not far from the Gulf of Mexico, from the Mexican Caribbean, known as the Mayan Riviera, and from the border with Belize and Guatemala.

The city has elected PAN mayors for some time now, but the state has chosen only one PAN governor. The same voters seem to prefer state officials (elected for six years, and much more powerful than city officials elected only for three, without reelection) from the PRI. Its governors have tended to be traditional, ruling-party *caciques*, with deep roots in the Yucatán countryside, corrupt and mistrustful of the center, but generally running a tight ship in their state. This was not always a conservative neck of the woods; during the early 1920s, it was governed by Felipe Carrillo Puerto, immortalized, at the request of his mistress, Alma Reed, in Orozco's New School mural in New York City. Carrillo Puerto was a Socialist and modernizer who attempted to free the Mayan indigenous peoples from the servitude and indentured peonage of the *henequén* period, and was murdered in 1924 for doing so . . . like all of Mexico's revolutionary heroes. *Yucatecos*, and the inhabitants of their capital city, have always felt distant from the rest of the country, and do not necessarily regret it. Today, they could continue to flourish on their own, isolated from the other Mexico's travails, flaunting or exacerbating their regionalism.

The problem is that this city of peace coexists with vast areas of violence, corruption, impunity, and absence of state control in other regions. Variety has made it increasingly clear that Mexico's national law enforcement, crime fighting, anti-narcotics efforts can only come to fruition if the country replaces the existing, complicit, venal, and incompetent local and state police forces with a national police, along Chilean, Canadian, or Colombian lines, that would allow it to recall the armed forces back to the barracks. But states like Yucatán, together with cities like Mérida, don't appreciate the idea. Nor do Mexicans in general: it would be anathema for them and their attitude toward the law to centralize the police and establish a single, national criminal code whereby every crime is a federal one. This would bestow upon the central state the possibility and capability of dispatching army troops for long periods of time to certain localities, declaring the equivalent of a state of siege, while the national police insures the security of the rest of the nation. How can a society that doesn't believe in the law admit radical change and on occasion extreme measures to enforce the law, especially if its "fairness" is not apparent to everyone?

Every Mexican president faces the same dilemma of choosing between the military and the police when he takes office. Upon arrival, he concludes that his predecessor bequeathed him a mess, especially as regards drug enforcement, and that he has to pull back the armed forces from police work, where the man before him irresponsibly inserted them. But he soon realizes that in Mexico it's the army or nothing. There is no police worth mentioning. He subsequently decides to leave the military in charge of drug enforcement, ramping up or down the intensity of its involvement, while relaunching the construction of a national police force. Since Mexican chief executives, like those everywhere else, cannot really concentrate on two major priorities at once, the war on drugs promptly overshadows the building of the police force, and when his six years are over, he hands the same quandary over to his successor.

I was a witness to this syndrome in the year 2000, when after Vicente Fox's election I accompanied him on a visit as president-elect to Washington. The outgoing Mexican ambassador organized a splendidly attended dinner for Fox, and among the guests was U.S. "drug czar" General Barry McCaffrey. The ambassador passed on his request to have a private conversation with me right after coffee, during which, wrongly believing that I had the president-elect's ear on all matters,

McCaffrey asked me to convince him not to fulfill his campaign promise to withdraw the armed forces from drug enforcement. His reasoning was straightforward and accurate, but partial. Removing the army, he argued, would create a vacuum that no police force would be able to fill for several years, and in the meantime, the cartels would inevitably flourish. I agreed to pass on the message with my recommendation, but I thought then that McCaffrey's advice—or strong suggestion—was contradictory. We would never have a national police force if we didn't implement a military retrenchment except for rearguard, sporadic, and pinpoint operations. We are still right there.

Mexico's security and law enforcement challenges cannot be solved with the current federal, state, and municipal police institutional scaffolding, copied from the United States. The state and municipal forces, roughly 400,000 strong but broken up into 2,500 cities and towns as well as thirty-two states, are irretrievably compromised with the drug trade, kidnappers, organized crime in general, and with petty, street-corner corruption. Mauricio Fernández, the mayor of San Pedro Garza García, an affluent suburb of the northern industrial city of Monterrey and Mexico's wealthiest community, revealed during his campaign in 2009 that even the more prosperous regions in the north of the country no longer could count on their police. According to Fernández, both his predecessor as mayor, and he himself as a leading figure of his community, reached deals with the drug traffickers who lived among the mansions in the hills overlooking Monterrey. That was why there were no kidnappings or killings in the town.

Fernández and the people of San Pedro and Mérida would not be delighted if their towns fell under the jurisdiction of a national police force that would gradually take over from state and local cops. They would not easily submit to a national code that would make most serious crimes federal offenses and eliminate state criminal codes except for misdemeanors. Right now, in Mexico 93% of all crimes are nonfederal, i.e., they fall within the purview of thirty-two states' laws; and 87% of *all* crimes (period) go unreported.[10] There is obviously a link between these two facts. The townspeople of Mérida and San Pedro would in all likelihood reject a militarized police force, more similar to the Chilean Corps of Carabineros (founded in 1921) than to the Royal Canadian Mounted Police. They, and others from cities and states with low crime numbers, would say that this is someone else's problem: NIMBY, however it translates into Mayan. While some governors would go along with the idea, this is the type of drastic, long-term measure that never makes everybody happy. It can only be achieved if there is a legislative majority (two-thirds of the Congress and statehouses) or a referendum in this regard, where inevitably at most a little more than half the people will be in favor, and a little less against.

The only way to combat victoriously Mexico's crime, violence, and drugs is by unifying the fight throughout the country, and that unfortunately calls for the center imposing its will on the states, in a manner not unlike Dwight Eisenhower's sending of troops to Little Rock, Arkansas, in 1958, or the Kennedys dispatching federal marshals to various points in the Deep South in the early sixties. And this implies accepting that whether the law is just or not, whether it is harsh or not, whether one likes it or not, it is the law: *dura lex, sed lex*. But it also requires passing laws that can be applied, and that people can abide by. Channeling everything into a war on drugs when the next-door neighbor is increasingly tolerant toward drugs, or even legalizing some of them, makes it difficult to extend credibility to the law, given the already widespread skepticism. The two go together, and simultaneously fly in the face of tradition. Mexico distrusts the law, and loves laws it cannot fulfill or immediately evade: hence the classic saying, *"Hecha la ley, hecha la trampa"* ("The minute the law is written, cheating sets in"). Either the attitude changes, or the consequences will endure.

### The Informal Economy

Consequences will also persist from the most egregious violations of the rule of law in Mexico, where the state's abdication of control involves a territory far broader and more significant for millions of Mexicans than drug lords' dominions: the immense extension of the informal economy. It is not our purpose here to delve into its origins—excessive regulation, insufficient growth, poorly aligned incentives, corruption—but rather to simply state its existence and demonstrate its links to the culture of lawlessness.

By government calculations (which are more narrowly defined than other assessments), in 2009, 13% of the country's GDP was generated by the informal economy, and 12 million Mexicans, or 28% of the eco-

nomically active population, toiled in this sector, with greater percentages in certain fields (commerce, restaurants, hotels) than others (manufacturing). This is more than the number of jobs provided by tourism
(the country's largest source of employment), emigration, agriculture,
the automobile industry, or any other activity. These are levels similar to
those of Colombia and Chile, and less than in Brazil or Venezuela. But
other estimates, by well-regarded experts such as Santiago Levy, who
created Mexico's much touted Progresa/Oportunidades antipoverty
program in the 1990s, estimate that in 2006, 25.7 million of the country's roughly 42 million members of the economically active population
belonged to the informal sector—approximately 57%. He believes that
since 2008 that share has expanded. Additional calculations hold that
between a quarter and half of the country's working population finds
itself in the informal economy, which accounts for between 12% and
20% of GDP.[11]

The variations have to do with definitions. There is a tendency
among nonspecialists to equate informality with illegality; in fact the
two segments overlap, but are not identical. There are many informal
workers who are not illegal, and there are certain illegal aspects to the
economic behavior of formal workers (i.e., doctors who don't report
cash payments by their patients to the Mexican equivalent of the IRS).
Our focus is on the illegal and informal *intersection*. Formal workers
can be defined as "those working in firms licensed with the government
and conforming to tax and labor laws, including minimum wage direc-
tives, pension and health insurance benefits for employees, workplace
standards of safety, etc."; informal workers are "owners of firms which
are largely de-linked from state institutions and obligations and their
employees, who are not covered by formal labor protections." But illegality is not limited to "the violation of laws regarding social security,
firing and severance pay, and labor taxes. . . . [It includes the violation
of] laws regarding payment of income taxes, registration with municipal authorities and other dimensions of illegal behavior (for example
not abiding by health regulations) associated with informality."[12]

When the business community or rightfully enraged citizens and the
media demand that the president crack down on student demonstrators,
peasants blocking highways, workers taking over mines and plants,
criminals flouting the law . . . he almost invariably responds the following way: "I can apply the law as strictly as you like, but if you want it

across the board, I would have to start with the informal economy, where millions of Mexicans earn their livelihood. Are you sure you want me to do this?" His interlocutors' response is always the same: perhaps some other time; for now, just throw the demonstrators, protesters, squatters, drug traffickers, or what-not out of town. While some mayors, in some cities, have made progress in relocating street peddlers and diminishing the incredible variety of "squeegies" on street corners, by and large the informal economy has expanded dramatically over the past fifteen years.

Formal employment grew approximately 30% between the mid-nineties and 2010, and wages in the formal sector have increased only slightly or stagnated.* But since the country's overall population rose significantly (from 83 million in 1990 to 112 million in 2010), emigration skyrocketed, but so did the informal economy's rolls, expanding by around 50%. Herein lies an important explanation for one of Mexico's most desperate plights: the share of GDP corresponding to wages and salaries has dropped from 39% to 30% between 1980 and 2010.[13] Labor productivity has remained basically flat over these same years. But actually according to the OECD, "labor productivity growth was slightly negative between 1987 and 2007 in Mexico." Between 2002 and 2007 it grew (1.1%), but overall "growth in Mexico has relied on the accumulation of production factors rather than on rising productivity." Since more Mexicans have entered the informal sector than the formal one, and productivity in the former is much lower than in the latter, the share of rewards to labor has dropped.[14] Why is productivity in the informal sector lower? The reason is simple: educational levels, wages, productivity, and investment are lower in the labor-intensive, capital-deprived informal sector than in the formal one.

In addition, since the nineties, when the political system began moving toward democracy and greater accountability, successive governments have increased social protection for the teeming masses in the informal economy, such as health insurance and pensions, through a makeshift, patchwork system. This implied that, up to a point, one could obtain nearly the same benefits in the informal sector as in the formal one, but without paying taxes or social security. Given the

---

* According to the OECD, labor compensation per hour in the total economy went from 3.9 U.S. dollars in PPP in 1996 to 5.7 U.S. dollars in 2006, about a 2% increase per year.

choice between doing so or not, Mexicans opted for receiving free benefits, even if they were slightly inferior in quality.

But the persistence of a large portion of the nation's economic activity outside the rule of law affects more than just wages, productivity, and employment. It gets much worse. We have already seen how Mexico has the lowest tax take of any country in the OECD, and a significantly smaller one than many Latin American countries like Brazil, Chile, or even Argentina. This is largely a result of low *income* tax collection (on *indirect* and *excise* or value-added taxes, Mexico is not too far behind), but also the product of one of Mexico's most peculiar fiscal features. Property tax revenues are practically nonexistent. The country collects under 0.2% of GDP in municipal levies, less than half as much as Chile, five to six times less than Colombia, Argentina, and Brazil, and a pittance compared to the U.K. (4.2%), France (3.2%), and Spain (3%).[15] When one recalls that 1% of GDP in Mexico is roughly equal to $1 billion (GDP was around $1 trillion in 2010), the difference in absolute terms between what the country obtains from property taxes, and what it should receive, given its level of development, is over $2 billion per year. This is just one consequence of the country's informality. The causes of this very low tax take can help us understand the other damaging effects of informality.

No government can impose duties on what people don't earn, spend, or own. It will inevitably encounter serious obstacles in taxing even fully legal revenue streams, transactions, and properties. But if properties are not registered, they are not only untaxable; they cannot be used for anything else—to obtain a mortgage and start a business, to bequeath to heirs, to buy and sell, to rent and move where there are better jobs. According to Hernando de Soto's Instituto Libertad y Democracia in Peru, which has carried out similar surveys in many parts of the world, from his native Lima to Cairo, 53% of all lots in Mexican urban areas are extralegal.[16]

This means that half of the homes and occupied land in Mexico's cities emerged outside of zoning regulations, and are not therefore registered either in the municipal zoning office or the public property rolls. In other words, the base for property taxes or cadastre is so low that it is impossible for the government to collect more revenue from people who at least formally, that is, legally, do not own their home or their slice of urban soil. One can argue—and various scholars have done so—that de Soto's view of the informal sector is somewhat illusory. Many of those who receive deeds proceed immediately to take out a loan, and end up losing their property because they squandered the money or invested it in a foolish enterprise. Nonetheless, the absence of property rights in the urban areas of what used to be called the Third World is a calamitous situation.

By adding the yawning gaps between cities and states within Mexico in relation to property tax collection—where the capital hauls in twenty-eight times more per head than the poorest states (Chiapas and Oaxaca)—we attain an idea of the difficulties Mexico's informal property structure generates for its strained public finances. Ultimately, this signifies that poor cities and states remain poor, and the more prosperous become ever more affluent.

It is true that this irregularity in property rights is prevalent throughout Latin America, where de Soto has detected similar or higher rates of illegality than in Mexico. With the exception of Peru, many of the smaller countries (Panama, the Dominican Republic, El Salvador, Guatemala, Haiti) and even some larger ones (Colombia and Brazil) experience higher rates of property informality than Mexico, though we can also surmise that Mexico's census machinery is probably more accurate than those of the poorer nations. But the weakness of the rule of law in Mexico explains the large differential in the property tax take, despite the pervasiveness of informality everywhere in the region.

What can be done? In the case of illegal automobile imports and registration from the United States, the dilemma also seemed intractable, and the impact was equally grave. The government's solution was to once and for all legalize all previous informal imports, and more or less indiscriminately allow legal used-car imports of increasingly recent model years. In a similar fashion, it is likely that the only exit from the overall informal economy conundrum lies in formalizing informal Mexicans, be it in their workplace, home, automobile, health care, or any other aspect of their everyday lives. A substantial amount of progress has been made over the past decade through the construction, sale, and ownership of new housing, as we saw in Chapter 2 regarding the middle class; but the magnitude of the untitled housing universe is still mind-boggling. Similarly, the creation of a national, single-payer, unified health system, financed out of the central fiscal treasury, would remove many of the incentives for lingering in the informal sector by

bestowing benefits on every Mexican, regardless of his or her employment status. If one can obtain similar benefits without paying taxes as
paying them, it does not take a Nobel Prize in Economics to understand
that most Mexicans will prefer the former option. This national social
protection system would also reduce the benefit costs of hiring—the
equivalent of around 30% of salaries—and thus encourage formal job
creation. And if far more jobs can be created by opening up opportunities for investment in the economy, then in principle Mexico could,
sometime in the century's second decade, begin to forsake the culture of
informality it has embraced since time immemorial. But behind this
culture looms the attitude toward the law. Without a fundamental
change in this devastating character trait, it will be singularly difficult
for these policy changes to occur.

A final anecdote resides in an unscientific but revealing study of
Mexico City's infamous *peseras*, undertaken by *Reforma* in 2010. *Peseras*
are neither single pirate taxis nor official metropolitan mass transit
buses; they are a bit of both, carrying between twenty and forty passengers, and are privately and often individually owned. The driver is paid
by tickets sold, so he has a built-in incentive to speed, load cargo as
often as possible, stop as frequently as he can, disobey traffic lights and
signs. Thus with the possible exceptions of policemen, these drivers
are—justifiably—the most loathed and insulted occupants of the capital's avenues. Of 417 surveyed *peseras*, 79% circulated with their passen-
ger doors open; 38% loaded or unloaded passengers in forbidden zones;
30% suffered a "dirty" or "informal appearance"; 21% carried a forbidden fee collector or helper; 5% raced with other *peseras*, used cell
phones, or carried passengers on the stirrup or the doorstep.[17]

This is not the end of the world. Other large cities suffer from analogous public transportation disasters, with kamikaze drivers, and
potential serial killers. They are both detested and tolerated the world
over. Pirate taxis and livery vans dot Manhattan's midnight landscape;
public transportation is chaotic in communities across the Third
World. But Mexico City boasts a world-class subway system (with the
drawbacks we pointed out earlier), it receives millions of tourists every
year, it is less than one thousand miles from the U.S. border, and it
aspires to be an international cultural center, all the while cohabiting
with this extreme form of illegality, informality, and impunity. The two
cannot indefinitely coexist.

## Civil Society Again

In the same fashion, Mexican attitudes toward the law are incompatible with any further organization of civil society, or with the construction of citizenship, as opposed to remaining a country of voting but isolated individuals. We have attempted to demonstrate that Mexicans proffer a better than average attachment to democracy today, compared to their own past, to other Latin American nations, and even to some wealthier countries. But this affection is directed at a narrow definition of democracy, as presented to them in polls regarding elections, political parties, and freedoms. When one moves on to more complex and wider definitions, including "legitimacy," or values that bind citizens to public life and their community, or even to so-called social capital, things change. The devotion to democracy collides with Mexican individualism, and with the rejection of any horizontal network of solidarity, association, voluntary work, or simple organization. The country has high levels of mistrust about its institutions; it lacks a sense of political representation and shows a deep feeling of political inefficiency and intolerance, as well as a generalized detachment from the law and a strong propensity for corruption.[18]

If we explore a bit deeper, we find that as in all Latin American countries, people trust institutions such as the Church above the media, the armed forces, and political parties. More importantly, in a qualitative query about Mexicans' "satisfaction with the workings of their democracy," the country ranked next to last in the region, with just 28% of its inhabitants describing themselves as very or somewhat satisfied. Only Peru did worse, with 22%; the regional average was 44%. To the question: "Is your country governed by a few powerful groups for their own benefit, or for all the people?" (a loaded question, of course, but equally distorted for all countries), Mexico came fourth to last with 21%, the subcontinental average being 33%. Without a comparative perspective, only 23% of interviewed Mexicans said they trusted political parties, and barely one-quarter placed their trust in Congress. Two-thirds believed that "people like me have no influence over what the government does"; more than three-quarters were convinced that "politicians are not very concerned with what people like me think"; only half felt that people are equal before the law; and 65%

concurred with the idea that "politics is so complicated that people like me do not understand what happens."[19]

It is worth recalling that until the early nineties, Mexicans lacked any political, institutional democratic experience. They did not enjoy the dubious luxury of Brazil's, Colombia's, or Argentina's elite democracy from the late nineteenth century, let alone Chile's, Uruguay's, or Costa Rica's more inclusive strain. Power was never contended for at the ballot box; citizenship in the broad sense of the term was never extended to the population; accountability had always been absent, and the rule of law, at least as far as individuals were concerned, rarely existed. So in fact, Mexicans are probably right in mistrusting authority, and in convincing themselves that any type of collective effort or associative endeavor will prove futile at best, counterproductive at worst. Yet this attitude unleashes a perpetual vicious cycle. The only way to acquire confidence in the power of civil society and the merits of associative efforts is by organizing and working along those lines; refraining from doing so—for whatever reason—strengthens the deeply ingrained skepticism of society, which in turn makes any new attempt arduous if not fruitless. The law is the only guarantee that things should work as they are supposed to; but if the attitude toward the law remains what it is, everything else will stay the same. The key to circumscribing individualism and encouraging civil society lies in subscribing to the power and the relevance of the law; otherwise, it seems almost impossible for anything else to change.

## A New Fit for Diversity

In fact, the country could discover in the rule of law the antidote to another of its anachronisms: the previous and persistent sublimation of its cultural, ethnic, political, religious, and geographical diversity, and the need to construct an innovative mixture of multiplicity for a new era. Mexico has been, since well before the Conquest, an incredibly diverse place. When the Spanish arrived, more than two hundred languages or dialects abounded, which of course was not the equivalent of two hundred cultures. According to French anthropologist Christian Duverger, the region known as Mesoamerica always combined unity and diversity, leading to its first *mestizaje*, with its multiple unifying traces of pre-Columbian civilizations and the linguistic, artistic, and cultural heterogeneity of their successive stages.[20]

The region extended, way back then, from the 21st parallel in northern Mexico all the way to northern Costa Rica, including parts of the Caribbean. It was not only a "mosaic of cultures," as it came to be superficially known, but more accurately, a site of "pluri-ethnical occupation," according to Duverger, long before the Conquest. Its fusion originated in the common consumption of corn, beans, and cocoa, the use of cotton and agave fibers for clothing, the absence of the wheel, the adoration of multiple gods, and the prevalence of stratified societies, but mainly, as Duverger says, in a shared way of "thinking about the world." It was the Nahua civilization, which over hundreds of years served as a bond between these different worlds, that eventually forged the "cultural crucible" that became Mesoamerica.[21]

The region was divided by topography, climate, and exposure (or lack of it) to the rest of the world. It was characterized by several overlapping splits—first, between the tropical zones along the coasts; the highlands, which were always the dominant geographical system; and the mountains and northern deserts. Then with time, after the Conquest, the ethnic subdivisions surfaced: light-skinned in the desert, uninhabited northern plains; *mestizo* in the highlands, indigenous in the south and Mayan areas; and African in the coastal regions. Afterward came the links with the rest of the world. Each region built its own: the islands in the Caribbean with sugar markets, the ports along the seas with international trade, the mines linked to Spain and the rest of Europe through bullion markets.

The Mexican locus of Mesoamerica only acquired the initial trappings of political unification with the Bourbon reforms toward the late eighteenth century, just before Independence, and the appearance of a self-functioning state toward the middle of the nineteenth century. Mexico's process of becoming a nation only got under way with the Porfiriato, when a single currency, a single market, a single army, and a single central authority emerged, slowly and painfully. On the eve of the Revolution, out of a total of 15 million Mexicans, 13 million spoke Spanish *and* their indigenous tongue; and the following ten years of warfare unleashed the old centrifugal forces that had been partly tamed during the Díaz dictatorship. It took another couple of decades—the twenties with Obregón and Calles, and the thirties with Calles and Cárdenas—

to rebuild and strengthen central authority, and assemble the institutions that ultimately converted Mexico into a unified nation. And it took the common, single, and simple version of history to create the ties among individuals that brought them together as a nation. Not much else did.

Without all of this, the country would not be what it is today: a middle-class society, with an incipient but vibrant democracy, an open economy, and one of the world's most thriving and multifaceted cultures. But an unintended and perverse consequence of its specific path to nation building was the suppression of much of its diversity. Despite its federalist pretensions, Mexico from the thirties onward, like before the Revolution, homogenized itself. It did so ethnically, through the *mestizo* cult; linguistically, as the token efforts at preserving indigenous languages or dialects proved futile; religiously, as the Catholic Church recovered power, in spite of its nominally legal inexistence until 1992; politically, through single-party rule, as heterogeneous as that party may have been; ideologically, as nationalism, the Revolution, land reform, and nominal anticlericalism converged in a "single thought" that crowded out other views but produced a powerful, socialized intellectual direction; and finally in economic terms, as the central state made most of the policy decisions, leaving very little to the market and regional diversity. The homogenizing drive was also partly rooted in the fear of Mexico's centrifugal tendencies being taken advantage of by the United States in the northern territories, as had occurred before.

But this was all an exercise in sweeping rubbish under the rug. In fact, Mexico's diversity never vanished, despite serious efforts at uniformity. Its challenges were not dissimilar to those facing other countries with new or acquired forms of diversity, as they seek an updated modus vivendi with the medley of regions, economic spheres, and cultures that are evident today.

In particular, Mexico must deal with the simultaneous challenge of being as richly diverse internally as ever, and possessing an immense, influential, and nearby diaspora that generates countless contradictory pressures and opportunities for Mexico, let alone the United States. It must do so without ever having been a nation of immigrants (at most it harasses Central American passers-through), and without knowing the experience of other immigrant societies. No country today has truly squared this circle of being richly diverse, having a diaspora, and flaunting a vigorous national identity, since previous arrangements have ceased to be fully relevant, and unprecedented situations still await accommodation.

Traditional European societies today struggle to come to terms with their new identities, which are often shocking to their native citizens. Among them are nations traditionally made up neither of immigrants nor emigrants, that combine national characters and identities in a strange hodgepodge of centralism and local resentments, national history, and local customs. The Spanish are Spanish to everyone who views them from abroad: a common history, a common language, religion, cuisine, and passion, bullfights and soccer, wine, and not a whole lot of hospitality. They fought the Moors into submission and final expulsion in 1492, when they also threw out the Jews and whatever Protestants might have dared to show themselves across their empire. Now, despite their desperate need for immigration to counter the lowest birth rate in Europe, if not in the entire world, they are resorting to *refoulement* on the high seas, paying foreigners to return to their homeland if they have lost their jobs (not an improbable occurrence given Spain's economic woes), and enduring some of the nastier racist incidents in Europe against Arab, African, and Ecuadoran immigrants. But viewed from within, the picture changes dramatically. Tell a Catalonian, or a Basque, or a Galician, that he or she is Spanish and the conversation quickly comes to an end. Few apparently homogeneous "old" nations suffer from centrifugal forces as powerful as those currently at work in the non-Portuguese section of the Iberian Peninsula.

The French, Germans, and British think they know who they are today, except for the mushrooming minorities of Arab, Turkish, Pakistani, and East Indian citizens (even in jus sanguinis Germany), who scarcely identify with "*nos ancêtres les Gaulois,*" Siegfried, or the Battle of Hastings. These societies supposed they had resolved such issues a long time ago; to a certain extent, they had. But the combination of building the European Union, globalization, and a mass influx of immigrants from radically different origins—religious, linguistic, ethnic, and political—has upset their apple cart. The third-generation French youth of long-removed Arab origins who burn cars in the *banlieues* of Paris and Lyon are outraged because they do not feel French and are not treated as French, yet they are, by all legal definitions, French. The other French on occasion respond, and often do, that the Beurs and the *hajib*-scarf-wearing female high school students may be legally French, but they lack the national character. Perhaps this is why French president Nicolas Sarkozy seemed so intent in 2009 on launching his national debate on rediscovering that character, by asking everyone in his country what it meant to "be French."*

China may have come to terms with these issues, after enormous efforts and sacrifices. With all its murderous crimes and excesses, Mao's revolution erected a nation and a national identity, but did so from solid preexisting foundations. More than 91% of the people of China are Han, and the country's ethnic, religious, or linguistic minorities (granted, upwards of 100 million individuals) are to be found, literally, on the margins of the Han nucleus of the country: on its borders with the rest of the world.[22] There are no immigrants, and the significant number of emigrants have their cultural and social status so clearly resolved that they are known not by where they went (sometimes generations ago) but by where they came from: "overseas Chinese." What we might call China's ruthless national cohesion rests, then, on a brutal political regime that reveres and reinforces it, drumming into every Chinese child a potent sense of cultural and ethnic superiority, as well as an underlying ethnic uniformity.

In the long term, the current competition between China and India may well continue to benefit China for one basic reason. Its unique response to the diversity challenge has so far proved successful, despite recent dramatic but isolated incidents involving the Uyghur minority. India, in contrast, continues to live, as V. S. Naipaul suggested years ago, "a million mutinies now." Suffice it to recall that sixty years after

---

* Even Israel, the quintessentially hyper-defined, virtually theocratic nation-state, is today grappling with its identity, which was formed by a thousand-year-old culture and religion (though not really a language, at least not until 1948), as well as by a Holocaust of unparalleled dimensions. Is Israel today a Jewish state whose territory is shared with—but whose identity is threatened by—a burgeoning number of non-Jewish Arab dwellers, as Benjamin Netanyahu's Likud and Arbel Liberman, the arch-conservative foreign minister in 2010, insist? Is a hypothetical single state, stretching from the Jordan River to the sea, and including Gaza and the West Bank occupied territories, as well as the right of return for both Jews and Palestinians, compatible with the existence of a Jewish state? If not, how can Orthodox Jews and secular ones, fundamentalist Arabs in East Jerusalem and moderate ones in Galilee, cohabit in two states, sharing a tiny sliver of land often less than a hundred miles wide? Can a national character and/or identity be constructed out of such ethnic and religious extremes of diversity, ranging well beyond what other highly heterogeneous nation-states (the United States, Brazil, Argentina, South Africa) ever experienced?

partition, there were more Muslims living in India than in what was originally known as East Pakistan and is now Bangladesh (138 million versus 127 million). The Muslim population of India is rapidly overtaking that of Pakistan itself (157 million). This has undoubtedly contributed to India's extraordinary cultural vitality, but has inevitably generated difficult domestic tensions.

The United States was able, years ago, to build upon its diversity—albeit with mass exclusions of various minorities for decades—but it is less and less certain that other societies, with similar characteristics but different circumstances, can succeed in the same way. The point is not that only homogeneous origins generate success, but that even the intention or the initial reality of foundational unity are short-lived. Construction of a national identity out of diversity in a globalized world—the task countries like Nigeria, South Africa, and Iraq, for example, face today—may not be as feasible as in the nineteenth and twentieth centuries.

Mexico must refashion its diversity in the light of the gaping regional inequalities that have emerged or grown in recent decades. It must restore it in view of its flourishing regionalism, in the light of past solutions' obsolescence, and given the importance of its increasingly binational diaspora. One possible exit from the current maze is the creation of a land of laws, where diversity fits and thrives, but which sufficiently unifies the country to prevent it from being torn apart by its very diversity.

Any journey across Mexico today conveys this sense of extreme variety. The north is industrious, modernizing, violent, lighter-skinned, and devoid of charm, but also fed by the energy wrought by its proximity to the United States and by the transient nature of many of its inhabitants. This is the region of the drug lords—but also of Juan Gabriel and Los Tigres del Norte (as well as most of the modern and popular music artists). Tijuana and Ciudad Juárez are places people pass through; Mexicali and Matamoros are settled, stable communities, every now and then plagued by crime and crisis, but largely prosperous and peaceful. Monterrey and mainly Saltillo, Chihuahua, and Hermosillo are, like others we have described, middle-class cities. They are not devoid of the stark dangers many similar cities face every day, but by and large they are a model for much of Mexico: state capitals with between 250,000 and half a million inhabitants, a local bureaucracy, public and private universities, industry (mainly in the automobile sector, mining, and agribusiness), strongly rooted business communities, and something of a cultural scene. But they totally lack the seductive powers of other regions; their cuisine is lackluster, their music nondescript, their art unoriginal, their literature often uninteresting.

Part of the center of the country resembles these areas, but with a strong Catholic, conservative, colonial past: Durango, where Joaquín Guzmán Loera, El Chapo, Mexico's most well known and wealthy drug kingpin, is said to hang out; Zacatecas, San Luis Potosí, Aguascalientes, and Querétaro, which are farther south, but equally inserted between the two Sierra Madres. This land is more *mestizo* and more colorful, with beautiful colonial layouts and city centers, rather peaceful today (except for Durango), with high levels of urbanization, industry, and uniformity, where the PRI stopped governing nearly decades ago, though on occasion it wins back a state governorship or a mayoralty, and where cities whose dimensions Mexico can manage, are consolidating their existence. With the exception of Zacatecas, almost half of whose native-born inhabitants live in the United States, this is a region unaffected by emigration.

Then there is the central lane of the country, which geographically is not homogeneous, but economically and culturally may be so. It starts in Sinaloa, on the Pacific coast, where tourists enjoy some of the best marlin fishing in the world, and prosperous businessmen export tuna and shrimp as well as winter vegetables to the United States. They also grow corn and wheat in the north of the state and in the south of Sonora, constituting the country's breadbasket. And of course, Sinaloa is a state devoted to cultivating marijuana and poppy for heroin in the highlands, contributing 60% to 70% of the cartels' profits, according to both the government and the U.S. Drug Enforcement Administration. It is a vital, dynamic, and folkloric state, home of the *narcocorridos* and *tambora* bands, tropical and *mestizo*, but also northern and light-skinned; people play baseball here, not soccer. Many die daily in Sinaloa, but they also come out ahead, and possess what Mexicans call the "culture of effort."

Jalisco, Michoacán, and Guanajuato are the Bajío: the traditional emigration and venerable Catholic states; Michoacán is Indian and *mestizo*, where the Cárdenas family hails from; Jalisco and Guanajuato are more export-oriented and industrialized. Guadalajara, in addition to the highlights we described a few chapters back, is also a city of jacarandas in spring and universities all year round, where more than 151,000 higher education students make it one of Mexico's premier cultural centers, as well as the home of some of its greatest creative talent, from mariachis and Orozco to the architect Luis Barragán and novelists like Juan Rulfo (from nearby Sayula). It leans toward *mestizo*, but is lighter-skinned than the rest of the country, and lacking the enterprising spirit of Monterrey, it is perhaps less of an unequal city than the northern industrial town, or than the capital of the country. In its eastern regions, Jalisco was the birthplace, together with upper Michoacán and Guanajuato, of the Cristero movement and war, the anti-anticlerical rebellion of the 1920s, and the semifascist, Catholic Sinarquista movement of the forties and fifties. For a revolt inspired by extreme Catholicism and a rabid, nineteenth-century anti-Americanism based on strictly religious feelings, it was no minor paradox that the war ended in 1929 thanks to negotiations carried out between the Church, President Calles, and the rebels, all at the U.S. ambassador, Dwight Morrow's weekend home in Cuernavaca. Morrow was not only Charles Lindbergh's father-in-law, and grandfather to Anne Morrow's kidnapped baby, but was counseled in Cuernavaca during those tense times by, among others, Woodrow Wilson's old right-hand man, Colonel House, and his right-hand man, Walter Lippmann.

This region, like every one of the others we have mentioned, has its own form of globalization or ties with the United States, old and new. Emigration began here, more than a century ago; many of Mexico's fruit and vegetable exports to the north proceed from here, and it is also where some of the largest automobile plants in the country are located. The area is well off but with deep and wide pockets of poverty, and it is plagued by drugs, at least in Michoacán, though no longer in Guadalajara, as was the case in the eighties and nineties. The tropical lowlands around Uruapan, Mexico's avocado capital, and Apatzingán, its melon center, are home to small marijuana plantations; its main port, Lázaro Cárdenas, hosted many of the methamphetamine labs established during the first decade of the new century. Michoacán is a deeply *mestizo* state, with strong indigenous roots, although the local Purepecha or Tarascan communities have all but disappeared. If this central belt were to continue eastward culturally, economically, and topographically, it would jut into Veracruz, Mexico's longest state, ranging up the entire Gulf Coast, which is almost a country in its own right. Veracruz includes a university capital, ports, cattle farming, and contraband; it is *mestizo* with hints of an early, ephemeral African presence dating back to just after the Conquest, and home to the marimba, *la bamba*, coffee, enormous fortunes, and the country's worst infrastructure.

Then comes the capital, the 21 million–strong metropolitan monster now comprising Mexico City itself, the surrounding towns in the state of Mexico (the country's most populous), and even the cities of Toluca, Pachuca, and Puebla, increasingly bedroom communities for the capital. This is where the largest concentration of power, wealth, people, and disparities lies: where the *mestizo*, colonial, and early industrialized Mexico of the forties and fifties coincides with one of the world's three or four largest, modern, trendy, cultural, and dynamic cities. It is a gargantuan metropolis, devouring everything in its path, living off government bureaucracy, industry, street peddling, petty crime, and services, with an airport smack in its heart. It attempts still to exercise a weakened and increasingly impotent economic dictatorship over the rest of the nation. This is where Mexico's bad news is generated, where over one hundred embassies and honorary consulates populate the affluent neighborhoods, and where the country's political, religious, economic, and intellectual elite dwell. There is no decentralization in this land: *fuera de México todo es Cuautitlán* (outside of New York, there is only Hoboken, one might freely translate this to mean).

And finally, but most interestingly, there is the poor, indigenous, still rural, and almost unglobalized Mexico, ranging from the Mixtec vortex in the states of Oaxaca, Puebla, and Guerrero, to Tabasco and the Mayan states of Chiapas and Yucatán. Here poverty still pervades everything, together with local customs ranging from collective village voting and *droit du seigneur* for men, but also the country's greatest artistic and culinary creativity. Some of the area's inhabitants have left for New York; much of Oaxaca lives off welfare, remittances, and drug cultivation. Rural violence is still a mainstay, having largely vanished from the rest of the country. These are Mexico's poorest states. Chiapas is the most rapidly expanding in demographic terms, and Guerrero perhaps is one of its cruelest, combining the modern brutality of Acapulco with the traditional vendettas of the Costa Grande (to the north of the resort city) and the Costa Chica (to the south). This is the Mexico—

mainly Chiapas, Oaxaca, and Yucatán—that fills the imagination of foreigners nostalgic for the country of the 1950s, that captivates left-wing activists from Italy and the Basque country to Greenwich Village, and that continues to provide much of Mexico's personality. The left doesn't dominate the region, as it has done Mexico City since the mid-nineties, but it should. López Obrador comes from this region; this is where the Zapatista uprising exploded (Chiapas) in 1994, and where the Oaxaca insurrection took place in 2006.

So what can tie all of this together? What can replace the old centralism of the twentieth century now that the gaps separating north and south, rich and poor, light-skinned, *mestizo,* and indigenous regions, globalized and introverted ones, and states exporting migrants and isolated ones are greater than ever? Mexico's regional divergences are growing. In 2006, the north had a per capita GDP 50% higher than the south, and almost 66% higher if rich states like Tabasco and Campeche (oil), as well as Quintana Roo (Cancún and tourism) were excluded. On a state-by-state basis, Nuevo León in the north had a GDP per capita in 2006 of $12,500 U.S. per year; outside of Mexico City (whose statistics are distorted because of corporate headquarters and government), it is the richest state in the nation, with numbers five times higher than Chiapas ($2,500 U.S. per capita GDP) or Oaxaca ($2,900 U.S.).[23]

On the one hand, only a sufficiently strong central government can provide public goods such as security, the rule of law, an open economy, democratic competition for power, and a relatively common foreign policy. It might be worth emphasizing, however, that emotional ties in the north to the United States, in the Gulf region toward Cuba, and in Chiapas and Tabasco to Central America will probably grow stronger with time. This national, unifying thread can rest on three pillars: a national police and criminal code; a national social protection, health care, and pension system; and national respect for the rule of law.

On the other hand, acknowledging and encouraging variations throughout the country, especially in relation to different patterns of globalization, is equally crucial. The border regions will always have their comparative advantage, which by definition cannot be extrapolated even with a major push in infrastructure. The natural resource zones—oil and gas, mining, fishing, forestry—will inevitably reinforce their own peculiar ties with the rest of the world. Mexico's tourism areas—numerous and also blessed with unequaled comparative advantage, like the Mayan Riviera, Baja, the northern Pacific coast, Yucatán—will continue to develop and strengthen their special bonds to the world and the United States. The sending states have specific traits that others cannot emulate: remittances, cultural nexus, communications, circularity. And the drug bastions, with or without eventual legalization, are implicitly pursuing their international intents and concomitant strategy. So what Mexico needs is a national arrangement where all of this becomes feasible and desirable: each fraction of the country cutting its own deal with the outside world, based on its vocation and features, with the center providing the necessary national public goods that allow direct bonds between the regions and . . . the United States and Canada. This combination of a stronger center and more energized and autonomous regions accentuating their own globalization just might do the trick.

Nothing else will, though the notion of a common embrace of the rule of law in Mexico seems quite a stretch. It would imply achieving a radical change of attitudes toward the law in the span of a generation, a transformation that can only originate in a major effort by the central state, which is precisely the source of the problem, not its solution. Midsize cities, states, and regions would have to begin collecting taxes (they receive everything from Mexico City right now), dismantling their own police forces, unifying their criminal codes, and adopting an education policy where adapting to the new economy and the requirements of the rule of law would be paramount. Mexico's local entrepreneurial, political, and intellectual talent is abundant, but the blueprint for this future has not surfaced, and the virtually monumental overhaul from the center has not begun.

Yet this radical, cultural transformation of Mexican minds outside the capital is not impossible, nor unprecedented. It is already under way, among the 12 to 13 million Mexicans who have left their home over the past quarter century, who live and work in the United States, legally or not, and who are still very much Mexican, but of a different kind. To these we will now turn, attempting to show, and conclude, that the traits of Mexico's national character, which served it so well for centuries, and so poorly today, are malleable. They can metamorphose into something new, different, and marvelous.

## CHAPTER 9

# The Future in Real Time

There is an old, somewhat silly but nonetheless self-deprecatory joke Mexicans often tell in regard to just how mean Americans can be. It proclaims that they are so nasty that when they took half of Mexico's territory in the nineteenth century, not content with just conquering *a* part of the country, they absorbed the "*best*" part: the paved, modern, irrigated, clean, and affluent part. What the joke could add, if one wished to be facetious, is that they also took the "best" Mexicans: those who don't litter, run through red lights or stop signs, skip work, or arrive late. The analogy is actually quite relevant: Americans—meaning Anglo-Saxons, Asian-Americans, African-Americans, and Mexican-Americans, among others—transformed California and the other territories from the largely deserted, sparsely watered, undeveloped, and abandoned Mexican provinces they were until 1848 into some of the richest subnational political entities in the world today. And the Mexicans who live there—both those who became Americans over the past century and those who arrived just yesterday—are neither better nor worse than the ones back home: they are just different. The question is how different, and why.

The 12 million or so native-born Mexican citizens currently living and working in the United States provide us with an extraordinary opportunity for a sort of in vitro experiment. They can be the focus of observation and study as a group of people who were almost identical to the 112 million Mexicans left behind, and who, of their own volition and because of force majeure, uprooted themselves and landed in a radically different environment that may or may not force them to change. In particular, that new working, living, worshipping, schooling, and socializing environment may or may not oblige them to jettison, more or less consciously, the national character traits we have described and hopefully understood over the previous eight chapters. If it turns out these Mexicans, over a relatively brief period of time, were able to transform themselves and, while retaining their customs and traditions, simultaneously acquire the cultural trappings of modernity, then there is hope for Mexico. Paraphrasing Lincoln Steffens's famous exclamation upon his return from the Soviet Union, we could say, "We have seen the Mexicans of the future, and they work!"[1] Conversely, there is a reason for despair if it turns out that the attitudes outlined throughout this book are so ingrained in the Mexican psyche that even such a dramatic displacement as the one endured by millions of migrants is insufficient to generate a metamorphosis.

A brief caveat is in order before we begin. Conventional wisdom has traditionally sustained that emigrants are the "best and brightest" a country has to offer. They are the boldest, most entrepreneurial, risk-taking, and adventuresome members of society, or in any case among the least economically favored. That is why some leave, and others— invariably a majority—do not. This factoid has not really been disproved over time and space. At most, nuances have been introduced to the effect, for example, that while this may be true for initial departures, for the migrating pioneers, with time, social capital, tradition, rites of passage, and transnational bonds take over and keep the immigration ball rolling. Subsequently, these factors make no distinction between the human qualities of the ones who stay behind and those who venture off into the unknown.

If so, even if we do conclude that Mexicans are changing, it might not be as a result of their migration, but rather of the self-selection process involved in creating the universe we are reflecting upon. It would be this specific process that made those specific Mexicans more susceptible to change, more sensitive to the need to do so, more adaptable to the external environment, and less reluctant to comply with strange, alien rules and patterns of conduct. Since not everyone can emigrate from Mexico to the United States (though some on the right in the U.S. and on the left in Mexico might think this is the case), then the ensuing transformation of the Mexican mentality would be a product of that self-selection process, not of immersion in a different context. And for our purposes, since the grounds for change are almost as decisive as change itself, if only the country's top citizens change, then the result is much less interesting than if everybody does as a result of external influences.

## How Many, When, and Where?

That said, let us begin with a brief and indispensable digression through numbers, history, and location. Emigration from Mexico to the United States began late in the nineteenth century, with American press gangs and *enganchadores* more or less kidnapping needed hands to work on the construction of U.S. railroads from the border to St. Louis, Kansas City, and Chicago, or to function as strikebreakers in places like Gary, Indiana. There were several migratory spurts and standstills over the next century, as well as alternating periods of mainly legal flows (as during the so-called Bracero Program between 1942 and 1965, or after the Immigration Reform and Control Act [IRCA] of 1986, and illegal ones (as during the 1970s and 1990s, through 2008).

The numbers, both in absolute terms and in relation to the two countries' respective populations, also varied, but never descended below 3–4% of all Mexicans, or 1–2% of the total number of people residing in the U.S. With time, those who arrived before World War II and during the Bracero period learned English, became American citizens, and started building a Latino middle class, mainly in California (where half of all Mexicans and Mexican-Americans in the United States still live), Chicago, and in the Rio Grande Valley in South Texas. They were, like all immigrant groups, the objects of discrimination, occasional deportation (as with Operation Wetback in 1951–52), repression during riots, and eventual assimilation. Pretty much par for the course.

Contiguity between the United States and Mexico, and continuity over the better part of a century, produced a few exceptions, however, to the rules generally governing previous or subsequent immigrant waves. First, migration from Mexico tended to be circular or seasonal: people came to work for three to six months in harvests of different crops, then went home for the off-season, and returned the following year, with or without papers. This meant that although with time some of the seasonal travelers would set down roots stateside, most of them didn't, and the dimensions of the Mexican universe in the U.S. did not seem to oscillate over time. Second, because of the back-and-forth movement, as well as the proximity of the sending country and the prolongation of the migratory movement for so long a period, Mexicans in the U.S. were able, up to a point, to live like Mexicans in Mexico. They spoke Spanish, went to mass, ate Mexican food, watched Mexican television, and enjoyed Mexican soccer games, concerts, and movies. But unlike other groups before them, this process did not cease when immigration withered, because it didn't wither; it went on and on.

In addition, the educational level of most Mexican immigrants remained dismally low, whether in comparison to previous flows of other nationalities, or to their contemporary colleagues, even from countries poorer than Mexico, like the Philippines or El Salvador. So Mexicans remained largely estranged from American social mobility and stuck in low-paying, low-skill jobs, without much chance of moving up the ladder, at least until the second generation. It was difficult but also somewhat unnecessary for the first generation to learn English, the principal instrument of upward mobility in the United States. Another characteristic might reside in the time span involved: a sixteen-year-old urban, lower-middle-class resident of Jalisco or Michoacán who "went north" in all likelihood would live in the U.S. for the following sixty years, perhaps eventually attaining legalization, but doubtfully learning English or moving up the social ladder. Only his sons and daughters would.

Several factors intervened in the mid-1990s to transform this steady state. Firstly, the so-called Rodinos, that is, the approximately 3 million Mexicans who were amnestied one way or another by the Simpson-Rodino or IRCA legislation, became eligible for citizenship in 1996 and 1997 (after five years of provisional residence and five years of permanent residence) and began bringing family from Mexico once they acquired American citizenship. Secondly, in 1996 the Clinton administration initiated an immigration enforcement policy that included far more money for the Border Patrol, crackdowns on the line in San Ysidro and El Paso, and expanding deportation, thus rendering unauthorized entry more expensive and dangerous (pushing it away from safe areas like Tijuana to the Sonora desert, for example), and also making coming and going twice a year less viable. Furthermore, the type of demand for Mexican labor in the U.S. economy also began to change, moving to services, construction, hospitality, landscaping, janitorial, and newer industries, all of which required year-long commitments and were spread out across the U.S. The unintended consequence of all these shifts was a virtual end to circularity and concentration in the "gateway states," introducing a process of dispersion across the United States.

Thus by 2008 there were roughly 6 million legal, Mexican permanent residents (of which one-third held dual citizenship), and about another 6 million unauthorized Mexicans. This was the equivalent of more than 4.2% of the total U.S. population, by far the highest figure ever (ten times as much as in 1920, for example), and 11% of the total Mexican population, also a record. Mexican-born immigrants represented 32% of all foreign-born individuals residing in the United States (a historic record); the overall foreign-born population reached 13% of all people in the U.S., the highest share since 1910.[2] The two historic peaks (the highest proportion of Mexicans abroad, and the highest proportion of Mexicans in the United States) wrought significant transformations in both the policy and rhetorical realms of the immigration debate in both countries. Most importantly, perhaps, Mexicans began settling in new areas, from Atlanta to Anchorage, from Little Rock to Raleigh-Durham, from Tucson to Hazleton, Pennsylvania, and working in everything from New York restaurants to Rocky Mountain ski resorts. Americans previously unfamiliar with Mexican immigration were unsettled by the novelty and many reacted the way people do when confronted with the unknown: with fear and hostility. Mexicans hunkered down, and accentuated their "Mexicanness" as their sheer numbers and breadth converted them into an exciting market for Mexican businesses delivering Mexican goods to Mexican consumers in Mexican neighborhoods.

Other consequences of continuity and contiguity encouraged this retrenchment, although they are certainly older than the anti-immigrant backlash of the early years of the twenty-first century. Since people kept coming practically forever—every other immigrant "wave" to the United States has experienced a beginning and an end, even in the case of China—a perpetual replenishment of the stock of Mexicans took place. And this entailed a replenishment of the "ingredients" of "Mexicanness": Spanish, Catholicism, tortillas, Cantinflas, and Pedro Infante yesterday, Salma Hayek and Gael García Bernal today, along with Los Tigres del Norte* and La Arrolladora Banda Limón, Chivas USA, and *telenovelas,* Mexican *barrios* in many major cities and many not so major ones, Mexican intermarriage and children growing up in Mexican neighborhoods. While this phenomenon led some scholars, such as the late Samuel Huntington, to question whether Mexicans would ever be assimilated like previous flows of migrants from other nations, it also allowed for an intermediate status to emerge for many immigrants from Mexico, somewhere between the seasonal circularity of the past and the full U.S. citizenship of the future. Mexicans north of the border cannot keep coming and going south, but can live in the north as if they were in the south. They can reproduce the Mexican experience in the old and new communities where they settle. This facilitates their adaptation to the end of circularity, but it also has a price: by refashioning their neighborhoods, homes, parks, stadiums, bars, and restaurants in the image of the old country, they may be also making the metamorphosis from the old Mexican attitudes to the new ones much more difficult.

According to the 2008 Bureau of the Census statistics, of the 12.6 million Mexicans in the United States 7.2 million were men and 5.4 million were women; the trend is toward equalization between the two sexes.[†] As of 2007, 31.3 percent of the Mexican foreign-born had entered the country after 2000, and 32 percent between 1990 and 1999.[3] In other words practically two-thirds of the total had arrived after 1990. The rest entered the U.S. mainly between 1980 and 1989.[‡] So as we stated from the outset, they constitute a substantial sample of Mexicans who have now lived in "another world" for quite some time,

---

* *The New Yorker* published an interesting article about Los Tigres del Norte, titled "Immigration Blues," by Alec Wilkinson, on May 24, 2010.

[†] Just under 2 million were U.S. citizens also, but 10.8 million had not yet taken advantage of the 1998 dual-citizenship legislation ratified under then president Ernesto Zedillo. This last number should rise in the next few years.

[‡] Although the flow may have diminished somewhat from 2006 onward because of the Bush and Obama administrations' toughening of border enforcement and the American economic crisis, as of 2010 there were at least 7 million Mexicans who had been in the U.S. for a minimum of five years.

who have actually spent much of their adult lives outside of Mexico. If the traits of the national character we have worked on are malleable, this is where we will discover its transformations.

Who are these Mexicans? Where do they come from, how old are they, what educational levels do they possess, where do they live and work? The U.S. Census Bureau provides some answers, and polls deliver others, but it is important to note that most of the figures must be taken with a grain of *chile*. By definition, any statistic based on questionnaires and originating with individuals possessing an illicit status must be considered less than robust; they tend rightly to fear pollsters, census takers, and interviewers in general. According to the Census Bureau, very few of these 12.5 million Mexicans are children—only 9% are under seventeen years of age. And very few are elderly: only 13% are over fifty-five. The large majority—nearly two-thirds—are between eighteen and forty-five. This is a very different age structure from Mexico's back home and from the United States. Moreover, their educational level is very low: more than 60% do not have a high school diploma. This is a direct consequence of the continued importance of rural areas in generating migratory flows from Mexico. While this has been changing over the years, as more and more migrating Mexicans are from midsize cities and seek jobs in nonagricultural activities in the U.S., the rural origins persist and remain important. These Mexicans reside preponderantly in California and Texas, and in two additional states, with one older community in Illinois, and another new community in Arizona. Despite the above-mentioned and novel dispersion, most Mexicans in the United States are still to be found only in four states, and more than half in only two. Similarly, there are just five cities with more than half a million Mexican-born inhabitants: Los Angeles, Riverside (California), Houston, Dallas, and Chicago.[4]*

* Mexico's population between eighteen and forty-five years old is 53% of its total population, whereas the figure for the United States is 52%. But for Mexicans in the United States, the number is 65%. About 57% of those who leave still come from the countryside, and more than 40% were previously employed in agriculture. Today only about 6% of the Mexican-born population in the United States works in farming, fishing, or forestry activities.

States with significant Mexican population (percentage of total population): California (37%), Texas (21%), Illinois (6%), Arizona (5%). Seventy percent of all Mexicans in the United States are still to be found only in four states.

In a nutshell, then, migrants are not a mirror image of Mexican society. They continue to be poorer, closer to the land, with less schooling and marketable skills than the average. They are not yet our new middle class from Chapter 2, although they are moving in that direction. The main difference between them and the rest of the country probably lies in the proportion of women who emigrate. Since the census numbers show no significant difference in employment levels between men and women, and more importantly, since only a very small number of migrant women work in agriculture in the United States, this probably implies that the urban-rural breakdown for women is quite different than for men. In all likelihood, women who go north are much more urban than men, setting the stage for the most important change in the Mexican migrant mentality.

### The Hearts and Minds of Stateside Mexicans

What do we really know about these Mexicans' attitudes and mindsets? Two aggregate, indirect conclusions regarding their behavior in the United States suggest several initial differences between them and their compatriots back home. First, in view of the low wages prevailing among Mexican workers in the United States, the volume of remittances indicates an extraordinarily high savings rate, far superior to what their countrymen put away in Mexico.[5]* This can be anecdotally confirmed by what many observers and narrators have emphasized repeatedly: Mexicans in the U.S. live under very adverse conditions (ten to a room), work two shifts if they can, spend very little on drink and food, and send home as much money as is humanly possible. Their savings rates equal those of industrial, migrant laborers in South China, and are way above those in the cities, towns, and villages in Mexico. Part of this propensity to save begins undoubtedly with the need to pay off the debt incurred with the *pollero* or smuggler, but it

* Remittances by five-year totals (in millions of U.S. dollars): 1980–85, $5,671.6; 1986–90, $9,371.2; 1991–95, $16,210.7; 1996–2000, $27,197.5; 2001–05, $73,770.4; 2006–09, $97,954.2. Ranking of countries with the highest remittance incomes in 2008 (in millions of U.S. dollars): (1st) India, $49,940.8; (2nd) China, $48,523.5; (3rd) Mexico, $26,304.3; (4th) Philippines, $18,843; (5th) France, $15,908.4.

continues afterward. Only after many years of channeling funds to family in their hometown do migrants even begin to cut back on remittances (for example, by founding a new family in the U.S.), but the stratospheric savings rate may well endure even after its original raison d'être has disappeared. The Mexican who splurges on his daughter's *quinceañera* or drinks away his fortnight's salary in one long weekend with his *cuates* is not easy to find in the United States. He may not even exist.

The second indirectly detectable trait has to do with the law. It has been widely reported that part of the remarkable drop in crime and delinquency in the United States since the mid-1990s can be attributed to the rise in immigration. As poor neighborhoods receive foreign laborers from everywhere, law and order improves, petty crime diminishes, and other more serious violations of the law—such as homicides, rapes, or home robberies—also drop. This apparently counterintuitive phenomenon has often been explained by the Catholic, conservative, family-oriented nature of many Latin American migrants (not just Mexicans), who avoid drugs and gangs, and by their law-abiding behavior in general. Which seems a bit difficult to believe when we know how little law-abiding Mexicans are in Mexico, how violent countries like El Salvador, Honduras, and Guatemala have become, and how many cities in Mexico from sending states like Guerrero and Michoacán are infested with crime and drugs. Moreover, the religiosity of Mexicans in the U.S. appears to be dropping below that of Mexicans in Mexico: 58% of the first group attributed importance to their religion, and 67% of the second group did. Nonetheless, the numbers are in principle indisputable, and this would seem to insinuate a change in attitudes.[6]

Several experts have highlighted this trend thanks to research undertaken during the first decade of the century. In his book *New York Murder Mystery*, the criminologist Andrew Karmen examined the trend in New York City and found that the "disproportionately youthful, male and poor immigrants" who arrived during the 1980s and 1990s "were surprisingly law-abiding" and that their settlement into once decaying neighborhoods helped "put a brake on spiraling crime rates." *The New York Times* reported in an article in 2006 that Robert J. Sampson, chairman of the Sociology Department at Harvard University, developed a theory that may be the most provocative yet. Could America's cities be safer today not because fewer unwanted children live in them but because a lot more immigrants do? Could illegal immigration be making the nation a more law-abiding place? Sampson doesn't deny that crime may be underreported in immigrant neighborhoods. Nonetheless, he is quick to note that as the ranks of foreigners in the United States boomed during the 1990s . . . America's cities became markedly less dangerous. But Sampson also notes the importance of another factor, one often stressed by conservatives: Mexicans in Chicago, his study found, are more likely to be married than either blacks or whites. "The family dynamic is very noticeable here," Sampson remarked.

In response to this *Times* piece and Sampson's study, columnist David Brooks noted approvingly, "As immigration has surged, violent crime has fallen 57 percent."[7]

According to Rubén Rumbaut and Walter Ewing in an essay titled "The Myth of Immigrant Criminality and the Paradox of Assimilation":

The problem of crime in the United States is not "caused" or even aggravated by immigrants, regardless of their legal status. This is hardly surprising since immigrants come to the United States to pursue economic and educational opportunities not available in their home countries and to build better lives for themselves and their families. As a result, they have little to gain and much to lose by breaking the law. Undocumented immigrants in particular have even more reason to not run afoul of the law given the risk of deportation that their lack of legal status entails. Although the undocumented immigrant population doubled to about 12 million from 1994 to 2005, the violent crime rate in the United States *declined* by 34.2% and the property crime rate fell by 26.4%. This decrease in crime rates was not just national, it also occurred in border cities and other cities with large immigrant populations—such as San Diego, El Paso, Los Angeles, New York, Chicago, and Miami. The incarceration rate also is lower for the immigrants from Mexico, El Salvador, and Guatemala who account for the majority of undocumented immigrants in the United States and who tend to have low levels of education. In fact, data from the census and other sources show that for every ethnic group, without exception, incarceration rates among young men are lowest for immigrants, even those who are the least educated. This holds true especially for the Mexicans, Salvadorans, and Guatemalans who make up the bulk of the undocumented population. What is more, these patterns have been observed consistently over the last three decennial censuses, a period that spans the current era of mass immigration, and recall similar national-level findings reported by three major government commissions during the first three decades of the 20th century.[8]*

In fact, there *is* a very powerful reason for Mexicans in the United States to play by the rules and obey the law: the penalty for doing so is exorbitant, i.e., deportation for those without papers, losing them for those with legal residence. This is why the incarceration rates for foreign-born Mexicans are much lower than for Puerto Ricans, Dominicans, and Cubans in the United States, for example: they all tend to be legal residents or U.S. citizens. Migrants everywhere save money and respect the law because their entire purpose in life is to take every advantage of every opportunity in the new land, and to reduce every risk and every danger of being forced to depart from it. So logically

---

* Another study, carried out by the Immigration Policy Center, showed that "among men age 18–39 (who comprise the vast majority of the prison population), the 3.5 percent incarceration rate of the native-born in 2000 was 5 times higher than the 0.7 percent incarceration rate of the foreign-born. The foreign-born incarceration rate in 2000 was nearly two-and-a-half times less than the 1.7 percent rate for native-born non-Hispanic white men and almost 17 times less than the 11.6 percent rate for native-born black men. Native-born Hispanic men were nearly 7 times more likely to be in prison than foreign-born Hispanic men in 2000, while the incarceration rate of native-born non-Hispanic white men was almost 3 times higher than that of foreign-born white men. Foreign-born Mexicans had an incarceration rate of only 0.7 percent in 2000—more than 8 times lower than the 5.9 percent rate of native-born males of Mexican descent. Foreign-born Mexicans without a high-school diploma had an incarceration rate of 0.7 percent in 2000—more than 14 times less than the 10.1 percent of native-born male high-school dropouts of Mexican descent behind bars." The prose could be more elegant, but the research and the conclusions seem categorical.

enough, Mexicans stay away from compromising situations, and instead of being vehicles of crime, drugs, prostitution, gang wars, and smuggling, rapidly become bulwarks of law-abiding conduct in their community. This may not last beyond the first generation, and there are obviously exceptions, but it should not be that surprising. Mexicans even refrain from acts they would never imagine abandoning back home, from littering and going through a red light to panhandling, cheating in the subway, or hustling in the bars or at soccer games.

Hence at least for starters, there is certainly a change in a couple of traits of the Mexican national character: saving and respect for the law. What is not clear is whether these transformations are so directly linked and driven by the migrant experience that they would vanish once it ceased, and if these new attitudes extend to conduct occurring other than in public places and work sites. From impressions and anecdotes, we also know that Mexicans in the U.S. are considered to be highly productive, hardworking, responsible individuals, at least as far as the workplace is concerned. They are punctual, assiduous, and tend to remain in the same job, if they can, for long periods of time. They obey American laws, with the exception of having entered the United States without papers—which given the more than century-old U.S. stance of don't ask, don't tell, or wink and nod, is not necessarily seen as a binding law by the migrants. This includes even laws that might seem bewildering: against jaywalking, loitering (back home and back then, as a teenager, this is what we did in Actipan: *ir allá abajo*, in other words, loiter on the corner and drink beer on the sidewalk outside the store), littering, speeding (a ban on which is as anti-Mexican as it is un-Italian), peddling wares on the street (a custom dating back to the Aztec *tianguis*). What we don't know is if all of this represents a product of subjecting Mexicans to the market, as often happens in the north of the country, or whether it is a bellwether signal of the mutation of the Mexican national character.

## Juan Gabriel: "No Need to Ask If You Can Tell"

Part of the solution to this riddle of why Mexicans are so law-abiding in the U.S. may lie in the Mexican north, and more specifically, in the border towns, which many equate with the country's contemporary version of the proverbial U.S. Wild West: cities like Tijuana, Matamoros, and Ciudad Juárez. We will dodge the issues that brought this city of roughly 1.5 million inhabitants to the front pages of newspapers all over the world in recent years—the murdered women of Juárez, the drug cartels, the generalized violence and gruesome killings, the intrusive though unavoidable and desirable forms of cooperation with Washington, even the confusing paradoxes. Juárez is one of the world's most violent cities, as tabulated by willful homicides per hundred thousand inhabitants a year; El Paso, a sleepy West Texas city (like the song), of barely 300,000 residents, is one of the safest communities in the United States. Safe and progressive: its city council voted, in 2009, to legalize marijuana, but the mayor, under pressure from Austin and perhaps from Washington, vetoed the ordinance, arguing, not inaccurately, that it didn't make much sense to support Felipe Calderón's war on drugs while simultaneously legalizing even one drug a hundred yards away from the most deadly front in that war. We will stick to what has really made Juárez famous, over decades, and which is more of a harbinger of things to come than the admittedly gory details of everyday gangland shootings.

Alberto Aguilera was born in Michoacán on January 7, 1950. His father went crazy soon thereafter, threw himself in a river, and was interned in an asylum, where he died later. His mother took her eight-month-old to Ciudad Juárez, where he grew up and became, twenty years later, Juan Gabriel, or Juanga, the most successful Mexican composer and singer of modern times, who has written more than one thousand songs and sold more than 100 million records. From the local haunt known as Noa-Noa, a seedy hole-in-the-wall club in Juárez, to the proclamation of October 5, 1986, as Juan Gabriel Day in Los Angeles, to his many concerts in the Palace of Fine Arts in Mexico City, at Radio City, and the Rose Bowl, and singing to nearly forty heads of state at the first Ibero-American Summit in Guadalajara in 1991, Juan Gabriel has sold more records, made more money, and become more popular than any Mexican musician in the United States or Latin America. But this is El Divo de Juárez's least interesting facet. As he himself put it: "*Lo que se ve no se pregunta*" ("No need to ask if you can tell"). Juan Gabriel is perhaps the ultimate Mexican character modernizer, and it is no coincidence that he is from the border, and belongs to the border.

He was burned in effigy in the mid-1980s, when having been named "Mr. Amigo" in Brownsville, Texas, he declared his support for U.S.-Mexican integration (though later he claimed he was misunderstood). This was not his most iconoclastic moment, though; his irreverence and modernism lie in his music and his mores. He created what came to be known as modern mariachi, that is, the recourse to the same instruments (bass, horns, and guitar), the harmony and melody of traditional Mexican mariachi music (of José Alfredo Jiménez, more than anyone else), combined with snappier, changing rhythms—*norteñas, rancheras,* and *redovas*—and even what later came to be called *grupera* music, along with small doses of *música tropical.* The result was a mixture of schmaltzy lyrics with interesting double entendres, a modernized version of the traditional mariachi, with shifting paces in each song and from song to song, with two bands—mariachi and metal—playing simultaneously, and a form of showmanship that no other Mexican star has accomplished. He injected modern rhythms into the classical mariachi, and produced a new sound, both popular and contemporary, a bit of what Presley did in the fifties by melding black rhythm-and-blues with white crooning.

While he has never truly come out of the closet, Juan Gabriel is not only gay, but stridently so in his concerts, chiefly in the *palenques* in midsize towns, but also in more solemn or monumental settings. It was said that during his performance before the heads of state in Guadalajara, many of them, including Fidel Castro, were shocked by his glittery garb and over-made-up eyelashes and eyebrows, as well as by the cadence and gyrations of his dancing. His voice, his walk, his gestures, his outfits, his bonding with the audience, are all obvious and provocative, especially among the macho men from the northern states he often tours. He dresses his mariachi players in purple, has them play pink guitars and basses, and dance to both rock and stripper-like rhythms. But what is absolutely remarkable about Juan Gabriel is how that macho audience gives itself to him in the *palenques* and concert halls, how the Mexican *charros* and *narcos* and *machos* of all sorts openly embrace his gay stridency, respond to it, and throw themselves at his feet, singing and swaying along with him in ways that they would never be caught dead displaying if it were not at a Juanga show. They swoon over him like teenagers, except that they are everything but that. But there are also teenagers and Mexican teenyboppers at his performances.

While he has been the victim of homophobic pamphlets and innuendoes, he was also, in the eighties and nineties, a teenybopper idol and the object of enormous devotion by fans of all genders, ages, and social classes.*

He is irreverent and on occasion outrageous ("I have no time to read. Reading bores me. I have never read a book"), and politically incorrect, one day supporting the opposition, then composing and singing a campaign jingle for the PRI candidate in the 2000 presidential elections. He is both philanthropic, supporting children's music homes in Juárez, and excessive in his attire, his cars, his weight, and his overall demeanor. He was always a greater composer than singer, but even now with his voice irremediably declining, he is mainly an extraordinary performer. In his own way, and because of where he grew up, he is perhaps the first post-Mexican Mexican, that is, the first modern Mexican. Today, at the end of every performance in a *palenque,* where people can get up close to him, over a hundred spectators wait in line to have their picture taken with him on their cell phone: they all want a picture, they all have a cell phone, and he pleases them all.

He is a reflection of the changes in attitudes and behavior that we have already surmised without much evidence, but which the scant available polling data bear out. If we return to the graph we used at the very beginning of this book, where traditional and secular/rational values are plotted on the vertical axis, and survival and self-expression values are plotted on the horizontal one, in other words where the most "modern" attitudes appear in the upper-right-hand corner, and the least "modern" ones in the lower-left-hand corner, we can detect, with figures from a 2003 poll taken both in Mexico and in the United States, some very distinct trends. Mexicans in Mexico are the closest to the bottom-left-hand corner, and so-called Anglo-Americans are the farthest from it; in between, but closer to the latter than to the former, are Mexicans in the United States with less than twenty years' presence there. They place even closer to the upper-right-hand corner than non-Mexican Latinos or Hispanics do. The experts who carried out the poll

* "For many decades, in Mexican pop culture, El Divo represented mushiness, talent, and fortunate findings, all at the same time. Indeed, it was cheap marketing having them well grounded not only for a gay surviving in a macho culture, but also as the country's icon of the repressed ones who worshipped José Alfredo—which is not inconsequential, nor can it be!"[9]

and who plotted the graph conclude: "Mexicans in Mexico show relatively low numbers on both axes, making them the most distinct group of all those surveyed (including Asian- and African-Americans). Conversely, Mexicans in the U.S., however tightly linked they may be to their families back home, possess a system of beliefs that is very different from that of Mexicans in our country, and seem much closer to the Anglo-American average."[10]

As if the scholars were reading our minds, they immediately move on to what they call social capital, or collective action and associative conduct, and provide remarkable figures. When asked to choose from a list of eleven types of organizations, ranging from churches to human rights groups, and including sports teams, unions, women's groups, and cultural activities, which ones they belonged to or did voluntary work for, Mexicans in the U.S. revealed a constantly and significantly higher rate of participation than Mexicans in Mexico, though still below the levels of American involvement. Anglo-Americans worked with 2.8 organizations, Mexicans in the United States with 2.0, and Mexicans in Mexico, 1.4. According to the experts: "Mexicans in the United States organize themselves, or associate with others, almost as much as Americans do, and much more than Mexicans in Mexico."[11]

This appreciation would tend to be corroborated by more rhetorical or impressionistic analyses of Mexican participation in hometown clubs (*clubes de oriundos*) in their communities in the United States, their involvement in the Institute of Mexicans Abroad set up by the Foreign Ministry in 2003, and in a series of demonstrations in favor of immigration reform and against discriminatory laws in 2006. Studies such as *Invisible No More: Mexican Migrant Civic Participation in the United States*, edited by Xóchitl Bada, Jonathan Fox, and Andrew Selee, suggest that Mexicans are more politically participatory in the United States than in Mexico, although it is somewhat difficult to establish whether this trend moves by spurts and stops, according to the political and legal situation of the day. It is a well-known constant for politicians of all stripes who seek the support of Mexicans in the U.S., either for votes, money, or influence with their families back home, that the more politicized Mexican groups in the United States tend to be infinitely splintered and atomized, and that they are most of the time simple letterhead associations with no real constituencies. The legal obstacles to organizing are real, of course, and therein may lie the explanation: illegal workers cannot join unions or vote directly in consulates, and to do so by mail, as Mexican electoral law requires, is simply too complicated (a small number of barely 40,400 Mexicans in the U.S. voted in the 2006 presidential elections, the first one in which they were entitled to do so).[12]

Finally, as far as attitudes regarding key issues such as trust or respect for institutions and the law, the pollsters inquired as to the perceived accuracy of three statements put to those interviewed in both nations—"In our country, citizens respect the law; the authorities respect the law; and legislators and public servants are accountable to citizens." Mexicans in the U.S. provided between two and three times more affirmative responses than Mexicans in Mexico. This was not a behavioral question, and so we don't necessarily know whether they respect the law more than in Mexico, but it does reveal how their cynicism about the law is dramatically transformed by their stateside sojourn. We do know that Mexicans in the United States tend to be somewhat less individualistic and mistrustful of others than their compatriots in Mexico. According to the same poll from 2003, 30% of Anglo-Americans stated "you could trust most people"; 20% of Mexicans in the United States said the same; and only 10%, a figure roughly equivalent to the ones we described earlier in this book, of Mexicans in Mexico replied affirmatively. In relation to institutions, in contrast to people, Mexicans in the U.S. also show far greater trust than their fellow countrymen back home, with the most striking, though not unexpected, result appearing in the case of the police: only 8% of Mexicans in Mexico trust the police in their country, whereas 40% do so in the United States, despite all the news about, and truth to, charges of discrimination and racial profiling.[13]

This last point leads us directly to the core of the argument over whether not-too-recently-arrived Mexicans in the United States have truly left many of their character traits back home and, over time, become different: not American in the case of the first generation, but no longer typically Mexican in the strict sense either. The case can be made that the alteration in the Mexican mind-set in the United States does not extend, as we said, beyond the workplace and public spaces (transportation, parks, stadiums, churches). From this perspective, in their homes, *barrios*, streets, and bars, the changes vanish and the age-old features discussed throughout this book reappear, from the obvious machismo in relation to women, to the traditional individualism, conflict aversion, fear of the "other," and cynicism about the law. In this view, the transmutation is only skin-deep, and is exclusively the product of pragmatic opportunism: if this is what the *gringos* want in their space, so be it. In ours, we will continue to be "the way we were." Without more time having elapsed, and more sociological data to pore over, it is difficult to ascertain how much truth there is to this skepticism. Further legalization of undocumented Mexicans is also necessary, in order to determine whether the public and private spaces of Mexicans in the United States are converging anyway, and so the distinction might soon lose its meaning. But with all these caveats, something seems to be happening. And it starts, as do many things in this perplexing country, with the women of Mexico.

## Where the Women Are

If sexual orientation is part of the Mexican transformation, gender is much more so. There seems to be little doubt that women constitute the Mexicans who are most radically transformed by their U.S. experience. Similarly, it is women migrants who register the most important changes in what are considered classic Mexican attitudes and conduct. Here is where Mexico will confront modernity directly, and emerge as a different people, or not. Because if these attitudes and behavior patterns (toward the law, savings, taking sides, making tough choices, the police, and collective action) are modified, the prime drivers and beneficiaries of this mutation will be the millions of Mexican women who have left their homes and taken advantage of their new surroundings to turn the tables and settle scores with the men in their lives: fathers, husbands, brothers, and sons.

We have already seen how the male-female ratio among Mexicans in the United States is approaching equality; furthermore, the data show that about 60% of Mexican women in the U.S. above sixteen years of age are formally married. We also know where women work, at least in aggregate terms: 11% in management and professional occupations, and 41%, by far the largest sector, in services.* In comparison, only 23% of male Mexican immigrants belonged to this category.[14] An ini-

---

* This is in relation to the 2,227,317 Mexican women over sixteen and fully employed (that is, not part-time, not seasonally, and not self-employed), tabulated by the U.S. Census Bureau in 2008.

tial conclusion that can be drawn from the occupational maps of male
and female Mexicans in the U.S. is that they do not coincide, or work
in the same fields, which among other things means that women do
not depend entirely, or at all, on men—in this case, husbands,
boyfriends, or lovers—for the job they have.

Women work in hotels, as nannies, doing housework, in supermarkets, and in some textile factories; men are in construction, agriculture,
restaurants, and landscaping, and temporary, handyman jobs. There is
information available to the effect that women migrants tend to be
about six years younger than male migrants (almost half of the total is
under thirty-four years of age); that they enjoy slightly higher educational levels (59% have less than a high school diploma; the equivalent
figure for males is around 62%) and hail from more urban areas, from
northern Mexico; and that they find work more easily. They also continue to earn, on average, about 30% less than men do; two-thirds are
"lower income" that is, they make less than $24,000 per year. We know,
though less precisely, that while in some cases men leave home first,
and subsequently "bring" their wives to the U.S., a large number of
Mexican women migrate on their own. According to a study based on
deportees in Baja California, 70% of all women attempting to cross did
so as a result of their own decision; only 10% in response to a request or
instruction from their husbands. They end up paying their own *pollero*
or *coyote*, walking with others through the desert, but not with a partner, some with their children, some not, and they settle the debt to the
smuggler by themselves, or with the help of friends in the United States
or family in Mexico. About a little more than half have children.[15]*

All of this adds a further element of independence to their experience. Not only do they have jobs generating their own income (on
occasion greater than their male counterparts, since women can make
more than $15 an hour doing housework in major American cities; no
busboy makes that kind of money); not only have they not incurred
debts to their fathers or their partners; not only do they toil in areas
where interface with their partners is minimal; but since there are a sufficient number of their peers in the U.S., they can live with them, share

---

* In a survey carried out at the end of the 1990s in Baja California among deported
women, 61% declared they had children; in another study, from 2004 in the United
States, 55% said they were parents. A Mexican study from 2009 revealed that 56% had
children. This looks like a relatively accurate ballpark figure.

housing and expenses with them, go out dancing on Saturday night with them, and help each other out with the children, when they exist. In essence, they do not need male partners in the same way they did in Mexico, or felt they did. In a way, they enjoy the enormous gains made by American women in gender equality over the past quarter century, even though they did not participate in the struggle for those gains, and even if back in Mexico those gains are barely beginning to become a reality for a large number of women.

But perhaps as importantly, the Mexican migrant's trust in the law and institutions—among others the police—revealed by polling data, implies that women have a credible and effective recourse against domestic violence, abuse, and extortion. It is a difficult choice to make, since resorting to the police for women with illegal status (a reminder: roughly half of all Mexicans) brings the risk of detention and deportation, even if it also brings punishment to an abusive, drunken, violent, and undocumented male partner. But just the threat of telephoning the police is real enough, and on occasion, it can be a legalized *comadre*, cousin, sister, or friend who calls, and the illegal victim disappears when the cops arrive.

When there are children (many born in the United States, but a significant number coming from Mexico), American rules also tend to dominate. While it is uncertain that low-income-neighborhood public schools in the United States are much better than middle-class-neighborhood public schools in Mexico, the latter end classes at 12:30 for the morning shift, with only four and a half hours of schooling. In addition to the devastating educational consequences of this short school day or *mediajornada*, it obliges mothers to either work only half a day also, or to enable their children to be cared for by others, if they have a full-time job. The fact that American elementary schools are full-day affairs, with children eating lunch in school and remaining there until nearly the end of the working day, has an enormous impact on women's lives. The state—through the public education system—takes care of the children while women work. This increases their income and self-assurance, and thus their independence from men.

It would be wrong to imply that these vast changes in Mexican women's experience in the United States take place in a vacuum. Back home many aspects of women's behavior and attitudes belie the macho stereotype whereby Mexican men are overwhelmingly dominant and

women irretrievably submissive. Female migrants from the Mixtec and
Juchitán areas of Oaxaca, for example, who represent a substantial portion of the migrant population in New Jersey, have a long tradition of
independence and strength. In the Tehuantepec Isthmus and Juchitán,
for instance, it is they who have traditionally run the show.

Similarly, one of the most initially enigmatic experiences I encountered campaigning in Mexico from 2003 to 2005 was that at practically
all income and educational levels, my town hall meetings—large or
small—featured a singular difference between men and women. When
men asked for the floor and began to speak, they tended to run on
interminably, without ever getting to the point, asking their question,
or concluding what almost always ended up being a more or less relevant full-blown statement; Cantinflas was alive and well at most of
these events. After centuries of silence, and decades of no one listening,
perhaps this irrepressible penchant for long-winded oratory was understandable. But women did not act in this manner, even though they
spoke nearly as often as men did. Concise, specific, and no-nonsense
clarity were the marrow of their interventions. It took me quite a while
to obtain a rational, coherent explanation for this strange occurrence,
but I finally did.

Men in Mexico, I was told, can count on a practically infinite
amount of time to talk: at work, at home with friends, at the bar, or
having breakfast, lunch, or dinner. They can pursue endless conversations on soccer, politics, women, boxing, or life, love, and death. There
is no real limit, either at work or at home, to the time they can dedicate
to *platicar*: it is a full-time occupation. Women do not have this luxury.
They have to tend to the men, to begin with; then to the children; then
to their work (40% of women in Mexico work outside the home); then
to the house itself and to the rest of the family, including even their
mothers-in-law, and if possible, to themselves (which men do not do,
especially once they are married).[16] They cook, clean, wash, make
money, shop, hustle, come and go to school, and dress and bathe the
kids.

So when they talk, whether among themselves, with the children, or
in public, they know time is money. They are conditioned by the need
to economize time and effort; they are accustomed to getting down to
business, because their everyday life does not allow them to conduct
themselves otherwise; hence their concision and capacity to synthesize

or summarize rapidly what they wish to say. Obviously I cannot vouch for the veracity or sufficiency of this explanation for contrasting gender loquacity, but at first glance it seems reasonable. What is undeniable is the way women manage Mexico's and Mexicans' everyday life, in what many have labeled *"el matriarcado mexicano."*

Upon this solid foundation emerge the changes wrought by the American experience. The combination could be sufficient to transform Mexicans in the United States from what they were when they quit their home turf, into something different both from the American world and the Mexican past. It should be enough to detonate basic modifications in Mexican individualism, in the proverbial fear of confrontation, of the new, the foreign, and the different, in the obsession with the past and the dislike for competition or choice, in widespread cynicism with regard to the law, corruption, and impunity. If the law is upheld and serves a purpose; if hard work without corruption breeds at least relative and partial prosperity; if impunity diminishes, because you cannot get away with anything, even if you can still get away with something; if the state does what it is supposed to (provide public goods, from education to security) and abstains from doing what it shouldn't (shaking people down and ripping them off, as well as forsaking them); then many of the traits described over the past few hundred pages lose their meaning, or raison d'être. We know, of course, that frequently ingrained attitudes such as these outlive their causes and origins, and the simple disappearance of the circumstances in which they came forth does not suffice to banish them from any psyche, much less a national one.

But there is hope, and certainly an agenda for the future. We can know much more than we do about Mexican women in the United States; much more surveying, interviewing, and research can be carried out. We can also try to determine what effect the evident changes in women's attitudes bring about in the men they engage with: fathers and husbands, brothers and sons. Do they get it? Or do they understand and assimilate their female companions' transformation in their interpersonal relationships, but not in their general views on life, work, politics, altercation, collective effort, and self-organization? We have, for now, no way of knowing, except for acknowledging that in this case at least we do not have to beware of what we wish for. If Mexican women in the United States become what they seem to be changing into; if

Mexican men in the United States follow this route, and their example; and if Mexicans in Mexico of both genders and all walks of life are capable, as the country slowly and painfully moves into modernity, to evolve in the same direction as their compatriots abroad, the country we aspire to will emerge, and it will be a better one for all.

### Mañana Has Arrived

These pages were meant to provide readers with a roadmap for Mexico: where it comes from, where it is going today, and where it might find itself in the future. That map is by definition insufficient. The obstacles Mexico faces in achieving modernity are many more than the traits of its national character; the list of those traits described in this book is by no means exhaustive; and the underlying pessimism of the narrative cannot be countered only through the hope of redemption by our diaspora. The dilemmas persist: doesn't the country's magnificent and no longer sublimated diversity contradict the very notion of a "Mexican character," or in any case, of traits common to all Mexicans? Did the two hundred years of independence and the early-twentieth-century Revolution and its consequences suffice to truly build a nation that today can cast off its psychological and cultural moorings without floating adrift? And, most importantly from the perspective of many inevitable critics and skeptics, even if all of this were feasible, is it desirable? Are the Mexicans devoid of the traits here outlined preferable to those who thanks to those traits have survived centuries of oppression and decades of corruption and lawlessness?

One of the most recent foreigners to subject Mexico and the Mexicans to a foreign regard was a Syrian francophile by the name of Ikram Antaki. She visited Mexico in the seventies simply as a sophisticated, French-educated Ph.D. traveler, met and fell in love with a Communist Party cadre from Michoacán, whom she married, had a child with, and accompanied to, among other strange places, Muammar Qaddafi's Libya and the Sandinistas' Nicaragua. She eventually fell out with Fabián Soto, as her husband was named, but stayed in Mexico and became, thanks to a friend who introduced her to the country's premier radio talk host during the first Iraq War, one of the most widely read, listened-to, and quoted analysts of the "Mexican experience." She had the intellectual horsepower for the mission; she came to know the country well, having never lived the cosseted and protected life so many foreigners do in Mexico; and she mainly developed the love for the country without which no external observation can ever achieve truth and relevance.

In one of her books on Mexico, she contradicts the saying we quoted back in Chapter 7: *"Con dinero baila el perro"* ("Properly paid, a dog will dance"). She said that in Mexico, even if properly paid, the dog won't dance.[17] And it won't be because Mexican dogs, i.e., everyone, do not respond to market incentives, to monetary or pecuniary stimuli, to rewards and punishments like citizens of other market democracies do. She was not the first observer to say this, by any means, and she was only right in part: some Mexicans, sometimes, somewhere, and somehow, do react the way others do in similar environments. What Antaki was saying, however, in singularly emphatic and blunt terms, was that there is no virtue, no advantage, no charm, no redeeming value in Mexico's rejection of modernity, whether it be viewed as punctuality, responsibility, civic culture, or obeying traffic regulations, and going to work every day. When she died prematurely in 2000, she was mourned by her countless fans in the general public, but hardly regretted by colleagues in academia or the editorial columns, who always thought she was too strident and candid in her radical denunciation of Mexican ways. In their own fashion, her critics were making a logical point, which one can share or not. We don't.

A Mexico where Mexicans dispense with much of their atavistic baggage and permit the country to achieve the full modernity it deserves is a better Mexico, though perhaps a less enchanting if also less frustrating place than the one we have today. If we are right, and the only way for the country to move forward is by jettisoning those chapters of its national character that we have highlighted, then the game is well worth the candle. It would be presumptuous of Mexican elites, and of their foreign friends, to decide for ourselves that a nation where we thrive and live wonderfully, and that bewitches the world, but leaves 40% of its people in poverty and a majority in precarious, lower-middle-class status, is preferable to the alternative. That alternative consists of something in between the Mexican world in the United States, the middle-class towns of Ciudad Madero, Los Mochis, and Mérida, Juan Gabriel, and the new beaches of Acapulco. It lies in the midst of the jobs provided by tourism and value-added manufacturing, in a freewheeling democracy where majorities win and minorities lose, in a disposition to choose among options and face the consequences, and in leaving history and fear behind.

This middle-class, modern Mexico will undoubtedly lack the magic and mystery of the one we have known until now. It could not be otherwise. And that new Mexico will be running risks: discarding proven defenses in exchange for uncertain benefits. Ultimately, the Mexican people, one way or another, will decide which future they desire, and their wishes, for the first time ever, will be respected. I hope that decision will be in favor of a Mexico that is more diverse in its regional identities, socially much more homogeneous, and as similar as possible to the rest of the modern world. In many ways, the less Mexico is different, and the more it is the same as others, the better for its people.

This conclusion and tone might seem radical or simplistic; after all, why can't Mexico, or any other country, conserve its specificity *and* simultaneously achieve modernity and well-being? It can, but only if its soul ceases to be a burden for its people, if its character and culture become instruments of change, and no longer of immobility. Which is not to say the country could persevere—or muddle through—in its present state: all of the transformations described throughout these pages have been accomplished by Mexicans as they are, not as some, among them myself, would like them to be.

But the perpetuation of that country would be a second-best choice, a default option. A better Mexico is one that leaves its demons and fears behind, and concentrates on its passion and personality. That Mexico is just over the horizon, but the last haul is the toughest one.

# Notes

## Preface

1. Alan Knight, "Mexican National Identity," in Susan Deans-Smith and Eric Van Young, eds. *Mexican Soundings: Essays in Honour of David A. Brading.* (London: Institute for the Study of the Americas, 2007).

2. "GDP (Current US$)," World Bank, Washington, D.C., 2010, data.worldbank .org/indicator/ny.gdp.mktp.cd.

3. Lawrence E. Harrison, *Underdevelopment Is a State of Mind* (Lanham, Maryland: Center for International Affairs/Harvard University Press, 1985).

4. "Fiesteros, apasionados, entrones y valientes: al 87% no le hubiera gustado nacer en ningún otro país," Demotecnia, Mexico City, September 15, 2009, p. 2, www .demotecnia.com/Historico/15092008.pdf.

5. "Visitantes internacionales, 2008," Secretaría de Turismo, Mexico City, 2009, datatur.sectur.gob.mx; "El sector turístico en 2007 generó 2.5 millones de empleos" (INEGI, Mexico City, December 2009), www.inegi.org.mx.

## CHAPTER I
### Why Mexicans Are Lousy at Soccer and Don't Like Skyscrapers

1. Juan Villoro, "¿Era para hoy?," *Reforma* (Mexico City), August 29, 2008.

2. Alan Riding, *Distant Neighbors: A Portrait of the Mexicans* (New York: Vintage, 2000), p. 5.

3. "Medallistas Olímpicos," Comité Olímpico Mexicano, (Mexico City), November 2009, www.com.org.mx/f/.

4. Club Atlético River Plate, official Web site, 2008, www.cariverplate.com.ar; Club Atlético Boca Juniors, official Web site, 2009, www.bocajuniors.com.ar; Club Atlético Peñarol, official Web site, 2009, www.capenarol.com.uy/sitio/; Colo-Colo, official Web site, www.colocolo.cl/; Sociedade Esportiva Palmeiras, official Web site, 2009, www.palmeiras.com.br/5518001428; Clube de Regatas do Flamengo, 2009; Santos Futebol Clube, official Web site, santos.globo.com/.

5. Club América, official Web site, www.clubamerica.com.mx; Club Deportivo Chivas, Guadalajara, official Web site, 2009, www.chivascampeon.com; Club Necaxa, "Historia de Necaxa," Mexico 2009, www.clubnecaxa.com/site/; Club Universidad

Nacional, Pumas, 2009, www.pumasunam.com.mx. There are two exceptions: Atlas, a team from Guadalajara that was founded by a group of students in 1916, and has resembled the South American teams since then; and Pachuca, founded in 1900 by the British mining company Real del Monte, that resembled the South American teams even more so than Atlas.

6. Octavio Paz, "Will for Form," in *Mexico: Splendors of Thirty Centuries* (New York: Metropolitan Museum of Art, 1990), p. 18.

7. Carlos Salas, "Reporte laboral de México: 2007 anual," Institute for Labor Studies for Global Policy Network, Mexico City, April 2008, p. 19, www.gpn.org/data/mexico/mexico-eng.pdf.

8. "El sector no lucrativo a nivel internacional," Mexican Center for Philanthropy, Mexico City, www.cemefi.org.

9. "The Comparative Nonprofit Sector Project," Center for Civil Society Studies, Johns Hopkins University, Institute for Policy Studies, information provided by the Mexican Center for Philanthropy, www.cemefi.org.

10. Federico Reyes Heroles, "El tamaño del corazón," *Periódico Mural* (Guadalajara), December 23, 2008; "La oportunidad del Bicentenario" in *México 2010,* María Amparo Cásar and Guadalupo González, eds. (Mexico City: Tauros, 2010).

11. *Encuesta nacional sobre cultura política y prácticas ciudadanas de la SEGOB* (Secretaría de Gobernación, Mexico City, 2001), p. 20.

12. Alejandro Moreno, *Nuestros valores: los mexicanos en México y en Estados Unidos al inicio del siglo XXI* (Mexico City: División de Estudios Económicos y Sociopolíticos Grupo Financiero Banamex, 2005), p. 131.

13. Ibid., p. 53.

14. Carlos A. Forment, *Democracy in Latin America, 1769–1900* (Chicago: University of Chicago Press, 2003), p. 330.

15. Sebastian Edwards, *Left Behind: Latin America and the False Promise of Populism* (Chicago: University of Chicago Press, 2010), pp. 29, 31.

16. "Conociendo a los ciudadanos mexicanos," Secretaría de Gobernación, Mexico City, 2003, p. 13.

17. John Womack Jr., *Zapata and the Mexican Revolution* (New York: Vintage, 1970), p. xi.

18. Jorge Portilla, *La fenomenología del relajo y otros ensayos* (Mexico City: Fondo de Cultura Económica, 1986), p. 136.

19. Ibid.

20. Samuel Ramos, *Profile of Man and Culture in Mexico* (Austin: University of Texas Press, 1962), pp. 28–30.

21. "The World's Billionaires," *Forbes,* March 10, 2010, www.forbes.com.

22. René Coulomb, "La vivienda de alquiler en las áreas de reciente urbanización," *Revista A,* no. 15, Universidad Autónoma Metropolitana, Mexico City, p. 43. I owe not only the figures, but much of the entire reasoning to Ileana Ortega Alcazar.

23. Alejandro Moreno, *Los valores de los mexicanos,* vol. 6 (Mexico City: Banamex, 2005), pp. 144–46.

24. "Total de vivienda por tipología 2004–2008," INFONAVIT, Mexico City, 2008.

25. "Poblaciones de control," CONAPO/ENADID, Mexico City, 2009, www.conapo.gob.mx/encuesta/Enadid2009/Index. Francisco Resendiz, "En México 2.2 hijos

por cada mujer: INEGI y Conapo," *El Universal* (Mexico City), May 28, 2010, www.eluniversal.com.mx/notas/683945.html.

26. *Reporte mujeres y hombres en México 2009,* 13th ed. (Aguascalientes, Mexico: INEGI, 2009), p. 275, www.inegi.gob.mx; "15 de mayo, Día de la Familia," CONAPO, Mexico City, May 15, 2010, conapo.gob.mx/prensa/2010/bol012_2010.pdf.

27. "PIB nominal durante el primer trimestre de 2010," INEGI, Aguascalientes, Mexico, May 25, 2009, www.inegi.org.mx/inegi/contenidos/espanol/prensa/comunicados/pibcorr.asp; "Agriculture, Value Added (% GDP)," World Bank, Washington, D.C., 2008, data.worldbank.org/indicator/nv.agr.totl.zs.

28. "Composición de la población ocupada de 14 años y más según sector de actividad económica (nacional)," INEGI, Aguascalientes, Mexico, May 2010, dgcnesyp .inegi.org.mx/cgi-win/bdiecoy.exe/615?s=est&c=13021.

29. "Comunicación social. Resultados preliminares del IX censo ejidal," no. 069/08, INEGI, Aguascalientes, Mexico, April 11, 2008; Imelda García, "Crecen ejidatarios; bajan las parcelas," *Reforma* (Mexico City), April 13, 2009.

30. François Chevalier, *La formation des grands domaines au Méxique* (Paris, France: Institut D'Ethnologie, 1952), p. 377.

31. "Comunicación social. Resultados preliminares del IX censo ejidal," no. 069/08. INEGI, Aguascalientes, Mexico, April 11 2008; "Estadísticas a propósito del Día Mundial de la Población. Datos nationales" (Aguascalientes, Mexico), July 2008, www.inegi .org.mx/inegi/contenidos/espanol/prensa/contenidos/estadisticas/2008/poblacion.asp?s= inegi&c=2609&ep=4. *Conteo de población y vivienda 2005.* INEGI, Aguascalientes, Mexico, 2005, www.inegi.org.mx.

32. "Creen que cancelación traerá más conflictos," *Reforma* (Mexico City), August 8, 2002.

33. Enrique Alduncín Abitia, *Los valores de los mexicanos: cambio y permanencia,* vol. 5 (Mexico City: Grupo Financiero Banamex, 2004), p. 25.

34. Iniciativa de Reforma el Artículo 17 de la Constitución Política de los Estados Unidos Mexicanos, a Cargo del Diputado Juan Guerra Ochoa, del Grupo Parlamentario de PRD, October 3, 2008.

35. Joaquín Gallegos Flores, "La deficiente tutela de los intereses colectivos y difusos en México," *Realidad Jurídica* (Mexicali, Baja California, Mexico), s.l.i., vol. 3, no. 1, January–April 2004.

CHAPTER 2

*At Last: A Mexican Middle Class*

1. "Pobreza por ingresos según entidad federativa, 1992–2008," CONEVAL, Mexico City, 2008, www.coneval.gob.mx/contenido/med_pobreza/4136.pdf; "Presenta CONEVAL metodología oficial para la medición multidimensional de la pobreza ante la comisión de desarrollo social de la Cámara de Diputados," CONEVAL, Mexico City, February 2010, www.coneval.gob.mx/contenido/prensa/6875.pdf.

2. José E. Iturriaga, *La estructura social y cultural de México,* 2nd ed. (Mexico City: Fondo de Cultura Económica y Nacional Financiera, 1994), p. 28.

3. Enrique Alduncín Abitia, *Los valores de los mexicanos: en busca de una esencia,* vol. 3 (Mexico City: Grupo Financiero Banamex, 1993), p. 82.

4. "El principio de la fundación," R. Ayuntamiento de Ciudad Madero, Tamaulipas, Mexico, 2008, www.ciudadmadero.gob.mx.

5. "Pemex es . . . de los líderes," *Reforma* (Mexico City), July 8, 2008.

6. "Población total con estimación, por entidad, municipio y localidad, según sexo," Censo de Población y Vivienda 2005, INEGI, Aguascalientes, Mexico, 2005, www.inegi.org.mx.

7. "Grado promedio de escolaridad," *Conteo de población y vivienda 2005*, INEGI, Aguascalientes, Mexico, 2005, www.inegi.org.mx; "Población de 5 años o más, por entidad y municipio, según asistencia escolar," "Alumnos inscritos, existencias, aprobados y egresados, personal docente y escuelas en educación básica y media superior de la modalidad escolarizada a fin de cursos por municipio y nivel educativo. Ciclo escolar 2008/09." *Anuario estadístico, Tamaulipas,* INEGI, Aguascalientes, Mexico, 2009, www .inegi.org.mx/est/contenidos/espanol/sistemas/aee10/estatal/tamps/default.htm.

8. "Enciclopedia de los municipios de México, estado de Tamaulipas, Ciudad Madero," Instituto Nacional para el Federalismo y el Desarrollo Municipal, Tamaulipas, Mexico, 2005, www.e-local.gob.mx/wb/ELOCALNew/enciclo_tamps, "Hogares en viviendas particulares habitadas, por entidad, municipio y localidad, según disponibilidad de computador," *Conteo de población y vivienda 2005*, INEGI, Aguascalientes, Mexico, 2005, www.inegi.org.mx.

9. *Niveles socioeconómicos por entidad federativa 2007–2008,* Consulta Mitofsky, Mexico City, January 2009, p. 4.

10. Everardo Elizondo, "Competitividad y estabilidad en México," Secretaría de Economía, Mexico City, 2004, www.economia.gob.mx.

11. Celia Yamashiro, "Volaris, un vuelo de bautismo," CNNExpansion.com, November 10, 2008, www.cnnexpansion.com/.

12. Data provided to us by one of the area's main developers.

13. "Income Distribution, Inequality, and Those Left Behind," *Global Economic Prospects* (Washington, D.C.: World Bank, 2007), p. 69. "Who's in the Middle?," *The Economist,* February 12, 2009, www.economist.com.

14. "Income Distribution, Inequality, and Those Left Behind," *Global Economic Prospects* (Washington, D.C.: World Bank, 2007), p. 73; Raluca Dragusanu and Dominic Wilson, "The Expanding Middle: The Exploding World Middle Class and Falling Global Inequality," in Goldman Sachs, *Global Economics Paper,* no. 170, New York, July 7, 2008, p. 7.

15. "Who's in the Middle?," *The Economist,* February 12, 2009.

16. "Burgeoning Bourgeoisie," *The Economist,* February 12, 2009, www.econo mist.com.

17. "Who's in the Middle?," *The Economist,* February 12, 2009.

18. "Income Distribution, Inequality, and Those Left Behind," *Global Economic Prospects* (Washington, D.C.: World Bank, 2007), p. 73.

19. "Ingreso corriente trimestral por tamaño de localidad," *Encuesta nacional de ingresos y gastos de los hogares 2008 (ENIGH)*, INEGI, Aguascalientes, Mexico, 2008.

20. Ibid.

21. "Gasto corriente monetario promedio trimestral," *Encuesta nacional de ingresos y gastos de los hogares 2008 (ENIGH),* INEGI, Aguascalientes, Mexico, 2008.

22. Ibid.

23. *Vehículos de motor registrados en circulación,* INEGI, Aguascalientes, Mexico, 2009, p. 281, 200.23.8.5/prod_serv/contenidos/espanol/bvinegi/productos/integracion/pais/aeeum/2009/Aeeum092.pdf.

24. Marcelo Neri, coordinator, "Consumidores, produtores e a nova classe média: miséria, desigualdade e determinantes das classes," Getulio Vargas Foundation, Brazil, September 2009, p. 74, www.fgv.br/cps/fc/.

25. "Ventas anuales 1981, 1992 y 1994," Asociación Mexicana de la Industria Automotriz (AMIA), Mexico City, May 2009.

26. "Autos importados ilegalmente 2006," Confederación de Asociaciones de Agentes Aduanales de la República Mexicana (CAAAREM), Mexico City, April 2009; "Ventas anuales 2006," Asociación Mexicana de la Industria Automotriz, Mexico City, May 2009; Ward's Automotive Group, "U.S. Vehicle Sales, 1931–2009," Penton Media, 2010, http://wardsauto.com/keydata/historical/UsaSa01summary/.

27. *Vehículos de motor registrados en circulación,* INEGI, Aguascalientes, Mexico, 2009, p. 281, 200.23.8.5/prod_serv/contenidos/espanol/bvinegi/productos/integracion/pais/aeeum/2009/Aeeum092.pdf.

28. "Hogares con televisión por cable" and "Hogares con televisión," *Estadísticas sobre disponibilidad y uso de tecnología de información y comunicaciones en los hogares, 2009,* INEGI, Aguascalientes, Mexico, 2009, p. 7.

29. Lilia Chacón, "Se abaratan TVs planas y crecen ventas," *Reforma* (Mexico City), December 6, 2008.

30. "Tarjetas de crédito emitidas al cierre del trimestre, 2002–2010," *Estadísticas de los sistemas de pago de bajo valor, tarjetas, tarjetas de crédito, tarjetas vigentes al cierre del trimestre,* Banco de México, Mexico City, 2010, www.banxico.org.mx/sistemas-de-pago/estadisticas/sistemas-pago-bajo-valor.html.

31. Ibid.

32. "Compra tu vivienda nueva o usada para crédito Infonavit," INFONAVIT, Mexico City, 2010, www.infonavit.org.mx.

33. "Créditos otorgados por período, programa y organismo," Consejo Nacional de Vivienda (CONAVI), Mexico City, 2010.

34. Ibid.; "Desempeño sector vivienda: cierre septiembre," Reunión CANADEVI, Mexico City, October 2010, canadevivallemexico.org.mx/download/plenaria/CONAVI281010.pdf.

35. "Créditos otorgados por período, programa y organismo," Consejo Nacional de Vivienda (CONAVI), Mexico City, 2010.

36. "Usuarios teléfonos celulares, México," Centro Latinoamericano y Caribeño de Demografía, División de Población de la CEPAL, May 2009; "Telefonía móvil usuarios 1990–2010 (mensual)," Comisión Federal de Telecomunicaciones, (COFETEL), Mexico City, 2011, www.cft.gob.mx/es/Cofetel_2008/Cofe_telefonia_movil_usuarios_1990_2007_mensual; "Serie Mensual de líneas telefónicas fijas en servicio residenciales y no residenciales 1994–2010", COFETEL, Mexico City, 2011, www.cft.gob.mx/es/Cofetel_2008/Cofe_serie_mensual_de_lineas_telefonicas_fijas_en_.

37. "Millennium Development Goals Indicators, Mexico," United Nations, July 2009, mdgs.un.org/unsd/mdg/Data.aspx?cr=484; "Usuarios estimados de internet en México 2000–2010 (anual)," Comisión Federal de Telecomunicaciones (COFETEL), Mexico City, 2011, www.cft.gob.mx/es/Cofetel_2008/Cofe_servicios_de_internet.

38. Yasira Pérez and Rodrigo León, "Crece el uso de nuevas tecnologías," *Reforma* (Mexico City), August 12, 2010.

39. "Número de asegurados, 1994–2008" and "Accidents and Illness. Executive Summary, December 2009," Asociación Mexicana de Instituciones de Seguros (AMIS), Mexico City, 2009, p. 6, www.amis.org.mx/InformaWeb/Documentos/Archivos/ResumenEjecutivoDIC09.pdf.

40. "Población total de alumnos, México," CEPAL, May 2009.

41. Ibid.; Instituto Nacional para la Evaluación de la Educación (INEE). "Población escolar de educación superior según nivel educativo (TSU, LUT, Normal y Posgrado) 2007–2008," *Anuarios estadísticos 2005–2008,* Asociación Nacional de Universidades e Instituciones de Educación Superior (ANUIES), Mexico City, August 2009, www .anuies.mx/servicios/e_educacion/index2.php.

42. "Pasajeros transportados por empresas nacionales en servicio doméstico regular 1989–2009," "Pasajeros transportados por empresas nacionales en servicio internacional regular 1989–2009," and "Pasajeros transportados por empresas extranjeras en servicio regular 1989–2009," *La aviación mexicana en cifras 1989–2009,* Secretaría de Comunicaciones y Transportes, Mexico City, August 2009, pp. 26–29, www.sct.gob.mx/uploads/media/Aviacion_Mexicana_en_Cifras.pdf.

43. "Pasajeros transportados pro empresas racionales en servicio doméstico regular 1989–2004, líneas aéreas regionales" and "Pasajeros transportados por empresas nacionales en servicio internacional regular 1989–2004, líneas aéreas regionales." Secretaría de Comunicaciones y Transportes, Mexico City, August 2009, p. 26.

44. "Opinómetro," *Milenio* (Mexico City), March 19, 2001.

45. Federico Reyes Heroles, "La oportunidad del Bicentenario" in *México 2010,* María Amparo Cásar and Guadalupo González, eds. (Mexico City: Tauros, 2010).

46. *Movilidad social en México* (Mexico City: Fundación Espinosa Rugarcía [ESRU], 2008), pp. 4, 6.

47. Nora Lustig, "Growth, Inequality and Poverty in Post-Reform Mexico," lecture given for "Whither Mexico?," Center for Latin American Issues, George Washington University, May 15, 2009, pp. 4, 21, 38.

48. "Población total, por entidad, municipio y localidad," *Segundo conteo de población y vivienda 2005,* INEGI, Aguascalientes, Mexico, www.inegi.org.mx/.

49. "Viviendas particulares habitadas por entidad, municipio y localidad según disponibilidad de televisión y computadora," *Conteo de población y vivienda 2005,* INEGI, Aguascalientes, Mexico, 2005, www.inegi.org.mx/sistemas/olap/proyectos/bd/consulta.asp?p=10215&c=16851&s=est#.

CHAPTER 3

*Victims and Enemies of Conflict and Competition*

1. Samuel Ramos, *Profile of Man and Culture in Mexico* (Austin: University of Texas Press, 1962), p. 4; Manuel Gamio, *Forjando patria* (Mexico City: Porrúa, 2006), p. 21.

2. Octavio Paz, *Labyrinth of Solitude* (New York: Grove, 1994), pp. 29, 31.

3. Gamio, *Forjando patria,* p. 21; Ramos, *Profile of Man and Culture in Mexico,* p. 11; Paz, *Labyrinth of Solitude,* p. 29.

4. Claudio Lomnitz-Adler, *Las salidas del laberinto* (Mexico City: Joaquín Mortiz, 1995), pp. 19–22; Roger Bartra, *La jaula de la melancolía* (Mexico City: Grijalbo, 1986).

5. José Vasconcelos, "La raza cósmica," in Roger Bartra, ed., *Anatomía del mexicano* (Mexico City: Random House Mondadori, 2005), pp. 64, 67.

6. Emilio Uranga, "Ontología del mexicano," in Bartra, *Anatomía del mexicano*, p. 157.

7. José Iturriaga, *La estructura social y cultural de México,* 2nd ed. (Mexico City: Nacional Financiera y Fondo de Cultura Económica, 1994), p. 93.

8. Federico Navarrete, "El mestizaje y las culturas regionales," in *Las relaciones interétnicas en México*, Programa México Nación Multicultural de la UNAM, Mexico, 2005, www.nacionmulticultural.unam.mx/Portal/Izquierdo/BANCO/Mxmulticultural/ Elmestizajeylasculturas-elmestizaje.html; Iturriaga, *La estructura social y cultural de México*, p. 95.

9. Guillermo Bonfil Batalla, *México profundo* (Mexico City: Random House Mondadori, 2005), p. 164.

10. Gamio, *Forjando patria*, p. 9; Bonfil Batalla, *México profundo*, p. 164.

11. "Resumen general de población, según el idioma o lengua hablado," *Censo de población y vivienda 1910,* INEGI, Aguascalientes, Mexico, www.inegi.org.mx/ sistemas/TabuladosBasicos/default.aspx?c=16769&sest.

12. James Creelman, "President Diaz: Hero of the Americas," *Pearson's Magazine*, vol. 19, no. 3, March 1908, p. 241.

13. Iturriaga, *La estructura social y cultural de México*, p. 90.

14. Andrés Molina Enríquez, *Los grandes problemas nacionales*, quoted in Bonfil Batalla, *México profundo*, p. 164; Ramos, *Profile of Man and Culture in Mexico*, p. 58.

15. Alan Knight, *The Mexican Revolution*, vol. 1, *Porfirians, Liberals and Peasants* (Lincoln: University of Nebraska Press, 1990), p. 6.

16. Iturriaga, *La estructura social y cultural de México*, p. 95.

17. Santiago Ramírez Sandoval, *El mexicano: psicología de sus motivaciones* (Mexico City: Grijalbo, 2006), p. 72.

18. Alexander Humboldt, quoted in Bartra, *La jaula de la melancolía*, p. 242.

19. Carlos Fuentes, "Tiempo mexicano," in Bartra, *Anatomía del mexicano*, pp. 257–58.

20. *Latinobarómetro Annual Report 2008* (Santiago, Chile: Latinobarómetro Corporation), p. 101.

21. Jesús Silva-Herzog Márquez, "Los buenos pleitos," *Reforma* (Mexico City), November 20, 2009.

22. "Estimated Mortality Rate (100,000 pop) Homicide," *Health Situation in the Americas: Basic Indicators,* Pan American Health Organization (PAHO), Washington, D.C., 2007, p. 8, www.paho.org/english/dd/ais/BI_2007_ENG.pdf; "Palabras del presidente Álvaro Uribe en la apertura de la Semana por la Vida y la Familia," Presidency of the Republic (Bogotá, Colombia), September 24, 2007, web.presidencia.gov.co/sp/ 2007/septiembre/24/05242007.html; "Homicidios dolosos. Comparativo internacional. Tasa por 100 mil habitantes." *Sexta encuesta nacional sobre inseguridad* (ENSI-6 2009), Instituto Ciudadano de Estudios sobre la Inseguridad, A.C., Mexico City, 2009, p. 110, www.icesi.org.mx/documentos/encuestas/encuestasNacionales/ENSI-6.pdf. According to other sources such as the WHO, Mexico's rate declined to as little as 8 per 100,000 in 2005 and began to rise again after 2007.

23. *Latinobarómetro Annual Report 2008,* p. 56.

24. Sherburne Cook and Woodrow Borah, quoted in Leslie Bethell, ed., *Historia de América Latina*, vol. 1, *América Latina colonial: La América precolombina y la conquista* (Barcelona, Spain: Grijalbo Mondadori, 1998), p. 174.

25. Nicolás Sánchez-Albornoz, "El debate inagotable," *Revista de Indias,* vol. 53, no. 227, 2003.

26. Andrés Lira and Luis Muro, "El siglo de la integración," *Historia general de Mexico,* vol. 1 (Colegio de México, 1981), p. 386.

27. Antonio Caponnetto, "Tres lugares comunes de las leyendas negras," Mexico, www.churchforum.org/tres-lugares-comunes-leyendas-negras.htm.

28. Gamio, *Forjando patria,* p. 154.

29. Octavio Paz, "Will for Form," in *Mexico: Splendors of Thirty Centuries* (New York: Metropolitan Museum of Art, 1990), pp. 7, 20.

30. *Estados Unidos Mexicanos. Cien años de censos de población* (Aguascalientes, Mexico: INEGI, 1996), pp. 17, 21; Leslie Bethell, ed., *The Cambridge History of Latin America V.C. 1870–1930,* vol. 9 (Cambridge: Cambridge University Press, 1986), p. 145.

31. Álvaro Matute, *Historia de la revolución mexicana, 1917–1924: las dificultades del nuevo estado,* (Colegio de México, 1995), p. 227.

32. Jean Meyer, *La révolution mexicaine* (France: Calmann-Lévy, 1973), p. 89.

33. Oriana Fallaci, "La notte di sangue in cui sono stata ferita," *L'Europeo,* no. 42, 1968.

34. *Primera encuesta nacional sobre la discordia y la concordia,* Consejo de Investigación y Comunicación, S.C., Mexico, December 2008, p. 21. Information presented by *Revista Nexos,* February 2009.

35. "National Survey," GAUSSC, Mexico City, December 2009.

36. Ramírez Sandoval, *El mexicano: psicología de sus motivaciones,* p. 41.

37. Enrique Alduncín Abitia, *Los valores de los mexicanos. En busca de una esencia,* vol. 3 (Mexico City: Grupo Financiero Banamex, 1993), p. 125.

38. Ibid., p. 130.

39. Aristotle, *The Metaphysics* (New York: Cosimo, 2008), book 4, chapter 7, p. 85.

40. *Diccionario de la lengua española* (Madrid, Spain: Real Academia Española de la Lengua, 2001).

41. Ramírez Sandoval, *El mexicano: psicología de sus motivaciones,* p. 85.

42. Fabio Morábito, *Lotes baldíos* (Ottawa: Les Écrits des Forges, 2001), p. 36.

43. *Primera encuesta nacional sobre la discordia y la concordia,* p. 20.

44. Uranga, "Ontología del mexicano," p. 2. Foul-mouthed expressions are actually common enough but are rarely directed at one's interlocutor face-to-face.

CHAPTER 4

*Finally, Mexican Democracy*

1. Miguel Carbonell and Enrique Ochoa, "¿Por dónde empezar?," *Enfoque* supplement, *Reforma* (Mexico City), December 10, 2006.

2. Rolando Herrera, "Se castiga sólo 1% de delitos," *Reforma* (Mexico City), August 29, 2009.

3. "Evolución de la Constitución Política de los Estados Unidos Mexicanos, por Artículo," Instituto de Investigaciones Jurídicas, Universidad Nacional Autónoma de México, México, 2009, www.juridicas.unam.mx.

4. *Encuesta nacional sobre cultura política y prácticas ciudadanas de la SEGOB*

*(ENCUP),* Secretaría de Gobernación, 2008, p. 58; "Cultura política de la democracia en México, 2008: el impacto de la gobernabilidad," Latin American Public Opinion Project (LAPOP), Vanderbilt University, Nashville, Tennessee, United States, 2008, p. 16.

5. Alejandro Moreno, "Concepto y valoración de la democracia: hallazgos de la encuesta mundial de valores 2005 en México," *Este País,* no. 181, April 2006, pp. 66, 67.

6. *Encuesta nacional sobre cultura política y prácticas ciudadanas de la SEGOB (ENCUP),* Secretaría de Gobernación, 2003, p. 10.

7. *Latinobarómetro Annual Report 2009* (Santiago, Chile: Latinobarómetro Corporation, 2009), pp. 22, 23.

8. *Encuesta nacional sobre cultura política y prácticas ciudadanas de la SEGOB (ENCUP),* Secretaría de Gobernación, 2008, pp. 37, 46–47. Most worrisome perhaps is the fact that voter participation of young people between eighteen and twenty years old declined between 2006 and 2009; only 40% of new voters went to the polls. Karla Garduño and Martha Martínez, "Generación 2010," *Enfoque* supplement, *Reforma* (Mexico City), August 8, 2010.

9. Private conversation with a former governor of the Mexican Central Bank, Mexico City, September 2009.

10. Private conversation with a former governor of the Mexican Central Bank, Mexico City, September 2009.

11. "Atlas de resultados electorales federales, 1991–2009," Instituto Federal Electoral, Mexico City, 2010, www.ife.org.mx/documentos/RESELEC/SICEEF/principal.html.

12. Ibid.

13. Ibid.

14. Marc Lacey, "Seeking the World's Biggest Meatball? Try Mexico," *New York Times,* September 7, 2009.

15. Carlos Elizondo Meyer-Serra, "Tráfico Guinness," *Reforma* (Mexico City), December 24, 2009.

16. Constitución Política de los Estados Unidos Mexicanos, Mexico, Article 6.

17. Código Federal de Instituciones y Procedimientos Electorales (COFIPE), Instituto Federal Electoral, Mexico, 2008, Article 233.

CHAPTER 5

*The Power of the Past and the Fear of the Foreign*

1. Octavio Paz, "Mexico and the United States," *The New Yorker,* September 17, 1979.

2. Luis González de Alba, *Las mentiras de mis maestros* (Mexico City: Ediciones Cal y Arena, 2002), p.13.

3. Santiago Ramírez Sandoval, *El mexicano: psicología de sus motivaciones* (Mexico: Grijalbo, 2006), pp. 61–63.

4. Christian Duverger, *El primer mestizaje* (Mexico: Taurus, 2007), pp. 641–47.

5. Emilio Uranga, "Ontología del mexicano," in Roger Bartra, ed., *Anatomía del mexicano* (Mexico: Random House Mondadori, 2005), p. 151.

6. *Historia: quinto grado* (Mexico City: Secretaría de Educación Pública, 2006), p. 155.

7. González de Alba, *Las mentiras de mis maestros,* p. 18.

8. Héctor Aguilar Camín, "Cuentos de la Revolución, 1," *Milenio* (Mexico City), November 19, 2008.

9. Octavio Paz, "Mexico and the United States," in *The Labyrinth of Solitude* (New York: Grove, 1994), pp. 362–63.

10. Sonia del Valle, "Pone SEP en duda 600 mil exámenes," *Reforma* (Mexico City), September 7, 2010.

11. Consulta Mitofsky, "Conocimientos históricos," Mexico City, August 2007, pp. 2, 4.

12. Octavio Paz, "Will for Form," in *Mexico: Splendors of Thirty Centuries* (New York: Metropolitan Museum of Art, 1990), p. 4.

13. Octavio Paz, "Mexican Masks," in *Labyrinth of Solitude,* pp. 32, 33.

14. "Global Views 2004. Mexican Public Opinion and Foreign Policy," Centro de Investigación y Docencia Económicas (CIDE), Mexico City, 2004, p. 13; "México y el mundo 2006: opinión pública y política exterior en México," Centro de Investigación y Docencia Económicas (CIDE), Mexico City, 2006, p. 24; "México, las Américas y el mundo: política exterior. Opinión pública y líderes 2008," Centro de Investigación y Docencia Económicas (CIDE), Mexico City, 2008, p. 29.

15. "Troubled by Crime, the Economy, Drugs and Corruption," Pew Global Attitudes Project, Pew Research Center, September 2009, p. 27; "Global Views 2004," pp. 26–27; "México y el mundo 2006," pp. 49, 54; "México, las Américas y el mundo," p. 32.

16. "Background Note: Mexico," U.S. Deparment of State, Bureau of Western Hemisphere Affairs, Washington, D.C., February 2010, www.state.gov/.

17. "Visitantes Internacionales, 2008," Secretaría de Turismo, Mexico, 2009, datatur.sectur.gob.mx.

18. José Antonio Crespo, quoting Benito Juárez in *Contra la historia oficial.* Debate. Mexico City, 2009, p. 275.

19. José Antonio Crespo quoting Matías Romero in *Contra la historia oficial,* p. 277.

20. Francisco José Andrea Sánchez, *Constitución Política de los Estados Unidos Mexicanos comentada,* 5th ed. (Mexico: Universidad Nacional Autónoma de México, 1994), pp. 147–48, www.bibliojuridica.org.

21. Fernando Serrano Migallón, "Concepto de nacionalidad en las constituciones mexicanas. Apertura e introspección," in Nuria González Martín, coordinator, "Estudios Jurídicos en Homenaje a Marta Morineau, T. II: Sistemas Jurídicos Contemporáneos" (Universidad Nacional Autónoma de México, 2006), www.bibliojuridica.org; González de Alba, *Las mentiras de mis maestros,* pp. 53–54.

22. Pablo Yankelevich, "Proteger al mexicano y construir al ciudadano. La extranjería en los debates del constituyente de 1917," *Signos Históricos,* no. 010, July–December, Universidad Autónoma Metropolitana–Iztapalapa, p. 64.

23. Demotécnia, "61%: 'No es correcto que haya jugadores nacionalizados en la selección,' " Mexico City, January 24, 2009, pp. 2, 4–5, http://www.demotecnia.com/.

24. "México y el mundo 2006. Opinión pública y política exterior en México," p. 25. "México, las Américas y el mundo," p. 26.

25. Yankelevich, "Proteger al mexicano y construir al ciudadano," pp. 68, 75.

26. Ibid.

27. Enríque Flores Magón and Ricardo Flores Magón, "Programa del Partido Liberal Mexicano y manifiesto a la nación," St. Louis, Mo., July 1906.

28. "Global Views 2004," p. 33; "México y el mundo 2006," pp. 66–67; "México, las Américas y el mundo," pp. 15, 68–69.

29. "Troubled by Crime, the Economy, Drugs and Corruption," Pew Global Attitudes Project, Pew Research Center, September 2009, p. 21. "México, las Américas y el mundo," p. 69. In general, when any poll includes a reference to jobs, wages, consumption of goods and services, when inquiring of Mexican opinion of the United States, that opinion improves remarkably.

30. Ibid., pp. 72–73.

31. "2008 American Community Survey 1-year Estimates. Selected Population Profiles, by Country of Birth: Mexico," U.S. Census Bureau, 2010, factfinder.census.gov/home/saff/main.html?_lang=en.

32. "México, las Américas y el mundo," p. 15.

33. "México y el mundo 2006," p. 58.

34. "National Survey," GAUSSC, Mexico City, July 2009, p. 22.

CHAPTER 6

*At Last: An Open Society, an Open Economy, an Open Mind?*

1. "Export Goods and Services. Imports Goods and Services. Members OECD," Organisation for Economic Co-operation and Development (OECD), Paris, 2008.

2. "GDP (current US$)," World Bank, Washington, D.C., 2010, data.worldbank.org/indicator/ny.gdp.mktp.cd; "Balanza de pagos. Exportaciones totales," Banco Nacional de México, Mexico City, 2009; "Balanza de pagos. Importaciones totales," Banco Nacional de México, Mexico City, 2009.

3. Ulises Beltrán, Oficina de la Presidencia de la República Mexicana. Banco de Información para la Investigación Aplicada en Ciencias Sociales (BIIACS), Centro de Investigación y Docencia Económicas (CIDE), Mexico City, 2010.

4. "Exportaciones totales de México, 1993 a 2009" and "Importaciones totales de México, 1993 a 2009," Secretaría de Economía, Mexico, 2011, www.economia-snci.gob.mx/.

5. "GDP growth (annual %)," World Bank, Washington, D.C., 2010, data.worldbank.org/indicator/ny.gdp.mktp.kd.zg.

6. *Perfil y grado de satisfacción de los turistas 2007,* Secretaría de Turismo, Mexico City, 2009, www.sectur.gob.mx/.

7. *Tourism Highlights 2009 Edition.* United Nations World Tourism Organization, Spain, 2010, www.unwto.org/facts/menu.html; "Balanza comercial. Comercio exterior. Viajeros internacionales (ingresos)," Banco de México, 2011, www.banxico.org.mx/.

8. "El sector turístico en 2007 generó 2.5 millones de empleos," INEGI, Aguascalientes, Mexico, December 2009, inegi.org.mx/; Bernardo Méndoza and Edgar Sigler, "Industria sin chimeneas sobrevive al desdén oficial," *El Universal* (Mexico City), December 2009.

9. "Balanza de pagos. Balanza comercial. Viajeros internacionales (saldo e ingresos)," Banco de México, Mexico City, 2009, www.banxico.org.mx/.

10. "Balanza de pagos. Balanza comercial. Remesas familiares," Banco de México, Mexico, 2009, www.banxico.org.mx/.

11. "Migración Nacional," Centro de Estudios Sociales (CESOP) y de Opinión Pública y Parametría, Mexico, October 2008, p. 39; Consulta Mitofsky, "EUA: 4 de cada 10 mexicanos tenemos un pariente en ese país," Mexico City, April 2008, p. 3.

12. "Net Migration," World Bank, Washington, D.C., 2010, data.world.bank.org/indicator/sm.pop.netm; "Exigen salvadoreños en el exterior derecho al voto," Notimex, Mexico City, November 26, 2008; "Dos millones de ecuatorianos viven fuera del país," United Nations Radio, June 2009; "La migración en Guatemala," Agencia Informativa Púlsar, Buenos Aires, Argentina, March 2008; www.agenciapulsar.org; "Migrations in the Mediterranean," *Med. 2009, anuario del Mediterráneo,* Instituto Europeo del Mediteráneo, Spain, 2009, www.iemed.org; *Migration and Remittances Factbook 2008* (Washington, D.C., World Bank, March 2008), siteresources.worldbank.org.

13. "Foreign direct investment net inflows (BoP, current US$)," World Bank, Washington, D.C., 2010, data.worldbank.org/indicator/bx.klt.dinv.cd.wd; Oscar Bajo-Rubio and Simón Sosvilla-Rivero, "An Econometric Analysis of Foreign Direct Investment in Spain, 1964–89," *Southern Economic Journal,* vol. 61, 1994.

14. "Balanza de pagos. Balanza comercial. Inversión extranjera," Banco de México, www.banxico.org.mx/; "Foreign direct investment net inflows (BoP, current US$)," World Bank, Washington, D.C., 2010, data.worldbank.org/indicator/bx.klt .dinv.cd.wd.

15. "Balanza de pagos. Balanza comercial. Inversión extranjera," Banco de México, www.banxico.org.mx/; "Foreign direct investment," World Bank.

16. The Economist, *Pocket World in Figures, 2009 Edition,* (London, 2009), pp. 122, 180; "GDP (current US$)," World Bank.

17. *Diccionario de la lengua española,* 22nd ed. (Madrid, Spain: Real Academia Española de la Lengua, 2001). Origen de las Palabras, Chile, 2010, etimologias.dechile .net/?gringo.

18. Artemio de Valle-Arizpe, *Historia, tradiciones y leyendas de calles de México II* (Mexico City: Lectorum, 2009); Origen de las Palabras, Chile, 2010, etimologias .dechile.net/?gringo; Rodrigo Martínez Baracs, "Acerca del origen de la palabra *gringo*," in *Biblioteca de México,* 62–63, March–June 2001, p. 7, www.somehil.com.

19. Conversation with Ulises Beltrán.

20. Consulta Mitofsky, "¿Qué país queremos ser?," *Nexos,* no. 385, January 2010, pp. 13, 15, 17.

21. "Encuesta Nacional," GAUSSC, Mexico, February 2010.

CHAPTER 7

*Illusory Laws, Lawless Cynicism*

1. Jorge Portilla, *La fenomenología del relajo y otros ensayos* (Mexico City: Fondo de Cultura Económica, 1986), pp. 126–27.

2. Fernando Mayorga García, "Derecho indiano y derechos humanos," Memoria del X Congreso del Instituto Internacional de Historia del Derecho Indiano, tomo II, Instituto de Investigaciones Jurídicas, Serie: Estudios Históricos, no. 50, Mexico City, 1995, p. 1039, www.bibliojuridica.org/.

3. Octavio Paz, "The Philanthropic Ogre," in *The Labyrinth of Solitude* (New York: Grove, 1994), pp. 396–97.

4. Ibid., p. 397.

5. Claudio Lomnitz-Adler, *Las salidas del laberinto* (Mexico City: Joaquín Mortiz, 1995), p. 145.

6. *Encuesta nacional sobre cultura política y prácticas ciudadanas de la SEGOB (ENCUP),* Secretaría de Gobernación, 2003, p. 16.

7. Samuel Ramos, quoting Carlos Pereyra, in *Profile of Man and Culture in Mexico* (Austin: University of Texas Press, 1962), p. 20.

8. Roger Bartra, *La jaula de la melancolía* (Mexico City: Grijalbo, 1986), p. 170.

9. Jaime Sánchez Susarrey, "ABC," *Reforma* (Mexico City), June 12, 2010.

10. Código Federal de Instituciones y Procedimientos Electorales (COFIPE), Article 220, Instituto Federal Electoral.

11. "Cultura de la legalidad," IPSOS-Bimsa, Mexico, May 2005, p. 6.

12. "Atlas de resultados electorales federales 1991–2009," Instituto Federal Electoral, Mexico, 2010, www.ife.org.mx/documentos/RESELEC/SICEEF/principal.html.

13. *Dictamen relativo al cómputo final de la elección de presidente de los Estados Unidos Mexicanos, declaración de validez de la elección y de presidente electo* (Tribunal Electoral de la Federación, September 2006), pp. 202–3, www.lupaciudadana.com.mx/.

14. *Encuesta nacional sobre creencias, actitudes y valores de maestros y padres de familia de la educación básica en México* (ENCRAVE), *Este País* (Mexico City), no. 169, April 2005, pp. 10, 12–13.

15. Ricardo Raphael, *Los Socios de Elba* (Mexico City: Planeta, 2007).

16. "El irrespeto a la ley en México," *Parametría,* México City, March 2006, p. 2; *Encuesta nacional sobre cultura política,* p. 11; "National Survey," GAUSSC, Mexico City, December 2009; Enrique Alduncín Abitia, *Los valores de los mexicanos. En busca de una esencia,* vol. 3, p. 71.

17. "Cultura política de la democracia en México: 2006," Latin American Public Opinion Project (LAPOP), Vanderbilt University, Nashville, Tennessee, 2006, p. 507; "Cultura política de la democracia en México, 2008: el impacto de la gobernabilidad," Vanderbilt University, p. 34; "Troubled by Crime, the Economy, Drugs and Corruption," Pew Research Center, p. 38.

18. "Cultura política de la democracia en México, 2008," pp. 39–40.

CHAPTER 8

*The Law of the Land, or the Land of the Law?*

1. *Encuesta nacional de adicciones, 2002* and *2008,* Secretaría de Salud, Consejo Nacional Contra las Adicciones, Mexico City; Rubén Aguilar and Jorge G. Castañeda, *El narco: la guerra fallida,* (Mexico City: Punto de Lectura, 2009), p. 19.

2. "Entrevista con María Elena Medina-Mora. Nadie debería ir a la cárcel por usar drogas," *Este País* (Mexico City), no. 226, January–February 2010, p. 28.

3. Richard Nixon: "Excerpts from President's Message on Drug Abuse Control," *New York Times,* June 18, 1971. Gerald Ford: Gerhard Peters and John T. Woolley, "128—Statement on Drug Abuse, February 23, 1976," *American Presidency Project* (online), University of California, Santa Barbara, 2010, www.presidency.ucsb .edu/ws/?pid=5609; Gerhard Peters and John T. Woolley, "368—Special Message to the Congress on Drug Abuse, April 27, 1976," *American Presidency Project* (online), University of California, Santa Barbara, 2010, www.presidency.ucsb.edu/ws/ ?pid=5875. Jimmy Carter: Gerhard Peters and John T. Woolley, "United Nations Fund for Drug Abuse Control Statement by President Jimmy Carter, September 22, 1978,"

*American Presidency Project* (online), University of California, Santa Barbara, 2010, www.presidency.ucsb.edu/ws/?pid=29832. Ronald Reagan: Gerhard Peters and John T. Woolley. "Proclamation 5123—National Drug Abuse Education Week, November 1, 1983," *American Presidency Project* (online), University of California, Santa Barbara, 2010, www.presidency.ucsb.edu; Gerhard Peters and John T. Woolley, "Informal Exchange with Reporters on Drug Trafficking, February 13, 1988," *American Presidency Project* (online), University of California, Santa Barbara, 2010, www.presidency .ucsb.edu/ws/?pid=35419; Gerhard Peters and John T. Woolley, "Remarks at a Meeting of the White House Conference for a Drug Free America, February 29, 1988," *American Presidency Project* (online), University of California, Santa Barbara, 2010, www.presi-dency.ucsb.edu/ws/?pid=35482; Gerhard Peters and John T. Woolley, "Radio Address to the Nation on Drug Abuse and Trafficking, April 16, 1988," *American Presidency Project* (online), University of California, Santa Barbara, 2010, www.presidency.ucsb.edu/ws/ ?pid=35685. George H. W. Bush: Gerhard Peters and John T. Woolley, "Remarks at the International Drug Enforcement Conference in Miami, Florida, April 27, 1989," *American Presidency Project* (online), University of California, Santa Barbara, 2010, www .presidency.ucsb.edu/ws/?pid=16974; Gerhard Peters and John T. Woolley, "Address to the Nation on the National Drug Control Strategy, September 5, 1989," *American Presidency Project* (online), University of California, Santa Barbara, 2010, www.presidency .ucsb.edu/ws/?pid=17472; Gerhard Peters and John T. Woolley, "Address to Students on Drug Abuse, September 12, 1989," *American Presidency Project* (online), University of California, Santa Barbara, 2010, www.presidency.ucsb.edu/ws/?pid=17509. George W. Bush: Gerhard Peters and John T. Woolley, "The President's News Conference with President Felipe de Jesús Calderón Hinojosa in Mérida, March 14, 2007," *American Presidency Project* (online), University of California, Santa Barbara, 2010, www.presi-dency.ucsb.edu/ws/?pid=24587. Hillary Rodham Clinton: Matthew Lee, "Clinton: US Demand to Blame for Drug Violence," Associated Press in ABC News, March 5, 2010, abcnews.go.com/International/wireStory?id=10018805; Ginger Thompson and Marc Lacey, "U.S. and Mexico Revise Joint Antidrug Strategy," *New York Times,* March 23, 2010, www.nytimes.com; Marc Landler, "Clinton Says U.S. Feeds Mexico Drug Trade," *New York Times,* March 25, 2009, www.nytimes.com.

    4. *Informe del estado de la seguridad pública en México.* Secretaría de Seguridad Pública, Mexico City, January 21, 2010, p. 10. The Latin American homicide numbers are from "Homicidios dolosos. Comparativo internacional. Tasa por 100 mil habitantes," *Sexta encuesta nacional sobre inseguridad* (ENSI-6 2009), Instituto Ciudadano de Estudios sobre la Inseguridad, A.C., Mexico City, 2009, p. 110, www.icesi.org.mx/documentos/encuestas/ encuestasNacionales/ENSI-6.pdf; "Tasas de homicidios dolosos en Centroamérica y República Dominicana, por 100,000 habitantes, 1999–2007," OCAVI, November 2007, www.ocavi.com/docs_files/file_378.pdf.

    5. "Homicidios dolosos. Tasa por 100 mil habitantes," *Sexta encuesta nacional sobre inseguridad* (ENSI-6 2009), Instituto Ciudadano de Estudios sobre la Inseguridad, A.C., Mexico City, 2009, p. 109, www.icesi.org.mx/documentos/encuestas/encuestas Nacionales/ENSI-6.pdf.

    6. "Población total con estimación, por entidad, municipio y localidad, según sexo," *Conteo de población y vivienda 2005,* INEGI, Aguascalientes, Mexico, 2005, www.inegi.org.mx/; *Delimitación de las zonas metropolitanas de México 2005,* INEGI, Aguascalientes, Mexico, 2005, pp. 37–38.

7. Daniel Cosío Villegas, *Historia moderna de México. El porfiriato. Vida económica*, 2nd ed. (Mexico City: Editorial Hermes, 1974), p. 626.

8. "Población total con estimación, por entidad, municipio y localidad, según sexo," *Conteo de población y vivienda 2005*, INEGI, Aguascalientes, Mexico City, 2005. www.inegi.org.mx/.

9. "Elementos activos de la policía municipal de Mérida," Departamento de Comunicación Social y Atención Ciudadana de la Policía Municipal de Mérida, Mexico, 2009.

10. "Informe del estado de la seguridad pública en México," Secretaria de Seguridad Pública, Mexico City, January, 2010, p. 5; *Quinta encuesta nacional sobre inseguridad,* Instituto Ciudadano de Estudios Sobre la Inseguridad (ICESI), Mexico City, 2008, p. 53.

11. Santiago Levy, *Good Intentions, Bad Outcomes* (Washington, D.C.: Brookings Institution Press, 2008), pp. 86–87; Luis Rubio and Oliver Azuara et al., *México 2025. El futuro se construye hoy* (Mexico City: CIDAC, 2006), p. 126.

12. Mariano Bosch and W. Maloney, "Gross Worker Flows in the Presence of Informal Labor Markets: The Mexican Experience" (Washington, D.C.: World Bank, 2006), p. 7, quoted in Levy, *Good Intentions, Bad Outcomes*, pp. 34–35.

13. "Total Population," *Country Statistical Profile, 2009*, OECD, 2009, stats.oecd .org; "Overview: Data on Informal Employment and Self-Employment," *Is Informal Normal? Towards More and Better Jobs in Developing Countries*, OECD, 2009, p. 2, www.oecd.org/dataoecd/4/49/42863997.pdf.

14. *Economic Surveys: Mexico, 2009* (OECD, 2009), pp. 102–3, 107.

15. Mario Fernando Larios, "La reforma del impuesto predial en México," Instituto Mexicano de Catastro, I Congreso Nacional e Internacional del Catastro, en Córdoba, Argentina, September 2009, p. 22.

16. "Evaluación preeliminar de la economía extralegal en 12 países de Latinoamérica y el Caribe. Reporte de la investigación en México," Instituto Libertad y Democracia, Peru, p. 5.

17. "Arriesgan micros a pasajeros," *Reforma* (Mexico City), April 5, 2010. And according to a survey by Met-Life quoted a few chapters back, 74% of Mexicans buy black-market movies, a higher percentage than in other countries. Mexico occupies fourth place for piracy in the world, preceded by Russia, China, and Italy. Deborah Holtz and Juan Carlos Mena, eds., *El sueño mexicano* (Mexico City: Trilce Ediciones, 2009), p. 271; Walter Jasso Anderson, "Piratería. De transa en transa, México no avanza," *Revista del Consumidor,* Procuraduría Federal del Consumidor (PROFECO), Mexico City, December 2006, p. 23.

18. Alejandro Moreno, *La decisión electoral. Votantes, partidos y democracia en México* (Mexico: Porrúa, 2009), p. 340.

19. *Latinobarómetro Annual Report 2009* (Santiago, Chile: Latinobarómetro Corporation), pp. 34, 37, 39; *Encuesta nacional sobre cultura política y prácticas ciudadanas de la SEGOB (ENCUP)*, Secretaría de Gobernación, 2008, p. 16.

20. Christian Duverger, "El primer mestizaje" (Mexico: Taurus, 2007), pp. 37, 38.

21. Ibid., p. 17.

22. "Country: China," *The World Factbook*, CIA, Washington, D.C., 2010, www.cia .gov/library/publications/the-world-factbook/geos/ch.html.

23. "Producto Interno Bruto por Entidad Federativa," INEGI, Aguascalientes, Mexico, 2006.

CHAPTER 9

*The Future in Real Time*

1. "Lincoln Steffens," *Encyclopaedia Britannica Online,* May 25, 2010, www
.britannica.com/EBchecked/topic/564894/Lincoln-Steffens.

2. "Decennial Censuses, 1900–2000," Census of Population and Housing, United
States, 2010, U.S. Census Bureau, www.census.gov/prod/www/abs/decennial/.

3. "2008 American Community Survey 1-Year Estimates. Selected Population Profiles, by Country of Birth: Mexico," U.S. Census Bureau, 2010, factfinder.census.gov/
home/saff/main.html?_lang=en.

4. Ibid.

5. "Balanza de pagos. Remesas familiares," Banco de México, Mexico City, 2010,
www.banxico.org.mx/politica-monetaria-e-inflacion/estadistics/otrosindicadores/
balanza-pagos.html; "Balanza de pagos, 1980–2008," Centro de Estudios de Finan-
zas Públicas, Mexico City, 2009, www.cefp.gob.mx/intr/e-stadisticas/copianewe
_stadisticas.html; "Workers' remittances and compensation of employees, received (cur-
rent US$)," World Bank, Washington, D.C., May 2010.

6. Alejandro Moreno, *Nuestros valores: Los mexicanos en México y en Estados Unidos
al inicio del siglo XXI* (Mexico City: División de Estudios Económicos y Sociopolíticos
Grupo Financiero Banamex, 2005), p. 158.

7. Andrew Karmen, *New York Murder Mystery: The True Story Behind the Crime
Crash of the 1990s* (New York: NYU Press, 2006), quoted in Eyal Press, "Do Immigrants
Make Us Safer?," *New York Times,* December 3, 2006, http://www.nytimes.com/2006/
12/03/magazine/03wwln_idealab.html?scp=1&sq=eyal+press&st yt.

8. Rubén G. Rumbaut and Walter A. Ewing, "The Myth of Immigrant Criminality
and the Paradox of Assimilation: Incarceration Rates Among Native and Foreign-Born
Men," Immigration Policy Center, Spring 2007, pp. 3–4.

9. Mauricio Tenorio Trillo, "Contra la idea de México," *Nexos Magazine* (Mexico
City), no. 390, June 2010, p. 60.

10. Moreno, *Nuestros valores,* pp. 98, 99.

11. Ibid., pp. 150–51.

12. Roberto Suro and Gabriel Escobar, "Survey of Mexicans Living in the U.S. on
Absentee Voting in Mexican Elections," Pew Hispanic Center, February 2006, p. 1,
pewhispanic.org/files/reports/60.pdf.

13. Moreno, *Nuestros valores,* pp. 145, 47.

14. "2008 American Community Survey 1-Year Estimates. Selected Population Profiles, by Country of Birth: Mexico," U.S. Census Bureau, 2010, factfinder.census.gov/
home/saff/main.html?_lang=en.

15. "Hispanic Women in the United States, 2007," Pew Hispanic Center, May
2008, pp. 18, 24, pewhispanic.org/files/factsheets/42.pdf; "2008 American Community
Survey 1-Year Estimates. Selected Population Profiles, by Country of Birth: Mexico."
U.S. Census Bureau, 2010, factfinder.census.gov/home/saff/main.html?_lang=en; Ofe-
lia Woo and José Moreno Mena, "Las mujeres migrantes y familias mexicanas en Estados Unidos," p. 7, bibliotecadigital.conevyt.org.mx; Richard Fry, "Gender and
Migration," Pew Hispanic Center, July 2006, p. 9, pewhispanic.org/files/reports/
64.pdf; "Enfrentan difíciles condiciones sociales madres mexicanas en EU," Notimex,

Mexico City, May 11, 2009, http://www.e-migrantes.gob.mx/wb2/eMex/eMex_2e9cf_not204_enfrentan_dif.

16. "Tasa neta de participación, 2008–2010," Secretaría del Trabajo y Previsión Social, Mexico City, 2010, www.stps.gob.mx/DGIET/web/menu_infsector.htm.

17. Ikram Antaki, *El pueblo que no quería crecer* (Mexico: Océano, 1996), pp. 100–101.

# Index

Jorge G. Castañeda was born and raised in Mexico City. He received his B.A. from Princeton University and his Ph.D. from the University of Paris. He has been a professor of political science at the National Autonomous University of Mexico, a senior associate of the Carnegie Endowment for International Peace in Washington, D.C., and a visiting professor at Princeton University and the University of California at Berkeley. He was Mexico's foreign minister from 2000 to 2003, and is now Global Distinguished Professor of Politics and Latin American Studies at New York University. He is a member of the board of Human Rights Watch and lives in New York and Mexico City.

A NOTE ON THE TYPE

This book was set in Adobe Garamond. Designed for the Adobe Corporation by Robert Slimbach, the fonts are based on types first cut by Claude Garamond (c. 1480–1561). Garamond was a pupil of Geoffroy Tory and is believed to have followed the Venetian models, although he introduced a number of important differences, and it is to him that we owe the letter we now know as "old style." He gave to his letters a certain elegance and feeling of movement that won their creator an immediate reputation and the patronage of Francis I of France.